SPIRITS OF PLACE

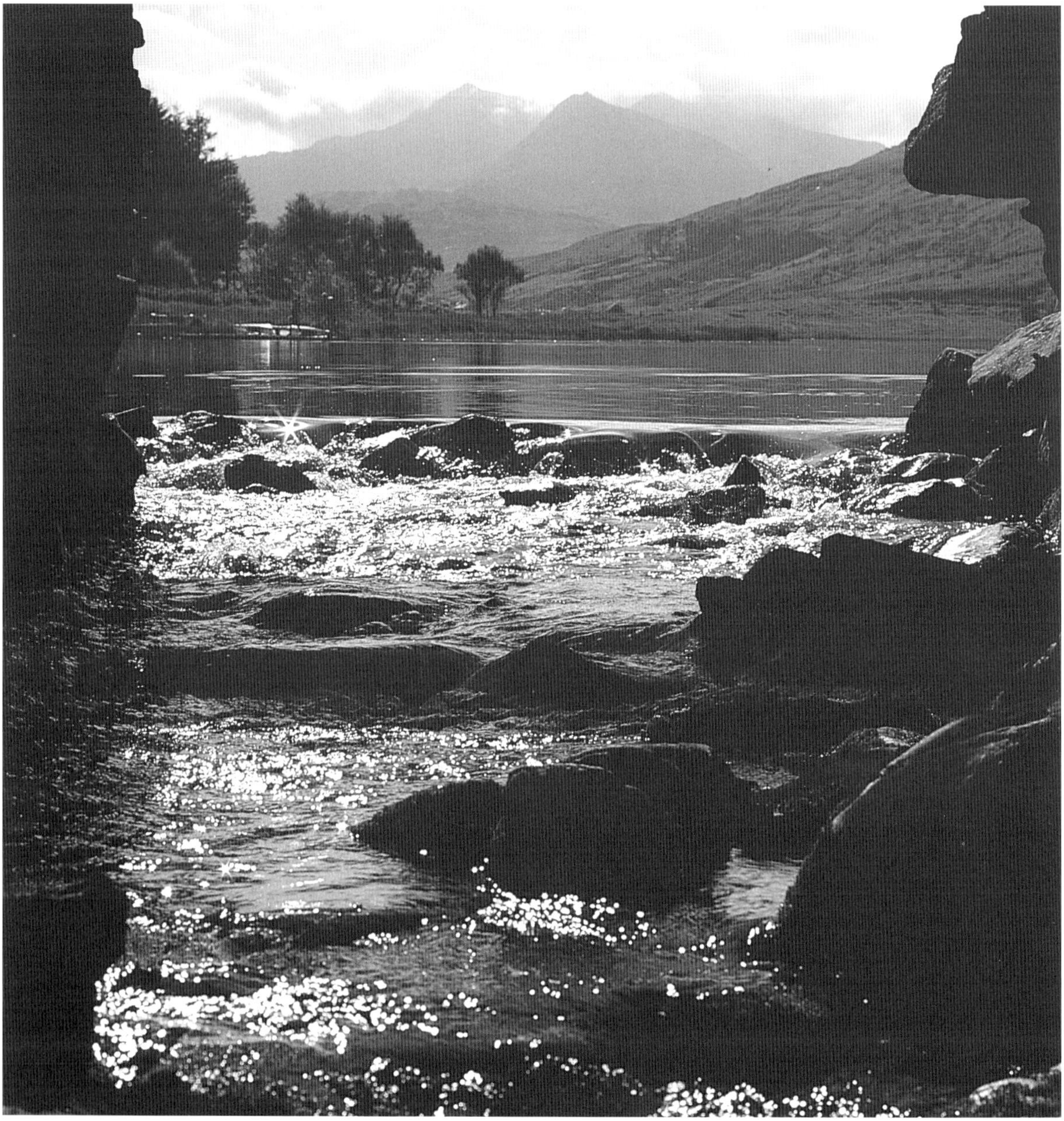

Spirits of Place

Travels, Encounters and Adventures in and from Wales

Jim Perrin

GOMER

First Impression—1997

ISBN 1 85902 482 3

© Jim Perrin

Jim Perrin has asserted his right under the Copyright, Designs and Patents Act, 1988, to be identified as Author of this Work.

All rights reserved. No part of this book may be reproduced, stored in a retrieval system, or transmitted in any form or by any means, electronic, electrostatic, magnetic tape, mechanical, photocopying, recording or otherwise without permission in writing from the publishers, Gomer Press, Llandysul, Ceredigion.

This volume is published with the support of the Arts Council of Wales.

Printed in Wales at
Gomer Press, Llandysul, Ceredigion

For Dermot Somers & Robbie Fenlon

. . . you never enjoy the world aright, till you so love the beauty of enjoying it, that you are covetous and earnest to persuade others to enjoy it. And so perfectly hate the abominable corruption of men in despising it, that you had rather suffer the flames of Hell than willingly be guilty of their error. There is so much blindness and ingratitude and damned folly in it. The world is a mirror of infinite beauty, yet no man sees it. It is a Temple of Majesty, yet no man regards it. It is a region of light and peace, did not men disquiet it. It is the Paradise . . . more to man since he is fallen than it was before. It is the place of Angels and the Gate of Heaven.

Thomas Traherne

Nid i ryw anheimladrwydd yr ildiaswn
O gwrdd ag ymyl gwisg yr Angau'i hun—
Na, heb fy ngwybod, mi ddarganfuaswn
Yno, gêl hanner etifeddiaeth dyn.
Presennol yw'r Absennol imi'n awr,
A'r Marw a'r Byw sy'n un gymdeithas fawr.

E. Prosser Rhys

CONTENTS

Foreword by Dafydd Elis-Thomas   8
Introduction   10

1: 'In the regions of the air'

  Ruins   17
  Caban   20
  The Quest for Llech Ronw   23
  Drinking with Dervla   28
  Peregrinations   32
  Llama Farmer   35
  The Diver   39
  Condry on Cadair   41
  'Father, I must whisper this . . .'   44
  Visions and Virians   46
  From the Waves   48
  For Arnold Pines   51

2: 'For all these, and for all these, peace'

  Mapmaker on a Western Shore   59
  Funeral Address for Paul Williams   66
  Urban Guerilla   69
  Heroic Mock-heroic   74
  Ability   77
  Bird Artist of Ynys Enlli   81
  Piper Errant   86
  Foot on the Heath   88
  'A man who used to notice such things'   97
  Dignity   100
  Angry Laughter   105
  No Home but the Struggle   109

3: 'Nevadas of Rapture'

Bog Trot 117
Eating Bear Meat 121
Adventuring on Llŷn 124
(Beinn a' Chaoruinn and) The Vision of Glory 129
Small Climbs in Germany 134
Contumely of the Conquistadors 139
Three Cornish Climbs 144
Day Trip to Dalkey 148
'In dreams begins responsibility' 153
Learning Curves 160
Judas Climbers and the Trees 167
Kaleidoscope of the Senses 173

4: The Bereft Lunatic's Embrace

Sketches from a journey through Wales 177

Acknowledgements 250

Foreword

The Welsh language, usefully, has two words to fill the space in its discourse of the English-language word 'landscape'. The one is geographical: *tirwedd*, for the very shape and contours of the land, as mountain range gives way to *nant* or river valley, down to estuary and sea coast. In Wales, it is quite possible, even for the not so fit, to journey from mouth to river source in an active day, though I wouldn't recommend that for the Wye or Severn. But then they, like so much of Wales, flow through England. The other word for the English-language 'landscape' is *tirlun*, the term used for the artistic work, which means quite literally, the picture of the land. Not the way it looks, but the way it is looked *at*. *Tirlun* is the picture taken of the land—originally the landscape painting, then the photograph, and now, probably, the virtual reality of it.

Cultures require landscapes in both senses. Much of the rather silly debate about landscape and the environment arises from the fact that the debaters only have one word for what they are talking about. Every landscape is both a shape and a shaped entity, presented and interpreted in a certain way depending on how it is regarded within a culture. Indeed, cultures can be seen as the ways of looking at and making meanings of the spaces and places which they occupy.

That, essentially, is what Jim Perrin does. He makes a literary and photographic art of landscapes. Though, like the landscape of Wales, no genre description can simply sum up his art or pin it down. It is travel writing, yes, but also ethnography. It is minute observation of habitat, but also exuberant participation in community. It is extravagantly condemnatory, warmly eulogistic, but nowhere more tender than in the elegiac mode. Here, as almost always in Welsh, elegies are not about cultivated or depressive feelings evoked around certain landscapes; they are, as in many of the following pieces, memories of persons in places.

Places are never inanimate, but rather they are always humanist and humanised. It is the people who *were* here, and the way they are remembered and understood by the people who are here today that conjure for readers the here and now of a particular place, and by inference, other places, that are continually discovered and rediscovered, made and remade, in these writings.

The boundaries between journalism, autobiography, fiction, travel writing and environmental campaigning are crossed and criss-crossed, because in the flow of words, as when *nant* becomes river, there are no boundaries. Boundaries are only for maps, and maps are only for finding places. When one gets there, the place

FOREWORD

inevitably finds you. Eryri found Jim, but he had family links anyway. Not that that matters. There is a whole generation of climbers who have moved to live and work in 'North Wales' because of the landscape. Their love of the landscape has brought them, because of their own libertarian understandings, to a love of culture and people and language. This in its turn has brought new energy and confidence into that language community itself. The constant reference throughout Jim's writing to Welsh-language literature is a sign of this.

But there is another metaphor as well. The Welsh *nant* as it turns into a river meets with the ebb and flow of the international, intercultural tides. Such tides enter estuaries below the freshwater, and as they interfuse, they create incredibly sensitive and fascinating habitats, an ecology always in movement. Such is Welsh cultural ecology and writing. When it gets over-defensive, or swims too easily with the tide, it loses its vitality. It is in that holding, if only briefly, of the moving facets that the fascination lies.

It is the making of signs, the telling of stories, which both interpret and explain, that give an understanding and meaning to difficult events. This is the art of the traditional story-teller. Before there was the historian, or the travel writer, there was the 'people's remembrancer', to quote Gwyn Alf Williams' resonant phrase. But before them, there was the *cyfarwydd*. He, usually, though sometimes she, was the person familiar with the old traditional material, who could always tell it in a new way. The stories of yesterday came alive as exemplars of the contemporary life of each generation. But always with magic. Jim himself not only understands the tradition of the *Mabinogi*, he is quint-essentially part of it.

But these words I have written are exactly not the way to write about these things. I have been trying to abstract from, or rewrite in a colder and more dispassionate way, what is alive in Jim's way of writing. Becuase if there is one sense which emerges for me from his work, it is that he writes at the same time particularly, for a particular occasion or of a specific place, but in a way that always speaks for other places and times. The particular, for Jim, is never parochial. And the spirit is not some abstract universal. They are always spirits of place. Jim, like the *cyfarwydd* of the *Mabinogi*, is always himself the heart of the performance that he gives. And it is out of my love for the kind of spirit which Jim has that I make, in that very traditional Welsh way, an introduction.

Dafydd Elis-Thomas

Introduction

In the fourteenth district of Pest I sit in an early evening bar with garish wooden painted furniture. Trams clack through the dusk outside and the damp leaves fall as I talk to Ferencz Dyözö, poet and lecturer at Budapest's university. The waitress taps her pencil on the table, commanding orders:

'Barna', I request from the menu, enjoying its pouting, plosive 'b', the roll of its 'r'. She smiles incredulously, lets loose a volley of words.

'She's scolding you for wanting peasant beer,' Dyözö explains. 'You're a Westerner—you can afford better.'

I tell him I chose it because I like the sound, receive this response:

'This name, Barna, was on what do you say? Balls for tennis table? When I was at school in the old days they were very strict. I remember the teacher taking one of these from me, her foot coming down. Phut!'

Re-shaping the memory, his hands describe a form crumpled as the expression on his face. The beer arrives in tall bottles, the waitress pouring it with a coquettish, disapproving rock of the head.

'It means brown,' Dyözö says as I sample it, malty and porter-like under the froth.

'It means the gap,' I respond, 'in Irish', and tell him of a place called Barna in the townland of Roundstone in Connemara, and a famine graveyard there with the low sun picking out quartz boulders on children's burial plots. In my memory they are puckered-white and grounded as his ping-pong ball.

'Here's to the birth of hope, then, and not its death,' Dyözö nods, an ache of a look in his eyes, 'and before you go, make sure you visit Lot 301.'

In the Fatal—a busy, cheap eating place down an alley off Vaci Utca—noisy parties face down heaped plates of meat, cabbage, fried potatoes, vegetables in batter, and drain deep glasses. Nick Thorpe, the BBC World Service correspondent here, talks about a recording he made the week before. At Lot 301—the name crops up recurrently—he fell into conversation with a man sitting quietly. Why was he here? The man's in his forties, a moustache, thick greying hair. It's his father's grave. He last saw him, as a six-year-old, the night before he was executed. For taking part in the uprising? No—he was a medical student—they caught him distributing leaflets. They hanged him—not by the drop, but slowly. Twenty-five thousand dead—the worst European war between 1945 and Bosnia. He and his grandparents would go at night to put flowers on the grave. Next day they'd be scattered. Those who were seen—children, old people, women—were clubbed by the soldiers.

Tomcsanyi Laura brings up the subject of Lot 301 in a students' coffee bar. This lovely, voluble, edgy young woman offers to take me there because for her it is *the* text in which to read the last half-century of her country's history. A three-quarter-hour tram ride from Blaha Lujza Ter past Lowry factories and shabby apartment blocks brings us to the Ujköztemetö cemetery on the eastern outskirts of town. We enter past flower-sellers and walk down a long road, its margins illuminated with the funerary culture of Catholic Europe. All Souls' Night has just past, each grave left starred by firmaments of coloured, melted wax where the children, the old people, lit bouquets of candles to flicker against the dark. There are no signposts, but each sector of the enormous cemetery is numbered. As we penetrate further—a mile, a mile-and-a-half—the place becomes progressively more unkempt and overgrown, reverting to the birch heath of middle Europe. Listing monuments catch our eye amongst impenetrable brushwood, the road narrows. We bear left, concrete-lap fencing of the perimeter in front, jag suddenly right and it's ahead.

Prone small slabs amongst the grass, some with names, are flowered with the wax All Souls' Night blooms. The larger grave of Nagy Imre—leader of the uprising—is hung with ribbons, each one for a streetfighter of '56. The ones who didn't escape west, who were executed, were buried here, face down, hands and feet tied, amongst the zoo animals and the criminals.

In one of Konrad György's essays there is an anecdote that implies the extent of an oppression Hungary now often seems to look away from or revise. In a working-class district of Pest in 1959 he comes across women weeping. They've just been given permission to collect clothes and possessions of children who fought in the uprising, and whom the authorities watched and left for three years until they were of age to arrest and hang. The memorial for these and the rest of the resistance dead is in a clearing amongst wooded heathland, below the flight-path of jets as they climb and heel over for Paris, Warsaw or Berlin. It's like a passage grave, like a portal-dolmen in form, built from great slabs and blocks of soft, white oolite, preternaturally light in this sombre setting, a chalky deposit adhering in the whorls of your finger when you touch. Underneath a huge capstone, its top elaborated with stone curtain and slender obelisk (the latter veined with incipient cracks), a passage leads to a natural boulder behind, its great weight come to rest. In the boulder is a niche. No names are carved. The monument's stone at front and top is fine-dressed, gives way to coarse-chiselling at its rear, then the rooted, native rock—from show through texture to gravity. Fifty yards away across the grass is a sunken, stone-lined recess like a well, in it a squat hexagonal black marble pillar, polished, worked, oddly threatening and repellent. You stumble across it as afterthought. Evil, it reminds you, is omnipresent, watching, concealed. The resonance between cenotaph-dolmen and the pit-phallus is intense. The sculptor has created in them something perfectly expressive of their place, as puzzling as the co-existence in humanity of heroism and brutality. Around the clearing, ash-trees are heavy-keyed, acacia and cotoneaster spread, rooks fly across an autumn sunset and the harsh call of a pheasant comes from the wood. Ordinary people sidle together, sharing stories they—and we—need to hear.

There is nothing obviously beautiful about Lot 301, but out of its matrix there issues something that adds to our moral, our aesthetic awareness. It is a necessary place and I record my sense of it here, use it to introduce this book, through a belief that for our humanity's sake we need to ground our imagination in place and the life or memory that inhabits there. Synge wrote of his own plays that the 'drama is made serious not by the degree in which it is taken up with problems that are serious in themselves, but by the degree in which it gives the nourishment, not very easy to define, on which our imaginations live.'

For me, that taking of imaginative nourishment crucially proceeds from a vital engagement with the hidden drama of place. Often a word can spark it off, as *barna* set off between Ferencz Dyözö and myself a kind of unstated moral contemplation that crackled between the vile inhumanities of Imperial England towards Ireland (the insolent assurance of which continues, of course, as Roisin MacAliskey or the Birmingham Six would testify), and those of Soviet Russia towards Hungary.

These considerations clarify out through the process of haunting induction into *elsewhere* to some part of which feeling the classical writers gave the name *genius loci*. I remember sitting at this table where I now write, reading an obituary by Bill Webb in *The Guardian* of a publisher—Irish but resident in London—by the name of Tim O'Keeffe. Into the text crept an account of the publication by O'Keeffe of Patrick Kavanagh's *Collected Poems*. It's a volume that hasn't left my bedside in twenty years. I have its contents almost by heart, love the peculiar rhythm of its author's thought, the quirky unexpectedness of his character. In the obituary, there was a sketch of Kavanagh 'in the corner seat of The Plough on Museum Street to where O'Keeffe regularly trooped across from his office to drink his lunch.'

So instantly I was with him in my imagination, the mental pictures floating across of Bloomsbury, the pub, the smell and tenor of jokey conversation, the shared sense of exile between Cork publisher and Monaghan poet. Involuntarily, I began repeating to myself an exquisitely and perilously balanced poem of Kavanagh's entitled *Kerr's Ass,* in which a remembered slight incident—the borrowing of a neighbour's ass to take butter from his home in Mucker to Dundalk market, triggers off the following:

> The winkers that had no choke-band,
> The collar and the reins . . .
> In Ealing Broadway, London Town
> I name their several names
>
> Until a world comes to life—
> Morning, the silent bog,
> And the God of imagination waking
> In a Mucker fog.

Another word-inspired journey's thus made, from a Welsh hillside down to London, then into a man's mind that has found itself recalling his early manhood in Monaghan. I know exactly the feeling he describes and you'll have your own parallels: the excited stilling of the breath, the calling-up of detail that brings with it a wave of feeling, has place alive for you once more and glowing: the mist-pearled miniature red cushions of sundew you barely noticed at the time; the filmy vapour in the valley-bottom condensing out as the autumn day fades; the swoop of ridge above that by some magic transforms from shape into movement into music into actual physical sensation in response. Riches from chance co-incidence of names!

Spirit of place is so ubiquitous in the life of our imagination, is preoccupied there with re-creation along the paths of feeling of those places we have been in the past. But there is more to it than that. The moral dimension of landscape I mentioned above has a vital function. Against landscape, pretension properly fades. How can you hold to your petty ego and its little fears and desires in the face of the waves? In endorsing the fact of our insignificance, time's passage or the mountain storm bring a sort of peace. In these spheres we should not be lauding a facile and notional heroism based on the urge to conquest and the instinct to survive, but rather recognising the response encompassing truth, insight and respect, and the importance to us of awe and wonder. Times come when it is proper to still yourself and go down into the profound interplay of consciousness where common humanity, human history, and something beyond both of those inform each other. On the coast of Llŷn I know a set of steps cut once into the rock and smoothed by centuries of feet. They lead down to the wave-margin and to a well.

If you listen, the clamour of voices here, of wave-sound, tide-race, the stilled pre-Cambrian magma—a drowned girl's scream, a pilgrim's prayer, slap of a launched coracle, the crack and hiss of cooling rock—are co-existent along the flicker of time. It happened here, and so much else besides. The distillation of these events is the spirit of the place. You drink and are intoxicated and reel from one scene to another and the film goes on into the action of which you too have now been absorbed, that you will view again and again, having once been there. And perhaps each new viewing will bring more meaning, in despite of our fixed and immediate world, that demands the concrete and material, cannot accept the necessarily evanescent or the wisdom of the old Scottish verse that runs thus:

> I would not find,
> For when I find, I know
> I shall have clasped the wandering wind
> And built a house of snow.

These essays in my third collection are about place, about its inhabiting people, its histories, and the activities focusing there. They were written variously over the last six years for newspapers and magazines, as eulogy, address, or radio broadcast (in substantially revised form for which latter medium one essay from each of my last two collections appears, for continuity and perhaps for a new readership). Freed from constraint of the hasty deadlines for which they were first produced, they are here re-cast, considered and refined. The majority have a Welsh setting or frame of reference, Wales for the greater part of my life having been country of my heart and home, and the place the well-being and essential identity of which concerns me passionately. If there are more pieces about Wales and the people of that country who've shown me kindness since I came to live here 33 years ago, there are fewer pieces about mountain activity and its participants than in my last two collections. I make no apology for this. Though the mountains thrill and attract me now as much as they ever did, there are ways in which they are used, aspects of the culture of mountaineering and effects upon (or projections of) its

INTRODUCTION

personalities that I find increasingly shallow and vitiating, and the Way that predicates itself on the summit is narrow. Strait that gate may be, but it does not necessarily lead to righteousness, or wisdom, or peace—qualities that we come the more intensely to desire the further we go through life. These essays are not celebrations of quantifiable achievement, but of spirit. They are also explorations of character and landscape and attempts to express the delight I've experienced in pursuing those themes—and the puzzlement and sadness at times also. I hope you find some points of contact with them, and some remembered pleasures here and there too.

Dinorwig, 1997

Om Giri

1: 'IN THE REGIONS OF THE AIR'

Ruins

In the corner of a field in front of my house there is a ruin. Most of the time I barely notice it. A spill of gleaming slate and a bank of gorse, lemon-bright and coconut-scented, obscure it from view. Its outline is broken up by the copse of trees amongst which it stands. Sometimes on autumn mornings the mist that settles on the lake below laps in waves across the field running up to the ruin, and then the ash trees stand rather gaunt and aloof to remind you of its presence.

This morning, I walked my dog that way. She started a rabbit, chased it to a hole beneath the row of blackthorn separating field and house. I went after her to look around, ducked in through the former doorway, sheep dung crushed into its hollowed step. Inside, abrupt dry angles of elder crowded between the walls, probing up past the roof-tree's tenuous span. The floor was a litter of fallen slate, twigs and sheep's bones, the elders themselves so old their boles were mossy, encrusted with scaly mauve lichen and bearded with spleenwort, which sprouts too from the mortar of walls built sound, but not so sound that do not now crack, lean, cast off their topmost blocks at the urge and heave of sycamore roots that have delved beneath them and sent trunk and branch striving skywards, putting forth the bronzey leaves of spring from lime-green buds since the winged seed first landed here amongst rusting bucket, nettle and skull maybe half a century ago.

The farmer at some time has used the place as cowshed or stable, but even that order of things has gone. There is scarcely any memory amongst the present people of the village of who lived here. Of their place in the scheme of a former time, as little remains as of the crushed fragments of shells in the rough lime render of the walls. From my neighbour I find that the house is called Tŷ'n yr Ardd, from the small enclosure in front of it where the local children pick damsons in September. The fruit trees are skeletal now, dead wood for the most part, but pink-tipped buds are still hopeful amongst higher branches, where a dunnock sings. Morfydd tells me further of the *llyn corddi*—the churn-pool—behind the house, where in childhood springtimes she and her friends would gather frogspawn. Her grandmother and great-aunt, Jane and Catrin Williams, were born there in the 1890s. Shards of recollection, and these great stones that effort of leverage raised are sinking back into the vegetable life, the house-corpse subsumed into the ash-copse. *There was a brother, went to America,* Morfydd says . . .

All over the Welsh hills, in Cwm Brwynog and Cwm Caseg, in

Nanmor and the Nant Pasgan, in Cwm Pennant and Bugeilyn and Cwm yr Allt Lwyd you find these former homes, always the same, with the moss and the sheep dung and the ash-trees, spleenwort and herb Robert growing from the walls, and memory falling from them fragile and fragmented as crumbs of mortar on the flagged floor. Always there was a brother went to America or Wrexham, *Lerpwl* or *Dinas Llundain,* Salford, South Wales or Patagonia, leaving behind him walls to go to ruin, forced out by lack of opportunity, economic necessity, even marital difficulty.

What happened to them and where they went and what they took with them and all the small component parts that made up the sum of their lives are as forgotten now as the words spoken within these broken walls. I know this from my own family experience. My people come from those colliery terraces with the clean hills of Wales at their back which look down on Wrexham from the shoulder of Ruabon Mountain to the south-west. They come from Rhos, with its fine Welsh and its score of chapels and its great choir, and they left there in the years before the Great War, in the way that working people did throughout the ages, to find jobs in Salford, and to live amongst the chemicals and the effluent and the smog with which the Industrial Revolution, throughout its progress, poisoned its people and its planet.

I think of my paternal grandfather and the change in his life, the decision formed of necessity to make his way from Rhos to Salford and what it entailed for him and for the millions like him over the century-and-a-half up to his time who had had to follow the same path.

For my grandfather as a youth, there would have been the heather changing colour season to season on Ruabon and Esclusham Mountains; the rare mornings when their hillside stood out above the cloud sea; the times after chapel when he and his companions might have ranged over the moor past Mountain Lodge, down into the lovely green limestone valley with the cranesbill trailing from the walls and the tang of wild garlic on the air at World's End before they clattered back, hobnails sparking, along Gwter Siani and past Llannerchrugog Hall as the stars came out to reach Rhos again.

How much of this did he miss, down there in Salford by the ooze and stench of the Irwell? He took his language and his culture with him. Each Sunday after his death my grandmother still went to the *Capel y Bedyddwyr* on Plymouth Grove in Manchester—she and it long gone—to sing the old hymns in the Tongue of Heaven. How can my grandfather not have taken also the memory of the sky and the wide moor and the clouds billowing out of Wales—all those

'IN THE REGIONS OF THE AIR'

... in Cwm Pennant and Bugeilyn and Cwm yr Allt Lwyd you find these former homes.

glimpses of freedom that the tyranny of economics and maybe also the closeness and scrutiny of a small community forced him to barter? I think of my grandmother in her chapel pew singing out *'Ar lan Iorddonen ddofn'*—on the banks of Jordan deep—and wonder if ever a glimmer of her sly Welsh irony passed between these banks of imaginary promise and those of the Irwell on which she lived. And the names of her childhood—*Fron Deg, Bryn Goleu, Llwyneinion*—how did Factory Lane, Barrow Street and the East Ordsall Road compensate for the loss of those? Or for the liberty of walking on a spring morning over Esclusham Mountain, the loping hare kicking rainbows from the dew, England still unknown and beneath the damp oblivion of the cloud behind her. And as, unknown to them, on a thousand hillsides frost and storm and rain tore at the integrity of their former roof and hearth, how often would the thoughts of all the displaced have hovered around the sentiment of this plea:

> *A ninnau boed byw*
> *Yn ymyl gwisg Duw*
> *Yn y grug, yn y grug.*

'Let us live too/At the hem of God's garments/In the heather, in the heather.'

Radio Wales, 1995

SPIRITS OF PLACE

Caban

On the afternoon of a bright Sunday, as the *gweddill dewr*— the brave and ageing remnant of a congregation were singing '*O fryniau Caersalem ceir gweled*' in the vestry of Capel Sardis, I idled my way into the quarry. It's only just down the road from my house, but I don't go there that often. Even on a luminous day like this, I find it oppressive. In the gloom of a November afternoon it becomes unbearable. I think of the men whose brief, hard lives were spent wresting from the mountain the rock from which were carved rank upon rank of headstones in Deiniolen cemetery under which they now lie. And it saddens me. I think of the contrast between their harsh barracks, close housing, and the ostentation of Penrhyn, Vaynol, Glynllifon, and it sickens me.

But that's to take an entirely negative view, and a sunny day's enough to put anyone in a good humour. It searches out the whole range of turquoise and purples in a rock slandered by the description of being merely grey. It highlights fold and fracture, bodies them

Quarrymen's terrace, Bethesda

forth as abstract shapes that you realise with a sudden shock were the defining geometries of quarrymen's lives. Where one *bargen*'s regular and true, another's splintered and bent—nature's accidents dictating even the sufficiency of a child's daily bread.

It's all past, it's all finished now. Lacey brilliance of parsley fern colonises gaunt tips, the tiny stonecrop spreads bulbous and globular amongst razor litter of the terraces, rosettes of lichen encrust and emboss. A pair of choughs tumble and scream. Scratched initials from the last century hide shyly in the darkness of tunnels. There are trees rooting everywhere; a tenacious birch sapling trembles on a cliff-ledge, sycamores obscure the angles of an incline, by the old *caban* an ash tree grows.

I know it was a *caban* because Rennell Pritchard, who worked here years ago, told me so before his death. Not that there's much left of it now. The slates from the roof, the table and the workmen's rough benches were taken long since. The lime render is flaking and loose, nettles grow in the hearth and the inevitable, the ubiquitous spleenwort feathers the walls. I'm struck always by how small it is. Ten feet by twelve feet—no more than that. The small window looking out on to Snowdon and the lake is frameless, glassless now, and the door's gone. Yet the place still breathes or even whispers. If I stood here on a day when the mist muffles every sound and is so dull even the generator hum that now permeates this mountain is deadened, I think the old echoes would creep back warily to the place that gave them birth. There would be voices here again.

What would they talk of? As I stand here now, a quarter-century beyond the quarry's closure, perhaps a hundred years beyond the *caban*'s time, I see paragliders circling on thermals like garish raptors with their prey dangling; on rock slabs, climbers in vivid pastels pad and poise, delicate-footed where the facemen's hobnails sparked. This roofless room draws me away from that modern and modish world to the preoccupations of another time. What would they have talked about?

In the archives of the university college in Bangor, itself founded from quarrymen's subscriptions, there is the minute-book of a turn-of-the-century *caban*. *Llyfr Cofnodion hen giniawdy Sinc y Mynydd, Llechwedd*, it's entitled, and it runs from St Valentine's Day 1902 to mid-April 1905. I don't imagine that the workers of Llechwedd were significantly more or less intelligent than their counterparts at Dinorwig. I suppose the topics raised in a single month—that of October 1902—are pretty much representative of the thoughts, the interests, the mind-set and the mind-play of workmen in the slate industry at the time.

There's singing—either serious solos, or more playfully the musical contortionism of setting the words of *'O Fryniau Caersalem'*—that hymn again!—to the tune of *Crug-y-bar*. There's recitation—of a poem, having only read it twice; of an abbreviated *'Dafydd Brenin Israel'*. There are competitions on grammatical themes—read a passage from which all the punctuation had been removed, spell difficult words, create new ones. There are discussions—should ministers of religion have a lifetime's or a defined term's appointment to office; should the measures of the 1902 Education Act as they affect Wales be opposed; is the taking of a wife a matter of choice, or a necessity?

There are lectures too: 'How much greater is a man than a sheep' runs the title of one of them; in another, Owen Morris talks about his holidays. All this took place in dank tunnels, in crude huts two thousand feet up a mountain, in rain and wind, as the men slaked their thirst with bottles of cold tea and ate probably no more than dry bread. Yet, does that range of subjects, that desire to play and perform, that involvement with the issues of the day, that eagerness to live the life of the mind hold sway in Hotpoint's or Ferodo's works canteens today? Was the breadth, the awareness, the pride evinced through them an expression of their proud knowledge of difference, of cultural resistance, of intrinsic superiority to the vain, philistine and greedy proprietors who allowed them so meagre a living?

I look across the abandoned terraces to where the rock-climber moves up his bald slab. Out of adversity he produces elegance and grace, moving with a purpose, reaching his goal. In the jumble of scree beneath him, pipework which drove the cutting machines is twisted as though cardboard tubing. The walls totter, inclines sag wearily, their work done. At their head, the wooden drums are scored deep by the hauling wire. One day, the buttresses that hold their axles will collapse and, freed, they will bound crashing down into the encroaching oakwoods, from which, on this bright day, rises the green woodpeckers' crazed laughter. And after that release, once again there will be silence, and the wind. As I walk home down worn steps, I see the congregation dispersing from Capel Sardis vestry, the few, leaning on each other. Behind them, the carpet-pedalled harmonium too has wheezed into silence. There will be no more *'O Fryniau Caersalem'* when these have 'crossed the bar'.

Radio Wales, 1996

The Quest for Llech Ronw

The story in outline runs thus: a destiny is sworn upon Lleu Llaw Gyffes by his mother Aranrhod, that he shall never have a wife of the race that is now on this earth. So Gwydion the enchanter and Math the king conspire together when Lleu is a man to create for him out of the flowers of the meadowsweet, the oak and the broom the most beautiful and best endowed maiden that mortal ever saw. She is baptised Blodeuedd, and she is married to him, and Math gives to them for land all the territory of Eifionydd and Ardudwy. So they live together in the uplands of Ardudwy at Mur Castell, which is now called Tomen y Mur.

I love the way in which, in the Four Branches of the Mabinogion, the narrative locates so precisely, the topographical detail attaches so firmly to the features of each story. In consequence of this, the landscapes themselves still resonate with the sense of character and action. And nowhere is this more pronounced than in the masterpiece of the art of the *cyfarwyddion*—the itinerant medieval storytellers—that gives the history of Lleu Llaw Gyffes and goes under the title of *Math Fab Mathonwy*.

Let's recount as much of the tale as concerns us here. Lleu and Blodeuedd are installed in Mur Castell; one day he leaves her to visit Math. A hunt passes by Mur Castell in his absence. At the dimming of the day, bloodied and tired, its members return past the court. Blodeuedd observes the duty of hospitality and invites them in. Its leader is a nobleman, Gronw Bebyr, Lord of Penllyn:

'Blodeuedd looked on him, and the moment she looked there was no part of her that was not filled with love of him. And he too gazed on her, and the same thought came to him as had come to her. He might not conceal that he loved her and he told her so. She knew great joy at heart. Nor did they delay longer than that night ere they embraced each other. And that night they slept together.'

How simply the storyteller manages the transition from creature of utility to object of desire, but in the moral frame through which he works there is always a cost to the consummation of desire, and an awareness of the instability it brings. Gronw and Blodeuedd conspire to kill Lleu. He enjoys magical protection. She finds out in the privacy of their bedchamber how to accomplish his murder: a spear worked at through the course of a year only whilst people are at Mass on a Sunday; a bath on the bank of a river, framed over and thatched, and Lleu must stand with one foot on the rim, the other on the back of a billy-goat—only thus, and with the spear, can he be killed.

Blodeuedd sends word to Gronw. The spear is made. She prepares the bath under the lee of Bryn Cyfergyr on the bank of Afon Cynfal; she secures the goat; she asks Lleu under pretence of fearing for his life to show her the position. Gronw conceals himself. Lleu, smiling no doubt from intimacy of the bath and his wife's foolish concern, raises his foot to the goat's back. The spear shears through his side. With a terrible scream, in the form of an eagle he flies away, leaving Gronw and Blodeuedd to hasten off to passion's bed.

But Math and Gwydion hear of the deed, and Gwydion searches through Gwynedd and Powys for the eagle. A sow leads him to the foot of a tree in Nantlle where she feeds on maggots and rotten flesh which rain down from an eagle in the topmost branches. Gwydion recites *englynion* to the bird:

> *Dar a dyf y rwng deu lyn,*
> *Gorduwrych awyr a glyn,*
> *Oni dywedaf i,*
> *O flodau Lleu ban yw hyn.*

('Grows an oak between two lakes/Shadowed is the sky and valley/If I speak true/From Lleu's flowers this comes.')

He lures the bird down, restores it to the form of Lleu, brings him back to health at the court of Math, and together they muster a force of armed men and set out for Mur Castell to seek redress. Blodeuwedd hears of their coming and flees across the mountains with her handmaidens. Always looking behind them out of fear, they fall into a lake, now called Llyn y Morynion, where all drown with the exception of Blodeuedd alone, whom Gwydion turns into an owl—Blodeuwedd, the flower-faced—bird of night and lonely voice.

For Gronw Bebyr, that which he gave, he must now receive, and so he stands in the place where Lleu stood when the spear was cast, to take the blow in his turn. But he asks—forgetting that the scheme was of his own devising—whether he might interpose a stone between himself and the spear's flight, since he was led to this pass by a woman's wiles. The request is granted, the stone raised, the warrior's arm draws back, his eye glittering on its target. The spear sails, pierces stone and flesh, breaks the deceiver's spine, and the story ends in these words:

> *Ac yna y llas Gronw Bebyr, ac yno y mae y llech ar lan Afon Cynfal yn Ardudwy, a'r twll drwydi. Ac o achos hynny eto y galwir Llech Gronw.*

Llyn y Morynion, where all drown with the exception of Blodeuedd alone.

('And so Gronw Bebyr was slain, and there the stone is on the bank of Afon Cynfal in Ardudwy, and the hole through it. And because of that, it is still called Llech Gronw.')

Thus the folk-tale—what of the stone, of which I can find no record in the books and guides, which seems to have slipped from between the leaves of this volume of the landscape's story? Does it still exist, in the lee of Bryn Cyfergyr, on the banks of Afon Cynfal?

'A large, old-fashioned house, standing near the church', is how Borrow describes the Pengwern Arms in Llan Ffestiniog, and it still fits the exterior. Inside, however, it belies the surface gloom and shows a bright, sunny aspect. I'd arranged to meet Antony Griffiths here on a fine May morning. An attractive young barmaid with a jewelled stud in her right nostril served us with tea, then balanced on a stool a foot or two away to adjust a clock on the wall. She glanced down to catch me in the benign study of her muscular calf, and smiled conspiratorially at the appreciation. Antony put on his look of amused disapproval. Spring was in the air. I'll bet the year was in its blooming when Gronw Bebyr met Blodeuedd.

Antony is the son of Bill Griffiths, who was the best field archaeologist of his generation in Wales. Antony himself has inherited his father's feel for the stories written in to the texture of a landscape. I can't imagine a better companion with whom to take up the quest for Llech Ronw, but the question was, where should we begin? I'd tried to find the stone, if it still existed, before, and without success. Neither of us knew of any reference to its still being in place on the banks of Afon Cynfal, and if Antony doesn't know of any mention of it in any of the topographical literature of Wales, then my instinct would be that none exists. Certainly I'd combed the banks of the stream in the past and found nothing that imagination could shape to fit the story's detail.

That doesn't mean there weren't clues. Blodeuedd bids Gronw be under the lee of the hill called Bryn Cyfergyr. So our first recourse is to the 1:25,000 map of Cwm Cynfal. There is no Bryn Cyfergyr marked on it, but what are these names: Nant y Beddau, Bryn Saeth, Bryn yr Helfa—stream of the graves, hill of the arrow, hill of the hunt—aren't those likely associations with Bryn Cyfergyr—the hill of battle, and with the story of Lleu, Blodeuedd and Gronw? And what's this? Llech Goronwy? It's not by the river. It's not marked in the Gothic script that would denote a site of antiquity. But it is on Sarn Helen as it leads up from Cwm Cynfal to Mur Castell, and with that name, we cannot but look.

What we find is this. A two-storied house, perhaps a hundred and fifty years old, in a salient of clear ground which thrusts in amongst the conifers. It faces north-west, looking across the Vale of Ffestiniog to the rough skyline of the Moelwynion. There are sheds, enclosures for animals, but we notice as we approach that it all has a seedy, deserted look. We peer in through cracked window pane. There's money been spent here on poor workmanship and poor taste, and now it's sagging into gimcrack decrepitude. Sad tokens lie scattered around. A child's soft toys, discarded and rain-sodden on the grass, speak of hasty departure. In a rotting outhouse, case upon case of empty bottles, and more of them peek up from beneath splintered floorboards. What dreams of bucolic bliss turned sour in this place, we wonder? What brutalities, what isolation, what betrayals? Blodeuedd's alone with three children and on the dole; Lleu's gone off to Birmingham with the family Giro to buy dope; Gronw's racing his Escort along the forestry tracks; the old engines power a tawdrier tale. Of the pierced stone, there's no sign.

We return along the tyre-adorned stream to the valley, try our luck with Bron Goronwy. We knock, a man comes to the door. Llech Goronwy? Oh, yes. A man from the Midlands, was it—bad feeling—he blocked off footpaths, threatened those who passed, wanted seclusion. He rolled his tractor and was crushed dead beneath it. A woman came with children, Dutch maybe, didn't last. The local dope-heads come and go, squat there, cause damage. Nobody knows who owns it now.

Yes, we urge, but the stone—what of the stone? Used to be in the wall of a field, he thought. Oh, yes, it still exists—or did. At Bryn Saeth they'd know. It's up there somewhere, not down by the river. We thank him, cross the river again and make our way back to Bryn Saeth. Outside the farmhouse a woman is on her knees chopping wood. Does she know where we might find Llech Ronw? *'Dacw, yn y gornel ym mhen pella'r maes.'* Yes, we can cross the field to it, watch the dog with the sheeps, use the gate there, look for it by the stream at the bottom of the wood.

In high excitement we hasten across the field and climb the fence into the wood's corner. At first we see nothing unusual. A little cascading stream flows down slabs velvety with moss and confettied with wood anemones. No stone. A trough, though, in the stream, a natural bath, rimmed, coverable. Planes of reality shift for an instant and I glimpse Blodeuwedd tethering the goat to a root. No stone! Antony sets off to climb the bank of the stream, but I stand quietly brooding on the story that is always on the verge of beginning.

At my feet!

I call to Antony. The stone! It is like a cleaver with a great eye, like a helmet, like a primitive sinister thing. Yes, Gronw Bebyr could have raised this to protect himself. It is a *llech*—a slab, foliate, four inches thick, five feet high, a shaped hole of six-inch diameter at head level. It lies prone amongst a drift of oak-leaves with earth only at the back of its terrible eye. We look around. Unobtrusive detritus of modernity—a blue plastic pipe, mossed concrete. But in the wall, by the stream, everywhere, blocks of white quartz not from this vicinity, and shaped stone.

Our trinity of passion melds to a stranger loss. The site was plundered, enriched by explanation. A spear quivers across eternal air, pierces its woman's place. The shrieks have been caught into silence. At twilight, Blodeuwedd floats down on hushed, pale feathers from her tree to grasp in needle talons the scurrying vole.

Radio Wales, 1996

Drinking with Dervla

This is a tale of three bicycles—or maybe four, if you count the Third Policeman's, but he doesn't really come into the story except as a principle, and we can ignore those for the moment. It takes place in Ireland—a place to which I go frequently, especially since the alternative, going the other way, is to arrive in England and I'm not sure I'd like that.

The first bicycle belongs to me. It has an engine. I started it up one morning and roared off to Holyhead to catch the ferry. On board, I bought a litre of the 10-year-old Bushmills and stowed it away in my rucksack, because I was going visiting. Several hours later my bicycle and I disengaged with difficulty after the long miles south through Arklow and Enniscorthy. As Flann O'Brien sagely remarks in *The Third Policeman*, 'People who spend most of their natural lives riding iron bicycles over the rocky roads of this parish get their personalities mixed up with the personalities of their bicycle as a result of the interchanging of atoms of each of them . . .' In our case, this metemcyclosis was well under way. If anyone had asked my name, I'd have told them it was Suzuki, and as for the bicycle, well, I can't answer for her, but I will tell you that there was a familiar at hand.

Our second bicycle—it will be some time before we get to the third—was very slowly traversing the pavements of Lismore with an aged man listing alongside. Would he happen to know where to find Dervla Murphy's house, I asked? He took off his cap, folded it carefully into the inside pocket of his gabardine coat, scratched a point not at the precise middle of his tonsure, exhaled several deep gusts of porter, and with grave due deliberation informed me that he did not, and was that the writer-woman? At which point a passer-by, an alert young woman with a good-humoured face like the Secular Mary's—all Ireland, you should understand, is ruled by two Marys, and my preference is for Mrs Robinson rather than the BVM—interposed herself between us: 'If it's Dervla Murphy you're wanting, turn in the arch here, go up between the bar and the ironmongers, round the back and you'll be grand.'

The man replaces his cap as he nods at and digests this piece of information, adding his assurance to hers that I'll be grand. I ease myself back into the saddle, trickle up the alleyway, and am confronted by Dervla Murphy. She's a sturdy, wiry woman in her sixties, her face tanned and very little lined, a scatter of iron-grey curls with a pronounced widow's peak, and eyes that are dark hazel, guarded beneath wild brows, piercingly intent and keen. She leads me into a book-lined room where we usurp cat-laden chairs. There's a round table, ethnic rugs, small vivid icons. I produce the whiskey, and the drinking concomitant on any visit to Ireland begins. Parameters of vocabulary are established—also important in Ireland, where every other word is a version of one not to be used in the politest company. We clash tumblers on a mutual detestation of certain politicians and all their works; and then, in a sonorous, deep voice with a high, grating, amused inflection on key words, she starts to interview me. I protest that it should be the other way round, but she presses on.

Is there otter-hunting in Britain, she asks? Not legally, I tell her, though the packs of otter-hounds still hunt mink, and as yet are capricious in distinguishing between the two. She recounts how, every morning from March to October, she goes down to the Blackwater to swim. There are otters along the bank, and if they see her approaching on foot, they disappear instantly, but if she swims round the bend in the river, they'll dive in and play around her, the whole family group sometimes within feet of her.

I tell her in response of watching badgers in a beechwood on moonlit nights, of the bounce and glisten of their coats, their innocent play and those beautiful markings accentuated in the silver light. She asks why I use the past tense. I explain that in the 1980s every badger sett I knew apart from two in the wildest places was dug, tell her the prices animals are said to fetch for baiting, conclude by commenting that though she will think it far-fetched, that seems to me the inevitable trickle-down effect of brutal and uncaring example in government. She retorts that it's the simple truth, and tragic that people are only now beginning to realise the effect of having had someone like 'T'hatcher'—she spits the word out with a glottal stop—in power for so long.

After this joint tirade, we eat—thick soup, moist soda-bread with nuts in it, crusty cheeses—and we drink a great deal—wine first, and then cider, the whiskey having gone. At two in the morning, by the cat-purred fire in the lamplight, the Guinness appears and I ask—by now not altogether coherently—about the relevance to her case of the black bicycle, which those of you who know Ireland will accept as one of the enduring symbols of the place—male, upright and motionless. All Ireland, I suggested, was contained within the frame of this bicycle, so when she mounted hers in 1963 and rode off on the solo journey to India that she describes in her first book, *Full Tilt*, had she determined to appropriate and subvert the image?

'How so?' she humoured me.

Because in her hands, I went on, the bicycle becomes female and

Dervla in her alley

subtle, like Irish society under the froth, it becomes the quixotic steed Rozinante, becomes a thirty-year continuum of living contradictions to the society from which she grew, becomes the means of expression and travel and escape from her Catholic and finely cultured, beautiful, barbaric, narrow, circumscribed and enchanted homeland of the black bicycles. I'd just finished when the two cathedral clocks of the place began to strike an asynchronous 3 a.m. We reeled out into a blackness riddled with stars:

'Sure, we're very drunk tonight,' she shot after me as I swayed away to my room, 'but we'll walk it off tomorrow!'

'C'mon, wake up, wake up!'

I'm shaken out of my slumbers, ordered on my feet from where I've collapsed fully dressed the previous night, and with barely time to pull on the motor-cycling boots which are the only footwear I have with me, and no time at all to gulp down any breakfast, am marched out before eight o'clock into a morning of towering clouds and brief illumination by the sun with the explanation that if we're not on the road soon we'll spend the rest of the day feeling very ill. I'm feeling very ill anyway, and Dervla Murphy's spirited commentary on the heritage industry, on Fintan O'Toole's notion of how the Irish are being made tourists in their own land, and on the history of Lismore castle is not falling on entirely receptive ears.

Beyond the Blackwater bridge we branch off up a steep, narrow lane rising as relentlessly as Dervla's morning conversation through woods. The hill-ridge of the Knockmealdowns ahead is dull brown and faded purple under its clouds. Much of the good land around us is derelict—undrained, untilled, a square field here and there shiny olive-green with Eurograss, which rouses Dervla to vituperative comment against Maastricht and the Common Agricultural Policy. We halt by a dilapidated farmstead. She eyes ruefully the tumbledown buildings, the nettle-grown midden, the litter of fertiliser bags and the pyramid of plastic-encased Euro-silage, gestures me on up the road and, as if to pass comment, goes into a gateway to pee. I come across a black bicycle lounging in a hedge, its owner painting a fieldgate obscured by vegetation in raincloud grey. I bid him good morning as Dervla joins us:

'This land's in poor shape,' she accuses him.

'Ah yes, it's in poor shape, but there's not many of the grants now, see,' he explains.

She flashes a frame of the basilisk glare he receives at me, to let me know what she thinks, and as we continue up the road tells me of the farmer by the house where she used to live, to whom she took her jug to be filled with fresh milk every morning until the day when he told her, crying with anger and frustration, that he was no longer allowed to do it. From this—when Dervla warms to a theme the examples come tumbling out—she moves on to tell of a lift she once had, hitch-hiking from London to one of the channel ports, in a refrigerated lorry. She'd asked what was being carried; bacon, came the reply, to Denmark, to have its stamp rubbed out, replaced with a Danish one, and be re-imported to Britain.

'Can you work that one out?' she challenges me.

'No, nor that one either,' I answer, pointing away from the good, idle land towards a digger on EU grant work draining a bleak field at the edge of the bog. We carry on walking under the ridge of the Knockmealdowns with Dervla swinging her shoulders and shuffling along at a pace of five miles an hour, to keep up with which I'm forced into a loping, suppressed run. After twenty miles of this we arrive at a pub by the name of The Cats, and since it's now mid-day and rain dogs us, we duly go in. She orders pints of Guinness and whiskeys and taxes the barman on the abortion issue, the referendum on which is about to take place. He's called Michael, and he tip-toes delicately round the point under her withering gaze, making most clear his respect for the clergy. She passes on impatiently to an interrogation about the nearby Melleray grotto, where the statue of the Blessed Virgin had been seen to move and heard to speak a decade ago.

Again, Michael blathers, tells us how the church distanced itself from the supposed miracle and Mary's 'message', but so as not to leave us with an impression of someone devoid of wonder, recounts the experience of 'a man he knew', a sufferer from Motor Neurone Disease, who had gone to visit Father Athanasius at Mount Melleray monastery, 'and he came away entirely healed, and hasn't suffered from that day to this.' Michael left us at this dramatically opportune moment, leaving Dervla to tell me that she didn't discount the healing potential in the laying-on of hands, and insisting that I finish up the third or fourth pint that we might go to the grotto.

It was half a mile down the road. There was an information stall, a toilet block, a vast car park and an immense glass-topped collection box full of high-denomination bank-notes. At the head of a wooded gully was the statue of Mary. Groups entered, gazed up at her expectantly for three or four minutes, retreated to empty purse and wallet into the box with quick, fervent glances back over their shoulders. A continual susurrus of subdued voices followed them, phrases recurring, voiced entreaties drifting into the glade:

The true sign of a democratic spirit

'Holy Mary . . . intercede . . . hour of our deaths . . . Breeda Guiney sufferin' terrible from the rheumatics.' I'm sent to ask where the donations go whilst Dervla disappears for a pee. The woman in the information stall smiles encouragingly as I sidle up, agrees that it's a lovely place, informs me how blessed they've been with the visit from the Queen of Heaven.

'And the money?' I ask. 'Where does that go?'

I snatch my fingers out of the way as the grille descends.

'It's all ploughed back into the grotto, and we're closing now.'

Dervla shuffles over. I report back the response.

'Does it fuck,' she snorts, and taps my beret with a knowing, odd look. She hauls us disapprovingly away. We return home by a short-cut of fifteen miles through Cappoquin. My feet ache but I dare not complain. After thirty-five miles taken at a near-run I drag off my boots, prick and drain hot blisters with a safety pin before re-joining Dervla for the anaesthesia of whiskey-talk. We drag off to bed long after midnight. Next morning at six she's at work. Long after that I emerge on to the street in search of a chemist. I ask for sticking plasters:

'What would you be wanting those for?'

'Blisters.'

'Where have you got blisters, now?'

'On my feet.'

'How did you go getting blisters on your feet?'

'I was out walking.'

'Oh, you were out walking! Who were you out walking with?'

'I was out with Dervla Murphy.'

'You were out wit' Dervla Murphy! No wonder you've got blisters—a young fella like you and her a seasoned walker. I'll sell you the plasters, and I'll give you some aspirin for the hangover, too!'

Radio Wales, 1996

Peregrinations

Along all the great walkers' highways of my youth there were scores of people whose rucksacks were every inch of them covered over with felt badges of the places they'd been, the journeys they'd completed, the youth hostels in which they had stayed. I used to admire them tremendously, maybe even covet them a little: I don't see them any more. But I was reminded of the fashion for them by a picture I came across in a history book I was reading the other day. It was of a thirteenth-century badge of the head of John the Baptist, of which relic Amiens cathedral had the care. What struck me was the similarity between this simple medieval badge, and those tokens of achievement sought after and worn to this day by those who complete the Welsh Fourteens, the Ascent of Snowdon, the Munros or whatever.

So by extension I wondered whether there might be a similarity of impulse between the medieval pilgrim and the modern recreational walker. How, though, can we know what comprised the medieval impulse towards pilgrimage, and equally how we can generalise about the motives of those who, in modern times, undertake significant journeys on foot?

Few aspects of the Middle Ages, in fact, were as well documented as the acts of pilgrimage which enjoyed their heyday in that time. In the centuries between the fall of Rome and the Reformation, from all the surviving sources on which history draws the sense comes down of a restless movement of scholars, poets, princes and the wealthier of the ordinary people backwards and forwards between Loretto, Assisi, Walsingham, St David's, Canterbury, Ynys Enlli, Santiago de Compostela, Jerusalem (the Crusades, remember, were effectively armed pilgrimages), in search of—what?

The simple—perhaps facile—answer is spiritual enrichment, and that in itself raises a beautiful paradox. These journeys of a distance, harshness, discomfort, danger and difficulty almost unimaginable to us cossetted dwellers of the late twentieth century were steps towards the state of Grace. Those who've studied the subject tell us that nomadic peoples do not go on pilgrimage. There is enough uncertainty already in their lives, runs the argument. These authorities say it's a phenomenon found only in settled communities that have reached a high state of cultural development. That ease, the reasoning goes, produces a reaction which desires insecurity, labour, the mortification of the flesh.

So the simple paradox runs that in the comfort of material things lies temptation and sin, in the austerity of the journey whose object is reverence lies salvation. And yet, I still get a sense from the records of medieval pilgrimage of something beyond all this—the unspoken reason, the passion unstated for which these hardships of the journey were to be endured. There's another way in which this comes out in the teachings of the Church, and that's through the bitter antagonism time and again displayed by it towards beauty, poetry, nature—all those unquantifiable, evanescent lures to the soul which steal through the defences of dogma and—literally—

annotate the margins of written religion from the so-called 'Dark Ages'. Paganism it was dismissed as, and the strictures against it came hard and early. Paulinus of Nola, at the beginning of the fifth century, gives the clearest statement:

'Not only pagan literature, but *the whole appearance of things as apprehended by the senses* is the lotus flower; so men forget their own land, which is God, the country of us all.'

To the early Church, instead of the austerity of Lucretius's rapture of denial that anything exists beyond the incandescent beauty of the world, there comes the self-absorbed quest for personal salvation; instead of the exquisite loveliness of those lines from Virgil's *Georgics* where he describes the blue smoke rising at evening from the little farms as, one by one, they're engulfed by the shadow of hills stretching across the plain—lines that are profound in their simple worship of divine creation—there comes consideration of how many angels can dance on the head of a pin.

As the great age of pilgrimage got under way, there came about in the teachings of the Church that was its chief promoter a curious disjunction between a journey's object, and the actuality of the landscapes it must traverse. The pilgrim's eye must not be seduced by the Great Illusion which is the World's glory. Yet how could the eyes of those travellers to Santiago de Compostela not have been ravished by the distant Picos or the wild coasts of Finisterre? What splendour of light illuminated for them the crossings of the Alps on the path to Rome? Did those who journeyed to Enlli not look on the curved lines of the sandbars, the clamorous birds, the clear water and the bronze-leaved oakwoods of spring beyond with a certain gladness as they followed their guides on the perilous crossing of the great Traeth? And years later, as they held their cockleshell mementoes to their ears, did they not hear with infinite pleasure the soughing of the waves against the cliffs, as surely as the London child looks on his or her Snowdon badge and sees again the great arm of land stretching out to Enlli and beyond, and both of them arriving thus at that truly religious sense of wonder at the actual, arriving at the wisdom that it is not the journey's object but the journey itself that matters, along the course of which the incidental can be the transcendent?

The objects, after all, change generation to generation. The paths up Snowdon have worn the slopes threadbare. Who can say that future ages will not return the mountain to its former solitude? Two holy wells I know on the pilgrims' path along the Llŷn peninsula would, six centuries ago, have been bustling and venerated; now one of them is trampled by cattle, drained by a plastic pipe, crowned by a broken fence; across the steps carved in rock down to

... trampled by cattle, drained by a plastic pipe, crowned by a broken fence: Ffynnon Ddunawd, Llŷn

the other—three pilgrimages to which equalled one to Rome—the slow, sun-tinted lichen grows like tattoos on a Jew's-skin shade. Life moves on, nomadically, leaving such places behind as were once accorded reverence, forever re-defining its objectives and the nature of its journeys, whilst the journey itself, in wonder of renewal and the renewal of wonder, winds ahead.

Radio Wales, 1995

Llama Farmer

There is an ancient path traverses the west side of Nanmor. It tacks loosely in and out of the relict oakwoods. Its worn stones like crude stitching fasten the peaty levels of a hanging valley to the strewn boulders of the hillside. I was out walking this path in the rain one day several years ago, when—most alarmingly—I ran into a llama.

It was the Peruvian and not the Tibetan variety, and it was eyeballing me from a distance of six feet. Which, given the known habits of these creatures, was not conducive to comfort and security. However, I stood my ground, he came over to make a closer inspection, tolerated my overtures of affection—a very tentative stroking of his muzzle—and soon decided that I was of no further interest. So he stalked away, casting a haughty eye this way and that. I thought it a very strange encounter.

There was a stranger one awaiting me around the next corner.

A man, short and powerfully built, dressed in waterproof leggings, balaclava and an old, waxed-cloth jacket, was plunging the blade of a long-handled spade into the peat, digging a hole, a sinister dark bundle waiting alongside. He felt himself being watched, turned round. I saw eyes glittering hazel with a strange grey rim to the iris, and a face of great mobility and intelligence.

'You're Paul Work, aren't you?' I quizzed. I introduced myself, helped dig the hole and bury the bundle—a sheep's carcase in a black bag (from which detail alone it was obvious this was no ordinary hill farmer, as bones whitening across every Welsh mountain slope attest). We talked for an hour and more bare-headed in the rain, and I took him up thereafter on his invitation to visit. He lived at Carneddi—place of stones—the hill farm the family of his wife, the writer Ruth Janette Ruck, bought in 1945, and about which she wrote two books, *Place of Stones* and *Hill Farm Story*, that have not been out of print since their first publication and are haunted, in one reviewer's colourful phrase, 'by the Heathcliff-like presence of Mr. Work'.

There is no more idyllic place in Wales than Carneddi. The farm track climbs from Traeth Gwyllt—the wild estuary—to the old house 500 feet up on the shoulder of Moel y Dyniewyd. It faces south amongst lovingly tended gardens, with a poet's plaque above the door. More of the llamas, their reputation for spitting ferocity quite undeserved, nuzzled you for food as you entered the yard. Sleek Welsh Black cattle, cowbells round their necks, swayed sonorously at Paul's call into their wooden stalls under the beams of a medieval barn where he milked them by hand. Even the farm dogs were peaceful apostates from the psychopathic tendency of their breed. If ever there was an argument for the beneficence of natural beauty, it located here.

After the first time I used to go quite regularly to visit Paul there. He was an intensely interesting talker, could recall even over distances of sixty years and more with the sharpest clarity details of events in his life. So these kitchen *conversaziones* at Carneddi, by the old brown Aga which had warmed new-born lambs by the hundred, became one of the pleasures of mine. One of the most interesting aspects of talking with older people is the sense of a different world and a differing set of values that comes through in their conversation. I always feel uncomfortable with the assumption to which younger people have a tendency that theirs is the only possible time, theirs the only possible activities, in which interest should be taken, and theirs the only values to which humanity might reasonably subscribe. This isn't to denigrate how they think and what they do, but merely to query the depth of their focus. I never had any such problem with Paul Work. He told of what interested himself; he sought out what interested others. And what he had to say interested me. For the most part, our talk would circle round a common devotion to the sport of rock-climbing. But since that pursuit's always had a lively metaphorical dimension, and since the characters involved, particularly in the phase of exploration in the 1930s to which Paul was witness, were particularly varied and idiosyncratic, it would embroider widely across that central thread.

Paul was born into a Cheshire family who farmed on the Welsh borders. His father died young and mother and children moved to Formby, on the Lancashire coast, from which the mountains of Snowdonia stand out against the sunset. There was another interesting family living in Formby in the 1920s. The father was George Zachary Edwards, a clergyman who'd retired because of ill health. His wife Helen was an artist and a woman of formidable intellect whose airing of Douglas's social credit theory on the distribution of the nation's wealth rather alienated her from the true-blue community of west Lancashire. Her daughter Nowell went on to marry Hewlett Johnson, the Red Dean of Canterbury, but it was the youngest of the family's three sons who exercised the most profound influence on Paul. His name was Menlove Edwards, and he became the most significant of rock-climbing pioneers from the pre-war epoch, and the finest of all writers about his sport. Paul's memory of the family is distinctly unsolemn:

'We called them Stalky & Co. and Menlove we called Beetle. They used to play trains with the hymn books and Menlove would always push them harder so that they'd fall off and disrupt the sermon.'

Paul could pull fascinating characters out of memory's hat almost at will: 'Have you heard of Millican Dalton,' he asked me once, and went on to explain that he was an eccentric, the self-styled 'Professor of Adventure', who lived in a cave in Borrowdale: 'He made his own clothes and equipment and he never washed. My mother was engaged to him for a while but she broke off the engagement eventually. She said that he had rather a strong goaty aroma. But Millican took no offence, and when she married my father he made them a tent for their honeymoon, in the gipsy style, with hoops rather than poles. Later he made me a rucksack that I used until well on into the thirties. In the winter he organised what I suppose would now be called instructional weekends in survival techniques. They took place in Epping Forest. My father painted a portrait of him in watercolour that I still have. So you see, from my mother I had a good grounding in the outdoors.'

I once asked Paul how he came to take up rock-climbing. He replied that as a child he had been disfigured, in consequence of which he discovered a preference for his own company. When pressed, he explained that the disfigurement had originally been an attack of ringworm, now easy to cure. In the inter-war period the remedy was less straightforward—a course of radiation, causing two large bald patches on his head that lasted throughout his schooldays. There was a moment's pause in his account, a temporary shadow from the recollection of emotional pain. He recovered and talked of his cricket coach at preparatory school:

'He was a man called Gardner, and couldn't lift his arm above his shoulder as a result of a climbing accident in which his skull had been fractured. One day he gave us a slide talk about mountaineering, and from that moment onwards I was sold. I climbed every tree on the school playing fields, was given the Abraham brothers' book, *Rock Climbing in North Wales* for my

SPIRITS OF PLACE

The Christmas Buttress climb on Moel y Dyniewyd

next birthday. I soon had its descriptions by heart, and when I was fourteen turned up at Idwal Cottage with another boy of the same age. When Connie Alexander opened up the hostel—for we'd arrived early—she burst out laughing at the sight of us. But she was kind to us, and soon I was a regular there, and became friendly both with Menlove Edwards and Colin Kirkus, who were the great Welsh rock-climbing pioneers of their time. I remember that we used at weekends to catch the Liverpool-to-Bangor bus, which stopped for ten minutes for a cup of tea halfway at the Central Arms, Corwen. Colin used to up-end bowls on the table and pick them up with the friction of those great, long, immensely strong fingers of his.'

'By how small a speck,' wrote James Boswell, 'does the painter give life to an eye.' In detail like the above, Paul brought alive for me the characters from the great decade in the development of climbing on the Welsh cliffs. They've gone—Kirkus shot down in his Wellington bomber in 1942, Menlove Edwards by swallowing cyanide sixteen years later. And Paul's gone too. The last time I saw him was four years ago. There were springtime birdsong harmonies as I drove up to Carneddi. White blossom on the blackthorn trees was scattered across the hillslopes. Paul's 73rd birthday had just passed. We had intended honouring a long-standing arrangement to climb his classic little route of Christmas Buttress on Moel y Dyniewyd together, on the crag above the sheep-pens where the falcons watch for unsuspecting pigeons traversing the wide shoulder of the hill. But rain threatened, despite the fitful sunshine which brought a flickering illumination to the flowers in his garden, and we sat there instead. Paul was tired, troubled by an old leg injury, not looking forward to the hip-replacement operation he was to undergo later in the year. So we just talked.

I remember we touched on the alarmingly high incidence of cancers downwind of the nuclear power station at Trawsfynydd, and shared sardonic laughter at official explanations of the same, that dismiss any connection between the two or ascribe it all, regardless of date, to Chernobyl. I taped an hour's conversation with him for a series on Radio Four, and when I played it back to my producer, he shook his head in pleasure at the hesitant rich *timbre* of Paul's voice. In front of us, Cnicht's sharp ridge played hide and seek amongst the mists. Paul's pet peacock spread its unearthly, glistening tail across an errant shaft of sunlight. I never saw him again. He went into hospital for his operation, cancer of the bone marrow was discovered, and in a matter of weeks he and all the wealth of his memory were gone. He was buried up near the top of Beddgelert's little cemetery on the side of Moel Hebog. I go there sometimes to put flowers on his grave, conscious of the privilege of having known him.

Radio Wales, 1996

The Diver

The first time I saw him, for a him I'm sure he was by his very cocksureness upon the water, was in late December. He was feeding in one of the deep lagoons the tide leaves around Trwyn Penrhyn. Not that red-throated divers are all that uncommon on the north Wales estuaries and mudflats—most winters there are a few, down from Iceland or the Hebrides, to be seen at Traeth Lafan or on the Dyfi, or here on the Dwyryd. But this was a magnificent specimen. The pearl braiding across his dark back glistened in the low winter sun, and despite this winter plumage he still had the rusty-red throat markings from which the name derives.

I sat and watched him fishing, often as little as ten or twenty yards away. Occasionally, if he caught sight of me and became momentarily anxious, he would sink down in the water, head uptilted at a suspicious angle, and then, with an arched, serpentine spasm of neck and body, would disappear underwater for minutes at a time to re-surface forty or fifty yards away. Frequently over the last few weeks I've seen him, up and down the estuary, never terribly cautious of my presence.

It's an enthralling place at this time of year for those who love to watch birds. The curlews gather now in great flocks, gliding down in wheeling formation on the sandbanks or coastal fields with graceful, droop-winged flight. At night they descant together in their bubbling, whistling, chuckling song until one soloist pitches up to the crescendo and every other bird's call then cascades after. It is the particular and identifying sound of the place.

But when the tide recedes, the curlews cease from song and play, and stalk stiff-legged and alert along the margins of the water, jabbing down their long-curved beaks, coming up with ragworms that they toss wriggling along the length of their beak and swallow down with a little shake of the head.

Farther out, on the sands where pilgrims needed guides to cross from Llanfihangel-y-traethau on their way by the Taith y Pererin to Ynys Enlli, the number of birds is at times spectacular. A flock of pintail, exquisitely elegant and several thousand strong, occupies the whole of a heart-shaped sand-island. Each bird faces in the same direction, as though spectating at some great event. But they are only looking out over the huge expanses of sand and shallow water where the two estuaries meet, and where tide and river have sculpted the estuarine sand into a lyrical, bas-relief eroticism of texture and curve.

Here and there, standing amongst the creases and wrinkles, or bushing together like the bodily hair of this great tidal matrix, are groups of geese. One congregation of barnacle geese sets up an angry Pekinese-dog yapping as two shelduck alight nearby and march—stolid in movement but gaudy in dress—across the perimeter of their territory. When the tide returns the geese will take off and wheel high in ragged skeins before they land upstream amongst the saltings, to graze and to scold at passing sheep.

Whilst all this communal activity is going on, the smaller birds are moving more or less quietly about their business. Here on Traeth Bach, oystercatcher and dunlin are always present, though seldom in the numbers to be found elsewhere. The latter stitch their patient trail hunch-shouldered along the tideline, whilst the oystercatchers, with dapper scurry and piping flight, race each other to the little draining eddies where handfuls of mussels are washed up.

In the empty middle of the estuary, where the geese squabble and preen, you have little time to stay and must time your visit cautiously. Slack water here turns with inexorable rapidity. The channel between you and the shore carried no more than a trickle moments ago. There is a hissing rouses you from your dreaming and suddenly it is a deep, black flood, widening, bubbling, spilling over the tidal flats. In minutes you can be cut off, with no option but to swim. The sense of danger adds piquancy to the vast sense of space, whose allurement draws you in.

From oak-wooded banks you can watch the whole drama enacted in perfect safety. There are abandoned slate-wharves here, now high and dry, masked by luminous, tawny stems of reeds and scarcely distinguishable from the glacier-scoured ribs of rock that once marked their entrance. Sit quietly on them and from every quarter come the seething territorial disputations of wren and shrew. So intense was this minuscule warfare yesterday that it devastated the peace of the place. Instead of idling there to watch the distant waders and the river's flow, I climbed round the rocks of the point, heading back to the car park at Abergafren.

On my way there I came across a dead bird, tossed aside from the path on the sheep-cropped turf. I picked it up, cradled it. It was the diver, its neck broken, its red throat blasted half away by shotgun pellets. There had been a man shooting down there that morning, on his car the bird-brained dog-badge of the British Association for Shooting and Conservation. This diver, whose grace and primitive mystery were a benediction upon the place, would have offered no 'sport', would have been a sitting target.

When I walked along to the tidal lagoons at Trwyn Penrhyn today, there were no red-throated divers there. The place was empty, apart from a pair of red-breasted mergansers out by the point, that took to their wings the instant they saw me.

Radio Wales, 1995

Condry on Cadair

I met Bill Condry amongst the oak and ash and the hand-tame chaffinches in the National Park picnic site below the northern slopes of Cadair Idris. It was a schizophrenic January day. There were bright salients of blue sky pushing in up the Mawddach estuary to break up a frowning grey heaviness of cloud which skulked across the hills to north and south. We didn't mind. Cadair's a pleasure in any weather. Not that we were making for its summit today. Bill was teaching me the Zen lesson that when a condition of achievement is placed on your pleasure, achievement becomes the object, not affirmation of the thing itself.

I don't know Bill Condry as well as I know Cadair, and I don't know Cadair half so well as he does, but the conjunction of the two was special. You, of course, may know quite a bit about Bill. You may have read his New Naturalist volume on the Snowdonia National Park—the best book ever written on its subject. You may read his 'Country Diary' columns in *The Guardian* on Saturdays. If you do, then no doubt you'll desire, as I desired, to meet the man himself.

He didn't disappoint when I first did meet him. On one marvellous walk round Cwm Brwynog he showed me saxifrages, roseroot, alpine chickweed, the Snowdon lily and all manner of other rarities I might have passed unaware within yards of the regular paths. Today's intention on Cadair Idris, he made quite clear, was botanising as well. He rounded on me sharply as we walked along the road to the start of the Foxes' Path, addressing me as 'young man', telling me that he was going to keep me away from those rocks and summits, was taking me somewhere to use my eyes and my brain for a change.

SPIRITS OF PLACE

Condry and Cyfrwy

If this sounds peremptory, it wasn't. It comes out soft-voiced and teasing in a Birmingham accent that's survived half a century of living in Wales, and the eyes watching for your reaction glint with good humour. Bill professes to detest rock-climbers. I think he suspects us all of botanical vandalism and competitiveness, of inattention to the mountain environment. There's no real argument between us on this. I know all too well that in many cases he's right. So I let him air his views to his own satisfaction as we walked along the road towards the Foxes' Path.

'I haven't been all the way up this path since 1923,' he told me, as we arrived at its foot.

Pressed to elaborate, he told of how, that summer, his father had sent his wife and children off to Tal-y-bont to camp in the rain, and how, after a couple of weeks, he'd joined them. They'd taken the train from Tal-y-bont to Arthog and walked up Cadair. Bill recalled him complaining bitterly at having to pay sixpence for a cup of tea in the refreshment hut on top because everywhere else it would have been a penny. He told me about the people on ponies, and the guide they saw in Dolgellau with 'Guide to the grand and sublime beauties of Cader Idris' stitched in bold letters around his hat.

On our way up to Llyn Gafr, Bill introduced me to a whole remembered cast of botanical characters who people this landscape for him. There's Price Evans, pupil teacher from the school at Upper Corris who became a headmaster in the north of England and acknowledged authority on the plants of Cadair. He's sketched in with the raindrops bouncing up off his gleaming bald skull, lying flat on his back having tripped, and continuing without a break his peroration on *Woodsia alpina*, or giving out a hint in a chance meeting with the most eminent geologist of the day that the rocks he's mapping can be traced easily by following the colonies of green spleenwort.

He talks of Mary Richards of Caerynwch—what she didn't know about the flora of Meirionnydd and Africa not being worth knowing—and of W.H. Mappin, to whose kindness he owes the house on Ynys-hir nature reserve where he and his wife Penny have lived for years. All these and more characters, talked about with a shining affection for their foibles, their knowledge and their humanity, bring us to Llyn Gafr, a plain and open little stretch of water whose quiet charms and loneliness grow in attraction by contrast with the scenic melodrama above. Once there, we head for the bluffs the reflection of which is stretched and joggled on the windy lake surface.

As we reach them, Bill confides that Dewi Jones of Pen-y-groes has found purple saxifrage flowering on Snowdon as early as the 26th of January, and as today's the 9th, I should keep my eyes skinned, because if we find any here in its southernmost location, we'll have beaten him by a fortnight. I rock with laughter, suggest that the genteel pursuit of botany is as riddled with competitiveness as climbing. Bill slaps me down for my levity, and calls me over to view something amongst the tangles of thyme across the rocks. I look down. There's the plant in profusion, but none of it yet in flower. I look at his face, and see by its expression that this does not matter. His hands, like a lover's, are gently, caressingly, parting the leaves, probing, turning to view. He shows me tiny white specks on the leaves:

'Lime, exuded, they say . . .'

His eyes shine at the wonder of this smallest thing, at the volcanic rich minutiae of potential growth, colour, beauty. And I think, as I see him stooped over it, that in the radiance of his response is praise and prayer.

Radio Wales, 1996

'Father, I must whisper this . . .'

Aberdaron is a place to which I go often. It feels so far removed from the twentieth-century everyday we're forced for the most part to inhabit. As you descend past the peeling lemony-beige of Salem chapel into its white simplicities clustered by the broad bay, you seem to be passing into a different world, not somehow *of* these islands. Particularly in winter, away from the high-seasonal visitor-tide with its detritus of ghetto-blasters, jet-skis and discarded takeaways, the landscape's more redolent of the essential western tranquility of Mayo or Connemara than that of Wales—a wind-blasted country of sunken lanes, bent thorns, the gorse flowering and old walls, with a breathing peace upon it. The church is the place's focus. Its strong, square bell-cot looks down on a beach of curved watercourses and black boulders; and on the sand, children playing. As I walk into the churchyard the first monument I see always moves me—a small grave plot with samphire growing, close by the orange-lichened wall. Within it, a plain marble cross on a three-tiered plinth bears this inscription:

'In loving memory of Joan Abbott Parry, daughter of Judge Parry of Manchester, born September 19th, 1888, drowned near St. Mary's Well, September 6th, 1904.'

On the west side the same facts, clouded with grey lichen, are repeated in not entirely correct Welsh. There is the name of the stonemason—Hugh Jones, Caernarfon—and nothing else. Who was this apparently motherless child? What's known about her death in this quiet place at the end of an Edwardian summer over ninety years ago?

The papers of the time—the *Manchester Guardian*, the *Carnarvon & Denbigh Herald*, are useful, but before I give you the story they tell, let's go to Ffynnon Fair, to St Mary's Well. Guidebook writers, with a vague, idle certitude which suggests they've never found the place, for the most part inform you that it's between the tides in the base of the rocky cove between Trwyn y Gwyddel and Trwyn Maen Melyn. It is not. It's in a natural niche of black Precambrian rock just above high water mark in the northern wall of the cove. You discover it by descending old carved steps and traversing a slippery fault where the waves rush and funnel at your feet. It is triangular in every plane, lined with viridian weed and fed by springs rising from the seamed strata. Sometimes with an onshore wind the waves sport and sluice into it, but always it clears itself and the water—cool but not cold, and perpetually flowing—is pure again. There is a washed-out purple in

'IN THE REGIONS OF THE AIR'

the rocks that the powdery grey cast of limpets and barnacles shows off to perfection. Creased and pillowy crags above are frilled with salt-crystals where the spray reaches; on the slopes beyond bracken is terracotta in the sunshine, burnt umber in the shade. Enlli crouches against the light, bull-headed, flat-tailed, like one of the small fish that cling to the sides of the well. This is the last scene Joan Parry looked on before death.

There is a family picnic party. It is a Tuesday, the last week of their holidays. As every year, they have been in Nefyn since July. The Judge and his three children, a cousin from Blackburn, Professor Napier and his family from Oxford, lunch over, are spread out amongst the rocks. The cousin is photographing, the father sketching, Joan is low down, watching the waves rush up the cliff, for the sea's high and exhilarating. A wall of water gathers on the receding tide, races back, plucks the child from the rock. In an instant it's over, she's gone—no sign but a cap floating out fast on the current towards the sound and its tide-race. Joan's younger brother runs to the Judge:

'Father, I must whisper this—Joan has fallen into the sea!'

Desperate searching, ropes sent for, the cove dragged, no trace. She's dead. At the morning session of the *Eisteddfod Genedlaethol* at Y Rhyl on Thursday, in the Great Pavilion the tragedy's announced, the lineage rehearsed: father a County Court judge and leading member of the Welsh community of Manchester; grandfather John Humffreys Parry, Serjeant-at-Arms and great radical, pro-Chartist and advocate of universal suffrage; maternal grandfather the educationalist and editor of Pope's poetry, Edwin Abbott; great-grandfather also John Humffreys Parry, first editor of the Transactions of the Honourable Society of Cymmrodorion (and no doubt before the silence of a standing condolence behind a few palms passed the whisper of his death at the hands of a bricklayer in a Pentonville tavern brawl). What might Joan have been, in that expansive time, with that mix of scholarship, humanity and jurisprudence in her ancestry?

Storms frustrated efforts at recovery. Fishermen who knew of these things offered the opinion that the body was trapped by weed in deep water at the scene; a reward of £20 was offered for its finding.

The Judge—no mention is made anywhere of his wife, the child's mother—returned to Manchester. Joan's sixteenth birthday came and went. A week beyond it, her corpse rose to the surface in the cove and was seen by two fishermen, her skirt of navy-blue serge fluttering in the wind. A line was cast, the body drawn ashore, brought up the rocks with difficulty and taken to Aberdaron

Ffynnon Fair

church for laying out by the women of the parish who were skilled in those matters. The Judge was summoned, travelled overnight and identified his daughter. An inquest was held next morning, three weeks after her death, where its cause was accepted as accidental drowning.

It was thought advisable not—as had been intended—to remove Joan's body to Manchester for burial, but to inter her immediately after the inquest in the churchyard. The light earth trickled on to the coffin and a weeping assembly sang the old hymn, *'O fryniau Caersalem ceir gweled'*. Beyond corruption of the flesh, beyond the lives of all who knew her, she lies in her small grave, towards which, as I stand here today, stretch shadows of children playing on the sand. At Ffynnon Fair, the rods of departing fishermen make a fragile, brief sign of the cross against the sun. A solitary raven alights momentarily on a ledge before flying west. I come here to remember her, at Imbolc, at the full moon, the women's moon of early February. And at moonrise, there is nothing here but the wave-sound.

Radio Wales, 1996

Visions and Virians

The present condition of my son gives cause for concern. He's just turned fifteen, and until last summer he was quite a pleasant, interesting kid as adolescents go, into mountain bikes and computers and building dens. All that's changed. He started hanging around the local climbing wall—I suspect initially because a girl at mention of whose name William goes bright crimson and professes to hate was always down there. Then he caught the rock-climbing bug. Talk with him now is a delirious babble of crimps and slaps, dynos and French grades—all the *patois* of the modern rock-ape. He hangs off any excrescence around the house like a great sullen lemur, mopes on wet days and is off into the quarries at every permitted opportunity, 'clipping, working and top-roping' God-knows-what. When I tuck him in bed every night he's propped up reading the Slate guide. He wants a climbing wall for his birthday . . .

Needless to say, all the members of the Llanberis climbing ghetto—The Crook and Radio Walton, Big G, The Creature, The Fugitive and the Lone Intoxicant—whenever they call in or he sees them around regard this as excellent sport, tease his incessant questioning into ever more ludicrously indefinable realms, so that

Opposite:
A Dream of White Horses

his fingers there on the bullshit edge he and his mates so eagerly grasp loosen their grip and he falls into the subversive void where the rest of us, knowing the folly of taking climbing seriously, have long been content to play. Alas, poor William, we know the state too well.

Me, I get parentally worried, remembering that inability to concentrate on anything as your mind runs over and over the moves of a climb. So what do I do? I insist he finishes his homework first, I don't let him go out too often on weekday evenings in case it affects his schooling (and sneakingly, I know that by not making it too easy for him, by giving him something to fret against, it sustains the allure). I can't share his enthusiasm for the quarries where he climbs mostly—the burden of their industrial history hangs too heavy for me to feel easy amongst them. But he—without that knowledge to trammel his enjoyment, rejecting empathy with those who worked here—takes them on the uncomplicated planes of egocentric recreation. In which guise I can appreciate their appeal, envy him the simplicity of that response, and envy him also at times—mornings especially—his growing strength and ease of body, as my own creaks and aches its way into decrepitude.

Also, I try to bring in the other dimensions, to fill in the gaps our mockery tears in his value-systems. So on Sunday, though rain was forecast, the wind blustering around and thick grey cloud scudding in across Anglesey, we set off to climb on the sea-cliffs near Holyhead. Our objective goes by the romantic name of 'A Dream of White Horses'. It's a rising traverse of 400 feet across a steep grey slab of rock which forms one side of the deep inlet known as Wen Zawn, near the North Stack lighthouse. There is a famous photograph taken of its first ascent in 1967—embattled, tiny figures and the flung spray of a leaping wave—that William has seen. So there is an element of apprehension in his mind to which I add by telling him about hanging belays above the surging water, rock little better than dried mud and stances that collapsed beneath you into the depths with a sulphorous roar, all of which exaggeration is the currency of those who climbed on these cliffs in the first phase of their exploration.

There is no one in Wen Zawn when we arrive. We creep down the descent route that crosses above its fearful void. I play mother hen, clucking over him, warning him about rock boots on wet grass, roping him to me where the path touches the cliff-edge by a 300-foot drop to the waves, explaining to him at the notch on the far edge of the slab from where the route begins that from now on we're *incommunicado* and tugs on the rope are our language. On the slab the wind's less. I concentrate on placing protection that won't pull out when tension comes on the ropes' long parabola. The moves are not difficult by today's standards—even the smallest holds will take most of your fingertips, and the hardest thing is to identify footholds from the dappled cast of rock. I take the hanging stance in the crack of Wen, backing up the belays on each rope, checking his figures-of-eight and clove hitches when he's across with me, ensuring the ropes will run free.

So it goes on. William relaxes, he's enjoying it, engaging with the differing demands of ropework, circumspect use of the rock, registering situation, relishing the huge drop beneath him from the security of big holds and an angle which puts little strain on his arms. For me, it is both pleasure and painful responsibility to see him habituating to this environment of deadly beauty in which so many of my friends have died. When we finish the sky's cleared, the hills of Wicklow are acid-etched on the horizon.

Back where we have left our rucksacks, ropes coiled, he asks to go down and look across at what he's done, where he's been. I look with him, see as if for the first time the slab's light, dusty grey, like new concrete, seamed and globuled as though some almighty artisan had applied a hasty scratch coat of rough render against the tide-roar; I see the patches of ochre and umber in the rock, the delicate pink tints that in summer pick up on the colour of tenuous clumps of thrift, I see the roughcast, quartz-splashed back wall where the grand design is broken into pieces, fragments, where the rock is splintered, hard and veiny as old timber, with the wave-surge amongst black boulders below. The sea's running diagonals merge into opalescent sky and the choughs tumble with a call like rusty springs as we turn to head out on the white track, amongst sepulchral stones, in the last light.

Radio Wales, 1995

Partridge, hand-tame, for gentlemen's sporting pleasure

From the Waves

I want to tell you of three bays, and a walk that I made between them. The bays are all in the vicinity of Carmel Head, north-westerlymost point of Anglesey. It has about it an indefinable atmosphere—the west of mood as well as of place—that overwhelms you in regions as removed as Iona or Achill, Pen Llŷn or Penwith. The first bay is Hen Borth, and it's typical of the small coves battered into this rough coastline. Great flat pebbles, browny-grey and heaped high as loaves in a Moroccan market, line the shore. Above, the cultivated land sweeps down almost to the cliff-tops. A dry, husky wind croons and trembles continually off the sea and through the fields of barley. Kestrels fly out of rabbit-holes and drift, red-brown shadows, over the rocks; coveys of partridge scatter at your approach, rabbits bolt and a peregrine's flight carves a scar across distance.

As you near Carmel Head itself, two beacons, white-painted to seaward, align themselves with that on the offshore rock of West Mouse to aid navigation through this difficult seaway. The light on The Skerries, which has shone since 1717, blinks out its two-second, ten-second rhythm. An old coppermine chimney lists crazily towards the ruined building beyond. You drop down green slopes studded in summer with sweet, round, nut-flavoured mushrooms that you can peel and eat raw, to the second bay, Porth yr Hwch.

There is a story located here, and it is one of the strangest I know. This coastline at the beginning of the eighteenth century was notorious for the smuggling activity that took place along it. On a stormy day one of these discreet outlaws was on the cliff-top above Porth yr Hwch, looking out for a cargo of contraband. He saw a raft drifting into the cove with two figures on it, half-drowned, and scrambled down to them. They were children, spoke no English. He took them to the farm of Maes by the church at Llanfair-yng-Nghornwy. One of them died. The other was adopted, given the name of Evan, and showed remarkable skill in the setting of bones, at first of animals, but as his reputation grew, in time of people too. He, and his son and grandson in their turn, became famous throughout north Wales as *meddygon esgyrn*—bonesetters. His great-grandson was the pioneer orthopaedic surgeon Hugh Owen Thomas, his great-great grandson Sir Robert Jones, who founded the orthopaedic hospital at Gobowen, and whose skill and invention saved the limbs of thousands of soldiers in the Great War. I find it so strange to think a lineage that did so much to alleviate human suffering should by chance have been cast ashore here, on this wild headland. But not so strange as I find the suffering humanity is still willing to impose here on mute creation.

The next of our bays is called Fydlyn. It is one of the most spectacular on the coast of Anglesey. It was bought as part of a holding called Mynachdy by the National Trust in 1986, using money raised by public subscription and from the National Heritage Memorial Fund, the Countryside Commission, and most anomalous of all, from—as it then was—the World Wildlife Fund. You would understand the anomaly if you were to visit Fydlyn. As you walk down from the headland, the path, the hillside, the reedy pool at the back of the cove, seem to move before your eyes, to

Carmel Head

SPIRITS OF PLACE

Fydlyn

sway, splinter into dynamic pattern, close again. Tens of thousands of partridge produce the effect. They are so tame you can pick them up, admire at the closest quarters their barred and red-eyed beauty. They are fed grain each day from a Landrover. Go and see them. Make sure that you do so before the fifteenth of September; for after that date until the first of February these tamed birds are shot.

I rather think that the National Trust does not wish you to witness this spectacle, for the interpretation boards it has erected in the area with initial financial assistance from the Countryside Commission suggest that you should not go to Fydlyn between these times: 'Please,' they so politely ask, 'do not walk this stretch of coast outside these dates.' There is a public right-of-way to Fydlyn. You have the freedom at all times responsibly to walk it, so I would ignore that, and its intention to discourage and mislead. I suspect that if the Worldwide Fund for Nature, as it now is, knew of the uses to which land bought from its funds were put, and of the prohibitions and discouragement to public access, it too might consider the position anomalous.

For my part, I'll withdraw from controversy and let the parties involved explain themselves, whilst I look down on the loveliness of the coast from Penbrynyreglwys, highest point of Carmel Head. There is a cairn there, and a twenty-by-thirty-foot ground-plan sketched out in the hummocky turf where a church of sorts once stood. The tormentil-starred bank of its former wall makes a good belvedere. You can think on such strange matters up here: healing dynasties from a western sea; the special providence of a sparrow's fall; the sable wings of sophistry that beat against the walls of prayer; Elijah's victory over the prophets of Baal on another hill of this name.

I did think on these things, but was distracted by a flurry and wheel of jackdaws from the demesne woods, that settled again querulously, and upon them my amused love. Perhaps some cowled monk, centuries ago, momentarily distracted from prayer may have glanced up to witness just such a sight from a lancet window through which, at an angle, streamed the morning sun. 'Our age,' Kierkegaard wrote, 'is essentially one without passion.' Not so! There are many with a passion for the freedom and beauty of these places, who seek to protect, celebrate and revere the life of nature that dwells there. The psychopaths who revel in its destruction are in a shamed and despised minority now.

Radio Wales, 1996

For Arnold Pines (broadcast version)

I may never have met Arnold Pines, but even about this I am not quite sure. Certainly, I've met people who knew him, even knew him closely. And I may have met the man himself. But this is not the point. Arnold Pines is dead. I read as much in an obituary column, and certain details set me wondering if I knew him. But I'll come back to this. On the day that I read Arnold Pines' obituary, a letter came in the post from Kevin FitzGerald:

'What with . . . a fresh fall of snow last night, and a general feeling developing that it can't be long now, and that I shall in consequence miss your novel, I am not in the best of moods . . .'

Well, I sit here today in my study, the novel unwritten, the Carneddau mist-shrouded beyond the window, rain dinning on the roof, washing away the last of the snow, and I'm beset with thoughts of death. If this sounds morbid or melodramatic to you, let me confess straight away that, like Montaigne, 'ever since I can remember, nothing has occupied my imagination more than death, yea, even in the most licentious season of my life.' As a climber, in fact, it doesn't seem to me proper to think about the mountains and our activities amongst them without considering the element of risk and consequent death they body forth. Acceptance of the possibility, even proximity, of death is at some level concomitant with the pleasures and rewards of mountaineering. You might not subscribe to Hazlitt's view that 'a life of action and danger moderates the dread of death.' But do you find no measure of agreement with him as he continues: 'It not only gives us fortitude to bear pain, but teaches us at every step the precarious tenure on which we hold our present being'?

You can scarcely disagree that the risk of death is indissociable from the thrill of climbing. The coward's thousand pre-deaths are all known to the climber upon the rock, as he or she weighs up the consequences and guards against the contingencies of a fall; and as for vicarious deaths, those too, and by the hundred.

I'm sometimes tempted to suggest to the British Mountaineering Council, since it purports to represent this strange and so-called sport, that it should erect a roll of honour. Just such a one as you find in schools, in village halls, on roadsides, in town centres or chapel yards throughout the land, always inscribed with the old, insidious lie about the men of these names having died for God, King and Country, that rightly would read, 'Betrayed by Mammon, obligation, the egoism and cupidity of politicians'. Only the mountaineering one would properly be inscribed to error, accident, insouciance.

The names come readily to the tongue. In the thirty and more years I've been climbing, the people I've met, known, been friendly with, who are now dead are many. No theory explains away all their deaths. What connection is there between the death of Lawrie Holliwell, whose abseil belay gave way on Craig yr Ysfa up there in the mist beyond my window, and that of Nick Estcourt, killed thousands of miles away in the Karakoram by a slab-avalanche as he crossed a snow-slope on K2? Or between Dave Sales, who died of a ruptured spleen after falling from the overhang of Quietus on Stanage, and Arthur de Kusel—Liverpool Arthur, a mop-haired manic ragamuffin of filthy personal habits and irrepressible laughter, who was struck repeatedly, jolted, screaming against the thunderous night. In the bright morning after the storm he was silent, charred by lightning where he crouched, foetal, burnt, in his bivouac on the Grand Capucin above Chamonix.

No explanations, no statistics encompass or suffice, no theories would have prevented these deaths. Yet the theories, of safety, of causation, are touted abroad. Consider for example the Cairngorm tragedy of November 1971 in which six teenagers died. An enquiry quite stunning in its assemblage of a cast almost totally unwilling or unable to answer the questions put to it, failed to reach even the simple and unavoidable conclusion that if you place a party of young people on a high, bare mountain summit in a blizzard, then no matter how well-equipped they are, in the course of a day or two most of them will die. It is in the nature of things. The mountains in winter are inimical to life. Even brute creation shuns a storm-swept mountain and cowers in its lair. Why then expect young, untrained human beings to survive? Why put them to the test? Which latter is really the crux of the matter. If they choose the test of their own volition, all to the good. But to persuade, instruct, inveigle them into following models of apparent competence—is that fair, or wise?

People die in the mountains because the risks of mountaineering can usually be minimized or abated, but they can never be excluded. There will always be occasions when the human animal, with all its aspirations to dignity, power and control, is reduced to a limp bundle of crushed flesh and rags. How then should we react to it, when any death could as easily be our own? Lawrie Holliwell was killed on a summer's day on that mist-shrouded cliff up there. His tape belay for an abseil pulled off a rounded spike. Yet I can remember more than a few occasions when I've used unsuitable, unsafe belays for abseiling. There was the time on the West Wing of Dinas Mot, retreating late in the day from the midway terrace rather than complete the scrappy upper pitches of a route. At the bottom, after a 150-foot abseil, only the slightest flick was needed to bring down the rope. Once, on Anglesey's sea-cliffs, I fished out from my rucksack a length of frayed bootlace and—in a spirit of devil-may-care brinksmanship—used it as an abseil loop. I shudder to think of it now.

Then there's the death-toll from soloing: John Taylor, Tony Wilmott, Jim Jewell—the two last killed on easy routes. My most frightening solo exploit was not the notorious drug-propped escapade when I came down from a cocktail of speed and cocaine 300 feet up Coronation Street in the Cheddar Gorge, but ten years earlier, in 1967, 120 feet above bouldery ground at the top of a route on Millstone Edge in the Peak District. With my hands on a detached dinner-plate of rock, both my footholds snapped off at the same moment. To this day, I have no idea why I didn't fall, what quirk of fate saved me.

What of accidents on dangerous ground above and around cliffs? I remember too well Hugh Gair—sweet-tempered, grey-bearded Hugh, starting out staid and sensible late in life on his first extreme

'I remember too well...'

climbs—I remember him falling from the dangerous, broken ground between the top of Llithrig and the foot of Octo on Clogwyn Du'r Arddu in 1968—300 feet through the air before landing terribly injured, his grey flesh mis-shapen, marbled with blood and the life-breath guttering out, on the path under the crag. A day or so before, I'd climbed Red Wall on South Stack with Bonington. Instead of abseiling in we had blithely scrambled down the usual abseil ridge and traversed across into the back of the zawn, unroped, on loose and slimy dreadful rock throughout the 300-foot descent. After Hugh's death I had wondered then, as so many times before and since, why Hugh, why not me? I am no more careful. I had no more reason to want to stay alive. Why him? Why not me?

Of course the question is pointless, too compounded with our emotions, too simple, too wistful. We indulge ourselves in imagining our own deaths: the things it would excuse us; the certitude at last of our friends' caring; the judgmental finality of it all by which we might come to know where we stood, the crushing irony being that we would not know. I recall the curious sensation Ken Wilson, then editor of *Mountain* magazine, produced in me through a chance aside in a conversation about obituaries that he and I had some time in the sixties: 'Oh, I suppose I'd give you three or four column inches in *Mountain*.'

Francis Bacon wrote that: 'Death hath this also, that it openeth the gate to good fame, and extinguisheth envy.' I don't suppose many would be too envious of 'three or four column inches in *Mountain*.'

These are private considerations, secret imaginings. We cannot easily joke about death and yet it has a jokey aspect. I remember Tilman—the century's greatest mountaineer-explorer—talking about it coolly, sardonically, treating the whole thing as a huge jest, not much to be feared, rather even to be welcomed, in a conversation I had with him in 1977 before he sailed—in his eightieth year and as an ordinary crew-member—for the Antarctic on his last voyage. At the time there were thoughts racing round my mind of what others who had sailed with him had said about what their reactions had been to his imperturbable manner in the face of peril. Ian Duckworth was a friend of mine who died in an accident in Scotland in the 1980s. As a young Marine lieutenant he'd sailed to Jan Mayen Island with Tilman in 1968, on the voyage on which Tilman's boat *Mischief* was lost. 'He's a bastard,' Ian told me, 'an absolute bastard. But my God, he's a hard old bastard!' From Ian there was no higher praise. Tilman is the only man I've known who was undeniably prepared for his death. The source of his serenity, good eighteenth-century man that he was, lay in his Christian faith. What of others who've not shared that faith? What of Jim Madsen's gloriously acerbic resignation as he slipped from his abseil rope at the top of Yosemite Valley's 3,000ft cliff El Capitan in '68? Falling past the climbers he was on his way to rescue, he calmly called to them, 'Ah, what the fuck . . .'

What does it matter? Of what account is our ceasing to be, our cutting apart the Gordian knots of life, our accepting future designs as by us forever unfulfilled, our transposition from the morass of experience to the flux of history? With all those questions goes the resounding affirmative response we can give to whether or not this activity of ours, that risks life and limb, is worth its occasional cost. Dr Johnson had it that 'the known shortness of life, as it ought to moderate our passions, may likewise, with equal propriety, contract our designs'.

Why should it? Why make of life such a thing as an examination question, where due, balanced, and just consideration be given to certain elements before reaching a well-balanced and judicious conclusion? Is that a better way than to allow your mental and physical capacities a passionate engagement with the contingencies of life? Should we, in mountaineering terms, keep well within ourselves, opting in considered fashion for what's been called a 'risk-free role', or should we explore our limits? Faced with that choice, the obvious rejoinder is that it is based on the curious idea that we may avoid death. Yet accident, by its very nature, is adventitious. There is no such thing, in mountaineering or anything much besides, as a 'risk-free role'. Death, at some unknown point along the way, is inescapable.

To those who do not bear that in mind, what can you say? 'Beware, the Struldbrugs are coming!' Who would want to be like Swift's terrible, anguished, ageing immortals? In mountaineering terms, they are the mountain rescuers, who gravely pontificate on the dangers of the hills, and all the while are unacquainted with them, only with their sometime consequences. In great danger, there is great joy. Life is then very light; it weighs upon us hardly at all and could so easily be blown away: such a delicate, tenuous hold in this short span between laughter and oblivion.

The rescuers, in their great beards and heavy boots, who stump along the roads with a dull emphaticalness, bearing stretcher and winch, bound down with heavy coils of rope and the weight of saving lives, will never know this joy of toying with death. All their pronouncements are virtuous and merciful rehearsals to place on a pedestal and praise that which we should treat with detachment, levity, disdain. Nothing so very dreadful about death, in the natural

'Such a delicate, tenuous hold in this short span between laughter and oblivion.'

SPIRITS OF PLACE

In great danger there is great joy.

order of things. Sorrow in parting, yes. Unfulfilment, yes. A certain selfish grief at the loss of the company of friends. (How dearly I have loved, and would wish still to be able to enjoy the company of, Biven, Tilman, Estcourt, Harris). But nothing about it that's so very dreadful. A shocking moment beyond recognition of accident and then release, resignation, and for a time, grief. To attempt to avoid the possibility of which is to follow the example of Aeschylus, of whom it was prophesied that he would be killed by the fall of a house. So he kept out of doors, only to be killed by a tortoise which escaped from the talons of an eagle flying above. Prudence, as the Greeks knew, is no guard against cosmic jokery.

And so to Arnold Pines. A month or two ago I went out one afternoon for a walk. Pen yr Ole Wen first, that great down-bound escalator of scree above the Ogwen tea shack. I limped along the exquisite ridge above Ysgolion Duon in hissing squalls of hail and a blustery east wind, stopped briefly on Carnedd Llywelyn to drink tea by the icy summit cairn and admire a coppery October sunset on Caernarfon Bay, then turned to descend over Craig yr Ysfa to Ffynnon Llugwy.

At the top of Craig yr Ysfa, a party of two had just finished Amphitheatre Buttress and another party was engaged on the final pitch—a couple of youngish men and one in his late 50s. There was a great deal of teasing and jocularity as the older man climbed. I sat and watched as they came up, then set off down slowly as I had torn ligaments in an ankle, cartilage trouble in a knee. The younger members of the party overtook me on the zig-zags down to Llugwy, but not their companion. Darkness was falling over the lake and only a glimmer of light remained higher up. I sat down by the path and looked for the older man; I could see him well above me, faltering down the scree, setting off little trickling falls of stone the component sounds of which were curiously sharp and amplified against the windless quiet of the cwm. I waited, and when he came up with me, offered him tea from my flask, stewed and foul though it was, thinking he might be tired. Then we set off together along the path, well suited to each other's hobbling pace.

On that walk down, I learnt several things about my companion, but not his name. I learnt that four years before he had been to Nanda Devi, that we knew some of the same people, that he was a doctor, lived in Hertfordshire. I gleaned something of the way he felt about being in the mountains, about the climbs he'd done, his family, and the times he would be back here. It was no more than a chance encounter, a half-hour's idling conversation as we walked down in the autumn darkness to the valley. At the road we parted, he a few yards left to where his friends were waiting, and I to walk along to Idwal Cottage and my car. I don't know who he was, but a few weeks later a 58-year-old doctor from Hertfordshire, who had been to Nanda Devi, died in a climbing accident on Tryfan. A hold fractured as he was soloing on easy ground, and he fell. His name was Arnold Pines, and he may or may not have been my companion of that evening. I don't know, and it doesn't matter.

The point is simply that someone died in a climbing accident on Tryfan, that his death was unexpected, its time and place unforeseen to him or to either of us as we walked towards its moment in the gathering darkness that evening. It seems best to end with another quotation from Montaigne, who would, surely, have appreciated the point:

'Did you think never to arrive at a place you were incessantly making for? Yet there is no road but has an end. And if society is any comfort to you, is not the world going the selfsame way as you?'

'Reading Aloud', Radio 4, 1993

'Is not the world going the selfsame way as you?'

2: 'FOR ALL THESE, AND FOR ALL THESE, PEACE'

'FOR ALL THESE, AND FOR ALL THESE, PEACE'

Mapmaker on a Western Shore

That night in Roundstone four years ago Mairead sang *'Amhran Muighinnse'* in a voice so plangent-sweet, halting and strange that it was impossible I should not go to the island that, in the song, is object of the dying exile's longing. But it was four years before I was next in Connemara, being fearful of the power that lies in the great beauty of the place. And then I went to Muinis.

No matter how loud I might have cried from Carraig na Blaoithe—the rock of the shouting—no boat would have crossed the sound from Mason Island to fetch me on the October afternoon on which I found my way to this westernmost point of Mweenish (as the anglicised, phonetic spelling has it). An old man was there before I arrived, sitting, watching. As I crossed the strand, he rose and returned to the road-end, slow and stiff in his gait, the flesh mostly gone from his bones, clothes hanging shiny-loose and the spirit of his whiskery, smoke-dark face not inhabiting the present. He had no words of English for me beyond a gruff 'Good day'. So I went on, and sat where he had sat and looked across the streaming water to where the roof-trees crowded naked above the sand. A peregrine harried an oystercatcher amongst the wave-tops, wheeling, plunging, rebounding after its prey as though connected by elastic. Frustrated, it spun free and flew, settled, was absorbed into basilisk shadow amongst grey stone. An onlooking heron amongst rocks by the shore peered after until reassured of the play's end, then returned to delving fish-rich pools.

Mairead's story-song; the rock's name; old man watching the tide-flow; a falcon amongst the waves, heron's presence and that spent island village on the farther shore—do you know what these things do? They map the identity of the place. Yet also, there is a graphic dimension:

'It was this strange geography, like a rope of closely interwoven strands flung down in twists and coils across an otherwise bare surface, that brought me to the region; I had a conception filling my head of the correspondingly strange map I could make of it, in which all the density of reference would cluster along one line between two almost blank zones, and that line so convoluted as to visit every square inch of the sheet. And having selected this particular stretch of coast because its near-unmappability perversely suggested the possibility of mapping it, I had felt the idea of walking its entire length impose itself like a duty, a ritual of deep if obscure significance through which I would be made adequate to the task of creating an image of the terrain.'

Opposite: photo John Beatty

Take up a map of Ireland's western coastline. From the mouth of the Shannon, follow the aquiline profile of County Clare round until the bare white forehead of The Burren lapses beyond Black Head into the flaggy shore at the back of Galway Bay, then runs ruler-straight out west through An Spideal, the wave-rock of the Aran Islands offshore, a breakwater to protect these raw beach-miles. Suddenly, before Ros an Mhil, this sureness of line and geological purpose fractures into infinite complexity. Another emblem there! Twenty miles to Roundstone now for the crow that arrows across the clear evening sky. For the foot-traveller? A bladder-wracked shoreline Pennine Way—two hundred and seventy miles of coast! Connemara—if you had been there, if you had looked across to Muinis from Ceann Gulam, if you had seen the Twelve Bens flicker their reflection across the wake of a fishing boat cutting into Roundstone harbour on a crystal evening, if you had sailed out to Bofin, walked through the mazey sculpted rocks of Goirtin round to Dog's Bay or seen Mason Island across the water, your heart would be lost to this place; and our mapmaker to further loss all too willingly would guide it on its desired way.

Connemara, Part One: Introduction and Gazetteer, Part Two: A One-inch Map; The Aran Islands—A Map and Guide; The Burren—A Map of the Uplands of North-west Clare; 'Setting Foot on the Shores of Connemara'; 'Mapping South Connemara'—all this is the work-in-progress. Aside from it, and as exegesis or considered masterpiece—consider it what you will—a book, *Stones of Aran: Pilgrimage*. This is the achievement, this last decade-and-a-half, of Tim Robinson. There is nothing else like it in contemporary topographical description of whatever medium.

'All this density of reference'! How do you represent landscape? I've long wondered that, attempted to come to terms with the difficulty of so doing in my own writing. The columns of outdoor magazines are filled with prescriptive, descriptive tracts in one or two dimensions, leading you out there, gesturing towards the hillswell and the long path beneath a whirling sky, picking up here and there on a scrap of history or anecdote. But how deeply *into* landscape do such words lead us? What *is* landscape? Is it the thread of a route by which we pass through it? Is it our subjective aesthetic—light, colour, form, integration, shade? Is it the sum of the changes man has wrought upon it, or the human associations? Is it the bone-structure geology beneath the vegetable skin, or the polished phrases of geomorphological time? There are clues. Listen:

'Each person entering the dark gallery finds a new surface, at first unintelligible, which is the record of his predecessors'

Tim Robinson

explorations and will be recreated or annihilated by his own investigations.'

This 'dark gallery' is literal—it existed in Camden in 1969. On the black floor are scattered pieces, shapes, black on one side, white on the other. The lighting is so dim that when their dark side is uppermost, only touch will discover them. People enter, explore, re-arrange: little children, critics, art students, civil servants and a religious fanatic; in a dark corner of the dark gallery, the shape-creator watches the shape-shifters at play amongst his work. It is called *Moonfield*:

'The "states" of *Moonfield* are not works of art, they are momentary records of people's visions, timidities, urges towards symmetry, towards chaos. The "work" has its being in a structured flux of activity; it is the process of exploration.'

The watcher in the darkened room, mapmaker in abstract, is Timothy Drever. He was born in 1935, read Mathematics at Cambridge, taught in Istanbul, became an artist in Vienna and London, and in 1972, as he writes of himself, 'domestic circumstances shook us out of our flat in West Hampstead, and we, my wife and I, took ourselves off to Aran.' Timothy Drever the artist and Timothy Drever Robinson the mathematician had gained the elemental rock on which the refining vision of Tim Robinson, cartographer and writer, was to be secured:

'. . . in a November beaten black by Atlantic squalls, it was an echo chamber for mental tumult. The two miles of walking or cycling to the village, on a road clambering along a bare hillside buffeted by gales, banged a new breath into our bodies. And the necessity for understanding our neighbours did the same for our minds, for the islanders are among the last native speakers of Irish and only a portion of what they have to say filters through their English. The terrain itself, boilerplated with rock, cut short without a foot's notice by vertiginous cliffs, forced one to clutch at handholds.

'Looking back on my first years in Aran, I see my rage to understand its geology, botany, archaeology, and so on as panic buying in a time of shortage. My zeal in exploring every briary track and noting the obscure name of stony fields—even before I had learned the language!—was observed by an astute postmistress, who saw that this mania could be turned to the community's advantage and suggested I make a map. I started that day, and now, 18 years later, I have mapped not only the three islands but two neighbouring areas, the Burren and Connemara—all the land visible from that uneasy foothold on alien ground. An absurdly literal response to a hesitation in the midlife pathless wood, no doubt. But from the overflow of that turbulent and cloudy experience . . . I hope some day to be able to read my own address in time and space . . .'

In 1986 I spent an afternoon at a book distributor's warehouse in Leicester, signing copies of my first collection of essays. When I'd finished, the manager handed me a map and asked me what I thought of it. This was not an Ordnance Survey map, with its delicate tints, standardised names, conventionalised graphics. It was a plain rectangle in black-and-white, and every square inch of border and card cover was filled with six-point type. In the empty white diagonal which stretched between the blocks of text swam the shapes of three islands—the Aran Islands—drawn with exquisite penmanship to a scale of 2.2 inches to the mile. The perspectives, the wealth of detail, the excited knowledge ringing out from it entranced me. I wanted to buy it, but it was the only one in stock and not for sale. The Aran Islands!—they were a place that, from the time of a youth steeped in Synge, Yeats and Lady Gregory, I had longed to visit. So I phoned my friend Dermot Somers, Irish writer and mountaineer, and proposed a visit with the intention of paying homage to the mapmaker and acquiring one of his extraordinary productions *en route*.

Tim Robinson and his wife Mairead lived at the time in a house on a tiny Irish Development Association industrial estate where their map-making business, *Folding Landscapes*, was based, in Roundstone. They had moved here in 1983, partly because Tim's phase of work which had resulted in the Aran map and the *Stones of Aran* book was complete, partly because of his involvement with mapping south Connemara which resulted in the Connemara map and guide published in 1990; and also, perhaps, for the greater accessibility of the mainland.

Dermot and I arrived in Roundstone on a late October afternoon of perfect stillness and golden clarity of light when the place had seemed as lovely as anywhere you might find on earth. Russet and tawny miles of peatbog stretched back to where the quartz parliament of the Twelve Bens argued around, mirrored in a calm sea. We searched out Tim and introduced ourselves. This is the impression I wrote down of him at the time:

'There is a suggestion of ritual in the measured gait, of asceticism in the cropped hair, rough clothes, strong nose. He has the self-absorption and diffidence of a man used to spending much time alone. Square-shouldered, there is a physical strength to match the mental power he expresses in gnomic, minimal utterances. It would, I think, be an impertinence or even an irrelevance to question him too closely about his life apart from his work—the attention is all outwards, he has attained a typological *persona*— mapmaker, wanderer—I do not *want* to intrude on the privacy of the man behind.'

Dermot went off to find Mairead and alert her to our arrival, leaving Tim and myself alone for an hour to talk. There are times when a person's conversation is so intense that the excitement rings within your skull. Here was a man committed to the task of reaping what harvest he could from the 'immeasurable richness of the world'. I remember quizzing him about the impossibility of his task; of his attempt to stretch the two dimensions of the map out to encompass history, geography, sense of place; of his direction *through* time, *into* pattern, *along* resonance. Again, the impression I had:

'His attentiveness, watchfulness, enquiry, is exemplary. And draws people to him with gifts. A local man comes with 'an old stone to show to the mapmaker from Roundstone'. Within a generation or two all that Tim records would have gone, the specific detail which grounds it in place lost. Scrupulously and critically therefore he records and explores, preserving both the history, present texture and his personal experience of a landscape, with a personal loom of connection, of mathematical pattern, woven through. The vision refines and perfects the task rather than completes it, and the acceptance of process here denotes a mastery. He says it was the geometries of limestone which appealed to him, drew him west. But out here the influences from outside this culture are most slow, least strong. And once here he—bringing his own uncorrupted and watchful gifts—has been led to commune with and conserve the experience of a people and enrich it with the uniqueness of his own attention. As with 'Moonfield', he is the watcher, but here the work, the people, the depths of shape, expand out and out and the gallery is shot through with light. He tells me, of Inishmore, that 'for an Islander to wander round the Island would be impossible.' Has he escaped, in this place, the alienation of that watcher in the darkened gallery, and in the daylight, with a whole community looking on, himself become the arranger of extant form?

Tim talked further of 'that mysterious and neglected fourth dimension of cartography which extends deep into the self of the cartographer', told me of his task in seeking 'to establish a network of lines involving this dimension, along which the landscape can enter my mind, unfragmented and undistorted, to be projected into a map that will be faithful to more than the measurable'. And he talked of magic—not conjurer's tricks, but the sort that produces great painting, poetry, cosmic jokes.

To an English audience this may seem precious, vague, insubstantial. So I would ask you to consider an idea by another poet who wrote in praise of limestone. W.H. Auden put forward the proposition that a good book reads you. The work of Tim Robinson does that, explores the adequacy of our responses to landscape in a way that no prescriptive or literal guide can ever do. It doesn't drag you along in some linear, cross-country dash the main purpose of which often seems no more than the placing of one foot in front of the other in order to collect the miles, as those books do. It invites you to ponder, enquire, recollect, explore. The labour of mapping a landscape like that of Connemara becomes visionary:

'. . . the shore drew me on by the mesmeric glittering of its waters; the days of walking became a drug, until I felt I was abandoning myself to the pursuit of this glittering for its own sake, that I welcomed every conceivable complexity of interplay between land and sea. I devoured distances, although I was working in finer and finer detail. Such a labour of body and mind is at first crushingly exhausting, rises to bliss as the activity fuels its own source of vigour, and then a point of satiety is reached rather suddenly, it is time to break off, go home, and lie for a spell under waves of tiredness.'

That October night four years ago, after the fashion of hospitality in the west of Ireland, Tim and Mairead invited Dermot and myself to eat, to stay. Dermot and Mairead took turn about in traditional *Sean-nos* singing of the old story-songs which recall longing, exile, community, death. I listened, noted the depth of Tim's knowledge of background and idiom, and the names imprinted on my

'FOR ALL THESE, AND FOR ALL THESE, PEACE'

Roundstone harbour and the Twelve Bens of Connemara

consciousness. None more so than Muinis. Now I have been there with his new map in my hand—to open up for myself this landscape, beyond even the echo of a song, into a quietistic receptivity to that which has borne upon it.

And that includes now the footfall of a broad-shouldered, quiet man walking, his boots grating-soft across the granite gravel and plashy on the soaked sward that sparsely clothes pink rock-ribs of this land. So quiet and soft is his step that in run of tide, breath of wind, stir of time amongst the forsaken lazy-beds a low sun picks out, this traveller can feel and transmit the strong, slow beat of a land's heart.

The Great Outdoors, 1991

SPIRITS OF PLACE

Funeral Address for Paul Williams

We come together at times like these as a community. We come to grieve together, we come together to celebrate, and we come to understand.

It would be easy for us, faced with the fact and the manner of Paul's death, to sound a note of psychological retreat, to consider ourselves as being all of us in thrall to a cruel sport.

But that's simplistic. It denies too much. Yes, climbing took away Paul's life, but it also gave him a life, and that life has left us a legacy of friendship and humour and memories. Through our celebration and our attempt to understand Paul's life, our own lives are enriched.

I would imagine that I speak for many of you when I say that my first reaction, on hearing the detail of his accident, was one of shock succeeded by anger. If he were to walk up this aisle now, and I half-expect him to do so, I'd want to kick his backside, lash him with my tongue like a parent whose child's just missed being run down on the road. I raged against him for dying thus, for the sheer damned stupidity of it, for having added another name to the apparently wanton carnage which besets our activity: in Britain alone, Tom Patey, Lawrie Holliwell, Tony Wilmott, Andy Fanshawe, Giles Barker, Jimmy Jewell, and now Paul Williams—each of them, and so many more besides, meeting a death that could so easily have been our death.

Many of us in this church will have soloed that actual route, will have pulled on that actual hold which gave way beneath Paul's weight just nine days ago. His death holds up a dark mirror to the way we live our own lives, and for that reason we need to think the more carefully about our responses to what we see in it.

Because it is a *dark* mirror. It dulls the brightness of things, makes us forget that the rock which took away Paul's life also redeemed his life, and will continue to do so now that he's become our memories of him.

Those of you who knew Paul well will have been aware of the shadows around him. This wise-cracking, ebullient macho man had more than his share of emotional fragility and insecurity to contend with.

I have a sense of where this aspect of his character came from—no more than that—and I don't want to dwell on it in this context. He was a friend of mine for twenty years and I found him—as I believe most of his friends and lovers found him—difficult at

Paul Williams

times. Yet it was the most reliable sort of difficulty, nothing much more than a combative questing after validation and affection.

He challenged our liberal attitudes and values by espousing deplorable and preposterous ones. He'd argue for hanging and flogging and conscription and repatriation, protest his adoration of Margaret Thatcher, display—and it *was* only display—the most appalling attitudes to women. He read the *Daily Mail* (God in Heaven! Shall I ever recover from having had a friend who read the *Daily Mail*?).

If you could be bothered engaging in argument against his wind-ups, which I can tell you could be pretty tiresome and irritating, you'd soon fathom that in some contorted way what he was about was the rejection of aspects of his own background and upbringing. His deliberate affronts to our sensitivities were his way of asking for the unconditional acceptance of our community.

And—bar the odd bout of piss-taking, to which we're prone and by which we test each other's self-importance quotients—he more or less got that unconditional acceptance.

Because ours is a community of interest. We recognised the energy Paul derived from that interest and put back into it, and we knew also his essential generosity and good-heartedness. He added hugely to climbing in the 23 years of his involvement with it. His picture recently was on the cover of *On the Edge*, soloing Cave Gully Wall on Stanage, which if I remember my history correctly was the climb from which Alf Bridge used to demonstrate his 'Art of Falling'. It struck me at the time that Paul's character was very much in the Alf Bridge mould.

Paul climbing Comes the Dervish, Vivian Quarry, Llanberis

Neither of them were the greatest pioneers or technical rock-climbers of their generations, but as facilitators, companions, masters of ceremonies, they were peerless. Bridge climbed with everyone—Kirkus, Menlove, Longland, Hargreaves—in that great period at the turn of the 'thirties.

At the turn of the 'eighties, Paul was doing just the same. The routes he did and the people with whom he climbed them are a whole period of climbing history encapsulated. Study the names, the routes that came out of those partnerships with Fawcett, Redhead, Moffat, Haston, Moran and countless others: Crimson Cruiser, Psycho Killer, Sultans of Swing, Atomic Hot Rod, Hitler's Buttock, True Grip, the Atomic Finger Flake—they speak to you of sunny days, great times, the most intense play. They're a legacy there for our re-creation, given the ability and application. And Paul lives on, will be remembered for the part he played in them and the zest with which he recorded them in those ridiculous and entrancing guidebook descriptions of his: 'rococo words for radical rock', 'a frantic, frictionless fight fraught with frustration', 'a dark, dank, slippery and slimy sluice, a gruesome grovel, compellingly uncompelling'. His guides were more fun, more expressive of the primal and joyful fingertip energy of climbing, than anything in their genre since those of Menlove Edwards.

They were criticised, of course. The snipers took his versions of history and his territorial expansionism to task, jibbed at how wildly over-the-top he could be. Personally, I'd rather someone who's willing to go over-the-top any day than Mr Cool cowering in the trenches, popping his head up when the action's over to carp at the way it was done. Paul was ready to do it, to put himself out, chance his arm. I don't hold with the view that mere enthusiasm is necessarily a good thing, but I do know that Paul's whole-heartedness gave something to our whole community that we will miss. He was a bridge-builder. He spanned generations. The young guys in The Foundry and the old farts in The Byron could both relate to him because he brought to them the reminder of the essential thing—the need for the cleansed moment when there is just you and the rock and the move being made and the sensuality, the totality of that experience, all trappings of ego and fear and vanity left behind.

Is it worth dying for, though? And doing so in front of Chris, his son, of whom he was so proud in so many ways?

I think the generous impulse, in attempting to answer those questions, looks not for criticisms but for consolation. Chris shared the last few hours of his father's consciousness, and in that time, which in future years he will treasure, all the things were said between them that most of us will leave unsaid to those who need to hear them most.

I think of my own father dying on a cancer ward, comatose with the stink of gangrene about him, and I know that Paul's was the better way.

I think of my dear friend T.I.M. Lewis screaming in the hospital night with his bowels eaten away, and I know that Paul's was the better way.

I think of that gifted, beautiful man John Syrett leaping in drink-sodden desperation into the darkness of Malham Cove, and I know that Paul's was the better way.

I know too that there will be times in future years when I'm walking down from Stanage, maybe, on one of those gold-and-purple autumn evenings after a day's soloing, and I will think that Paul would have loved to have been there, and I will remember him so intensely that he *will* be there with me, in that jokey, jibing, garrulous old way of his. Or I'll be coming down from Cloggy with

'I will remember him.'

the sun streaming through the gap and all the hills outlined against it, and a word or a phrase will remind of him so that he's back there with us again. Because, in the times we spent together, he so loved these places and was so alive amongst them, he is less dead now than you suppose, will be back whenever and whenever, and as vividly as we can imagine him.

This was a good man, who did good things. I don't believe any of us who knew him ever caught him out in a mean-spirited action, and of how many people can that be said? I shall miss him. I shall recall him often. I am glad that he was my friend.

Hathersage Parish Church, 1995

Urban Guerilla

There's a figure waiting for me in the doorway of The Apollo at Ardwick Green. Manchester's inner-city traffic swirls and rumbles past. The man framed in the dingy white of a tiled doorway doesn't know my car, scans the road, large head a little lowered as if apprehensive. I get the first glimpse of character—the crucial psychic polaroid—as I circle the roundabout and pull up alongside. Don Lee, Secretary of the Peak and Northern Footpaths Society, strides over, stiff and a little nervous. I order unruly terriers, ecstatic at a new presence to sniff and lick, into the back. We drive 200 yards along the road and at Don's command turn into a rough, unmade lane leading to a footpath running along a barbed-and-spiked, back-of-factory enclosure.

'So here we are, half-a-mile from the centre of Manchester . . .'

The style's ordered and formal. Neither of us knows quite what to expect from the other, so Don is using precision and the orderly presentation of facts as his opening gambit. He's tense with me, brandishes efficiency and grasp as a protective front.

'You might not think an open space like this of much importance . . .'

'You might be wrong to assume that, Don,' I respond. 'I grew up a mile from here when spaces like these were waiting on the demolition of the slum terraces to come into being. I know their worth. I wouldn't be choosing so apparently inappropriate a subject if I didn't.'

A clash of searching glances between us modulates into assent. The style eases. He explains that from this point you could walk, if you were so minded, by paths and through grassy oases out to the fringes of the city and beyond on to the Pennine moors: 'I know, because I've done it, and not just here either. You could plan half a dozen routes out from the city to take you into Cheshire, or to join the Pennine Way, or to the Lancashire moors and mosses. Not many people are aware of that . . .'

He leaves the comment hanging in the air, and I tap into it by telling of what for me, as a slum-kid in the Manchester of the 'fifties, were redemptive: bare spaces beyond which, for once, the horizon reared up; a green; or maybe only a clump of fern in a wall or a tree in the garden of a decayed-genteel house or rosebay willow herb spreading across the omnipresent bombed sites. These were assertions of life beyond smoke-stained brick and oozing mortar, were all that I had to relate to a countryside of which I had only heard or read about: 'So you see, Don, a place like this gives me an instant jolt of recognition. There's almost more of an emotional charge for me here than if we'd gone out and found the most beautiful place Derbyshire could offer. I get no peace from it, but it's an image which has power over me. It's where I began . . .'

My diatribe over, Don continues quite gently: 'Aye, but look at it. It used to be three times this size. If it had been undeveloped for twenty years we could have claimed it as an open space, but after nineteen-an'-a-half years, they fenced off two-thirds of it for a factory yard. I'll show you the same all over Manchester and I'll tell you why . . .'

Don's fifty-one, a little over medium height, slender build, emphatic northern accent. He's got the type of large cranium with which Dickens and Mrs Gaskell always invest their fictional autodidacts—massive cerebral weight on narrow shoulders. A pencil-slim ladykiller moustache lines his upper lip and the eyes are grey, narrowed, very watchful. From this space at the back of The Apollo we drive on to a sporadically busy industrial road behind Gorton's magnificent Pugin friary—one of Manchester's great Victorian buildings. We pull up opposite a small park. On a bank above the pavement, weeping willows are showing the first lemony-greens of spring, masking harsh contours of high-rise flats beyond:

'Kniverton Road recreation ground, Bennett Street, West Gorton!' Don announces. 'The city council are putting seven million pounds into the redevelopment of sink housing—are you acquainted with that term?—hereabouts, but to finance it, and because they're very conscious of the dangers of being rate-capped, the park must be sold off for exclusive private housing . . .'

He bestows a loving, lingering glance on the trees, and continues: 'There'll be no replacement public space. There was a chance, but that got sold as well. In connection with this scheme there'll be sixty closures of footpaths. Now that doesn't only affect what we were talking about before—the routes out to the countryside—it also means more difficult access to bus stops, schools, pubs. They've managed to sell the idea to the public on the grounds that it will add to their gardens. Most of them don't have gardens, and here's one for all of them . . .'

He sighs, then tells me about, and quotes from, a recommendation from the Committee of Ministers of the Council of Europe to its member states:

'Local authorities should consider it one of their priorities to create and encourage others to create and respect public space in towns. Partnership between local authorities and community groups is invaluable in creating and maintaining open spaces.'

'Fat chance!' Don snorts. 'And even here, where there's a Labour authority, mind . . .'

I ask about his background. It's in insurance, dealing with claims, from which he went on to information management in the Manchester public transport system, eventually taking redundancy on deregulation in 1986, and starting to teach on Workers' Educational Association courses in Environmental Education. He now runs a varied and absorbing 'Footpaths Programme' for the WEA each year: 'Torchlight safaris through deepest Manchester', 'Bolton's river valley rambles', 'Kinder's ancient crossings', 'Towpath treks'.

'I've done seventy or eighty courses so far and I'm developing them all the time. The WEA gives me a free hand . . .' He gives me some of the course literature. Its quality's immediately evident: scholarship, density, moral commitment and rhetorical mastery: 'Though some might argue that the little ways we explore are unimportant and of no intrinsic worth in themselves, such arguments fail when the otherwise-isolated paths are joined together to form independent and interesting, traffic-free and quiet inter-urban walks that in my opinion can far surpass the sanitized and deodorised proliferation of managed rural walking trails and tours.'

I ask where the campaigning zeal that's led him to the most important executive position in the Peak and Northern Footpaths Society—Britain's oldest amenity society—originated. He told of a walk taken with a girlfriend on her eighteenth birthday to Lyme Park in 1961: 'We were following a footpath marked on the one-inch map when we were attacked by a dog which the farmer set on us at Plattwood Farm. I was bitten and went to the police, and the farmer was merely reprimanded for what was a deliberate and apparently frequent action. Now the point is that I was a stroppy

Footpath de-Construction

junior claims clerk at the time and the walk we were following had just appeared as one of those Saturday rambles in the *Manchester Evening News*. Do you remember them?'

I recalled for him ones that I'd painstakingly followed in my youth, linking together parks, towpaths, urban footpaths and open spaces leading out to the country, implanting the possibility of escape.

'Aye, well the chap who wrote them—they appeared under the name of Perigarth—was called Arthur Smith. He was vice-president of the Peak and Northern—there's a memorial to him on top of Shuttlingslow—and he published a book in 1951 called *Fifty Weekend Walks around Manchester* that it's my ambition to revise and see back in print. Anyway, Arthur taught me all the dirty tricks you have to use to keep these paths open. He taught me that you have to be obnoxious at times, to stand on your rights, to accept that you're not going to be liked and that there'll be people out to get you—that you're not going to end up as one of the forelock-tuggers with their time-served OBEs if your intention is to buck a system that seeks continually to expand at the expense of the individual and his or her freedoms.

'Now I'll tell you one of my favourite tactics. It's to hold what I call "roving reviews" of problems. I'll get forty or fifty people out to a site, they'll study it, and then because they're fired up by actually seeing it they'll write in and lobby their local papers and councillors and something'll get done. There's nothing officialdom likes less than being wrong-footed, and there's nothing I like more than catching them like that. I tell you what I did recently. There's a farmer up at Mellor who's trying to stop use of a footpath across his land, so I went up there and had a conversation with him. "Where d'you think you're going?" he asks. Along the path, I tell him and he tries to kid me it takes a different route, so I show him the map and tell him where it goes and he has a good shout at me, but two hours later I'm back. He looks up and sees 61 people marching over the brow of the hill. He's livid, of course, yells at us that where he's saying is the footpath but it's not; says he'll report us to the council, but on Monday morning 61 people have beaten him to it because we're right and he's wrong. I'm not having my students buggered about by the likes of him! Why do they do it, I'd like to know? Footpaths are for everybody. The first one I ever saved is in Denton. We went to court on it in 1968 against the council—I like taking the big boys on: "It'll never be used," they said. If you go there today, there's a footpath sign and a well-tended and popular path leading down to a river-valley. The way people lie in the service of the arbitrary exercise of power—it's bloody criminal.'

'FOR ALL THESE, AND FOR ALL THESE, PEACE'

You may think that I should be keeping appropriately objective authorial distance here, letting Don speak for himself and letting you, as readers, form your own opinions on him. You'll do the latter anyway, but I want you to know that to me, his company and his actions were both educational and inspirational. We went from Gorton to Longsight, through acres of derelict land with gaunt Regency houses marooned amongst it, stucco peeling from their rotten brickwork.

'This path here—Manchester footpath number 121 . . .'

We've walked to a heavy locked gate with prohibition imaged and verbalised all across it.

'British Rail tried to get rid of this a few years ago and we saved it then. Now they've given it time to die down and they've come back and blocked it. They think they're above the law, those bastards, and they're going to get a shock.'

We circumvent the gate and walk the path, Don outlining for me the local history—a mound of rubble that's the remains of Tank Row, where D.H. Lawrence's mother once lived. He looks out across the waste ground, soliloquising, almost unaware of my presence:

'Private housing again—asset-stripping by the council—you name it in the inner-city, they're flogging it off.'

The talk and the tour go on. We visit a narrow former field path which once led to Withington church. The hedgerow trees now stand forlornly behind larchlap fencing which blocks the arrow-straight line to the still-visible tower. We stop in Platt Fields Park at the William Royle memorial and Don tells me of Royle's fight to

Don Lee, Platt Fields

preserve these city open spaces in the first decade of the century. He talks of plans to sell off for private housing parts of Wythenshawe and Heaton parks, of the idea of making an Edwardian theme park with its associated costly fripperies and admission fees out of the latter. Unerringly and unconsciously throughout the day, he's been traversing the ground of my childhood. In the wet dusk as the rush-hour pulses around we pull up in a car-park by the great crescent blocks of flats in Hulme which are the classic example of town-planning disaster in post-war Britain. Erskine Street, the slum terrace where I lived from the age of five to its demolition, lies somewhere underfoot. The occupants of a sleek, black Volvo with tinted windows watch us coldly and the shuttered eyes of the crescents above give nothing away. In front of us is a stretch of grass, a few trees, a young black woman hurrying through the rain along the path.

'They want to build here. For Heaven's sake, what else is going for this place? If this were Hampstead, and not Hulme, there'd be thousands objecting. But the people here don't speak up, and those above them sneer at how they'll misuse it, and the next step in that argument is Strangeways.'

I let my imagination erase the green space and look at other detail around. In the inner courtyards of the Crescents, fires of a gypsy encampment flicker, trailers circled around it. Dogs and children range loose in the twilight, silhouetted against flames. A frail, greying prostitute hovers in the cold, spring rain by the Kingdom Hall of Jehovah's Witnesses. Neon-emerald of an Irish pub flashes out *'Cead Mile Failte'*. Traffic drains from the city, buses lurch past. A word of farewell and Don slips out of my car, in seconds is lost to view.

The Great Outdoors, 1992

Heroic Mock-Heroic

The figure in farmer's corduroys unfolded from a corner seat in the smoking room of the Penygwryd Hotel, swayed upright, from a great height extended a hand down, informing me in measured, booming tones as I took it that 'You shake the hand that shook the hand of William Butler Yeats'. Thereafter he dissolved into a wheezing chuckle, pulled me down to sit beside him and teased, pricked and reminisced over a notable range of conversational topics: grass husbandry, Cardinal Newman, Isaac Disraeli's *Curiosities of Literature*, Ireland during the original Troubles, rugby and mountaineering as metaphors for life, Mrs Thatcher and Women's Suffrage traduced—on and on into the small hours of the morning, enchantingly.

Thus my introduction to Kevin FitzGerald, and if in any way he sounds pompous I do him a disservice. The parody of Browning was pitched at a level of self-mockery. Kevin took nothing about himself and very little about his fellow-humanity—other than its capacity for cruelty and self-delusion—at all seriously. Behind the grave facade of Kevin Columba ('Two men whose sanctity wasn't widely accepted at the time of my christening') FitzGerald was a mischievous Irish spirit of irreverence. He was once bearded in his club, the Athenaeum, in front of a fellow-member by some mountaineering-pundit-on-the-make who had contrived an invitation for himself:

'I see what you are, Kevin—you're a typical member of the Establishment!'

'Good Lord, Kevin!' exclaimed the fellow-member, rising to his defence, 'The Establishment's not going to like this . . .'

Whilst it may not have relished the idea of his typicality, it delighted in his character. He spoke as people no longer speak, or perhaps have never spoken—in grave, parenthetical perorations through which, as hyperbole mounted upon comic hyperbole, the realisation slowly grew that his natural bent was for the mock-heroic, that his whole intent was to hold up the clearest, gentlest mirror to human pretension and folly. He was drawn, therefore, to this most presumptuous and egotistical of human activities, mountaineering, about which he left a small body of essays—'Your lovely hills are very dangerous', 'Meet me on the Miners' Track', and 'The Assault on Slab Recess'—that inflate the dialect of the tribe in order to celebrate easy companionship, incompetence and the lack of all difficulty and motivation. Utterly subversive, they are so charmingly performed that there was never the slightest possibility of their gently mocked objects ever taking offence.

That was the slightest part of his life's output, proud though he was of it. Somerset Maugham had introduced him to Heinemann in the 'thirties with the recommendation, 'He's no novelist, but by God! He can tell a story.' So stories he told—eight of them published, all thrillers: *A Throne of Bayonets*, *Quiet Under the Sun*, *It's Safe in England* and others—by Chandler out of Buchan and Stevenson, about any one of which authors' work (but especially the latter's), with the preface of that wheezing chuckle he could enthuse at length with precise recall.

On our first meeting he was already approaching eighty. We had corresponded for several years. His letters were quirky and encyclopaedic, humane, always encouraging to others, modest about himself, pungent with lived-through advice. Health and sight both failing fast, he was working strenuously at memoirs which finally appeared when he was 84 under the title *With O'Leary in the Grave*. Immediately hailed as a minor comic masterpiece, serialised on Radio Four, re-issued in Oxford paperbacks, for the outrageous vivacity of its characterisation it found its way on to many peoples' shelves of essential books. The portrait of Kevin's father, the self-made grocer Michael FitzGerald, belongs with the great obsessives of literature. By comparison, Philip Gosse in Edmund Gosse's *Father and Son* seems almost listless, and much less benign.

It was to literature that Kevin owed his foremost allegiance. Professionally, he farmed in Tipperary and Canada, then worked as General Manager for ICI in Ireland and later as its Head of Agricultural Publicity. Recreationally, he played rugby for London Irish and was a member of the Alpine and the Climbers' Clubs. Emotionally, as his master at The Oratory School ('established by Newman', he would remind us) wrote, 'FitzGerald was a boy the whole of whose interests lay outside the normal curriculum.' He had a passion for good writing, worshipped Dickens, Browning, David Jones. Not to know this is to understand nothing about him, and it is a joy to me that he finally produced, in his blindness, a small masterpiece. It's so hard to accept that I'll never again hear the exquisitely turned periods of his talk; that there'll be no more letters telling of how he never found anything to beat the pleasure of ploughing with a pair of horses on a fine October day in a vanished Ireland; no more aphoristic asides such as his comment that 'England has never learnt that there is only one Irish problem—England'; no more of his elaborate teases: 'I suppose all you extreme climbers will vote for that disastrous example of the ultimate, Mrs Thatcher?'

His health had entirely gone twelve years ago: 'What with . . . a fresh fall of snow last night, and a general feeling developing that it can't be long now . . .', he wrote. In reply, I sent him my first edition of *In Parenthesis*. 'I shall live another ten years on the strength of this', he promised and more than fulfilled. His wife Janet, founder of *Woman's Hour*, died six years ago. He struggled on in his beautiful thatched house in Chinnor beneath the Chiltern escarpment, corresponding genially with friends, a Burmese cat, Thomas Lack, for company. At the first snow of this new winter on his home hills he finally gave up the most generous, rich and anachronistic ghost I ever encountered.

The Guardian, 1993

Ability

'The story goes,' I told him, as we drove up to Llanberis after meeting at Bangor station, 'that you were in The Radziel and a woman came in collecting for charity. Apparently she told you it was for "those poor disabled people with artificial limbs". "What, like this?" you're supposed to have said, reaching down and rapping a leg with your knuckles. "Or like this . . .?", doing the same to the other, at which she fled in tears.'

'I wouldn't have done that,' Norman protested, 'I wouldn't have made her cry.' And then, after a pause, he added, 'But I might well have mildly taken the piss . . .'

Once you get to know Norman Croucher, often billed as 'Britain's most famous double amputee', the possibility that he had indeed 'mildly taken the piss' clarifies out into near-certainty. Which isn't to imply that flippancy is his stock-in-trade. Far from it—where other people's welfare is concerned, or the mechanics of his own achievements, he is as serious and practical as the world out there might require. It is the pomp and inflation of ignorant adulation that he both refuses and undercuts. His proportions are soundly worked out.

We were to go climbing in Wales. He had arrived in the late afternoon of a perfect summer's day, was shortly to go off to the Alps and then the Himalayas, had not touched rock for a couple of years, so the urge for activity was upon him. After a hurried cup of tea at my house, we were on our way to do a climb which had been a long-standing ambition of his—Via Media on Craig Aderyn, probably the best medium-grade slab pitch in Snowdonia.

I don't like heroes, was pleased to find that on the way up to Gorffwysfa Norman fussed and worried as anyone might when faced with the return to climbing after a long break. But he tempered the apprehensiveness with a shrug-of-the-shoulders-oh-what-the-hell attitude that told me in his view the experience, and not the heroics or the impression he might create, was what mattered, was what he would enjoy, was what he had come for.

As we drove up the Llanberis Pass, he imparted something of the routine of his life. He lives with his wife of twenty-four years, Judy, in Ealing, where he drinks at the cricket club and, along with the Kinnocks, is one of the local celebrities. He told of how, when he had first moved there, the local MP had written to him congratulating him on his climbing and mentioning that he had had a one-legged uncle who climbed:

'Sir George Young's your MP, isn't he?'

Norman Croucher

'That's right—he's Geoffrey Winthrop Young's nephew.'

Heading for the Teyrn Bluffs, just across the pipeline from Winthrop Young's Climb, the resonances were perfectly pitched. We crossed the marshy ground at the head of Llyn Teyrn, squirmed under the Cwm Dyli pipeline, and scrambled down to the base of the slab.

'That pipe looks new,' Norman mused.

'It is,' I told him. 'It's only been there a couple of years. Do you remember the two old black ones which were there before?'

'That's right, there were. So why didn't they do away with it altogether, or at least bury the thing.'

'Cheap electricity's the answer to the first—sod the cost to the environment so long as it keeps down the cost to the consumer. As to the second, they said it was too expensive, bedrock all the way, couldn't be done. But when they came to put in the new concrete support cradles, they found on average there was thirty feet of peat on top of the bedrock, so it could easily have been done. But since they were very important people who told the original lies, they couldn't eat humble pie and be seen to change their minds, so we're stuck with the thing until the end of the next century unless . . .'

'Unless what?' asked Norman, sensing mischief in the pause.

'Well, my plan's to form a British chapter of the Monkey Wrench Gang and blow the bugger to pieces. That'd make them sit up and realise they can't get away with desecrating any bit of wild country they can get their hands on . . .'

'They'd send you down for years,' chided Norman.

'Like Sarah Tisdall? And anyway, how can you commit criminal damage against a thing which itself is criminal damage?'

He rolled his eyes. We got ready to climb.

Norman hadn't brought any rock boots, and intended climbing in the old green trainers he was wearing. But he had a secret weapon. Out of his sack he fished a pair of sticky-rubber knee-pads and proceeded to strap them on with a complicated system of webbing.

'I'm pleased with this idea. I made them myself, but I don't know if they work yet. We'll soon see, though.'

I laced up my own rock-boots with a guilty awareness of the advantages and mobility feet and ankles bring. Remembering the first time I'd done the climb, back in 1964, an echo of precise-edged delicacy tingled in my mind. I wondered how Norman's knee-pads would cope.

It's only a small crag a mile or so from the car-park, easy to get at, a little ruined by the serpentine pipe-presence at its side. But it's still a wild place, and a good one in which to formulate an impression of your companion, of his reaction to the environment.

'FOR ALL THESE, AND FOR ALL THESE, PEACE'

Between his preparations, Norman was quiet, looking around himself, breathing in the atmosphere. He was happy and at ease. The manner of his preparations told you more—methodical, analytical, unflustered. This was a man well in control; one whose business was to endure. You see it in the set of his face and the stubborn, awkward dignity with which he carries his body, thickset and strong above the two prostheses—aluminium under the trouser-legs, steel behind the smile, pained concentration in the eyes. I felt an instinctive confidence in him. Wherever we'd been, I'd have banked on him to survive.

He's done more than just survive in the thirty-one years since he lost his legs. His mountaineering record is outstanding by any standards: Mont Blanc, the Matterhorn and the Eiger; Muztagh Ata, Aconcagua, Huascaran. I don't think Norman would want it to be dwelt upon, but he deserves our making the imaginative effort to appreciate the scale of those climbs for a man with artificial legs. Grasp the remoteness of those summits, and understand the obduracy of the man.

The legs went when he was nineteen. A chapel-reared Cornish boy, he was far from home, working in Salisbury, drinking in pubs for the first time in his life, sleeping rough in a wood. On his way drunkenly from pub to wood one night he fell down a railway embankment on to the line. A boy passing by homewards from the pictures heard his cries for help. When Norman woke in hospital, there were stumps below his knees:

'I think it made it easier knowing that I only had myself to blame. If it had happened in a car accident and had been someone else's fault, perhaps I would've been bitter. But there's never been the reason to allow myself that luxury. I've just had to get on with it, and that's been a good thing.'

It was time for us to get on with the climbing. Norman paid out the rope with competent familiarity, and I set off up the centre of the slab. The route is perfect simplicity. A sweep of rock, dappled with lichen, tinged with red and bristle-tufted with pink-and-dark-green heather, soars up to a narrow apex. At its highest point it probably reaches 170 feet. There are several described routes on it, but they're beside the point. There are no real features—a low-relief gangway here, a slashed crack there, a stiffening of angle at two-thirds height seize the imagination of the guide-writer more than that of the viewing climber, who will want to go from bottom to top by the smoothest and straightest way. It's a place for Comici's philosophy that the perfect climb runs straight as a drop of water might fall. Once you've committed yourself to that theme, the route's discreet wealth unfolds in movement and texture.

SPIRITS OF PLACE

The movement is that light, dancing slab-delicacy in which the calves ache and fingertips scour smooth but the arms don't tire. The texture that dictates terms to this movement is crystalline. The rock is gabbro-like, rough and abrasive, little flat fingerholds and quartz-gemmed pockets everywhere across it—small enough, far enough apart, to keep you thinking and working, diffident enough never to announce their presence till you're upon them. It's one of those sensual climbs which, like good sex, you want never to come to an end. But inevitably it does, so with only the faintest trace of post-coital *tristesse* we'd better leave the analogy there, and allow Norman his turn to climb.

The green trainers were the problem. Within twenty feet one of them had fallen off. Unphased, Norman somehow caught it, jammed it back on, and shouted up his resolve to do the rest of the route for the most part on his knees. Now grasp the reality of this. You lose eighteen inches of height, and the ability to use small footholds. For 150 feet of Very Severe climbing, it's a case of smearing all the way. From my perch, I can see the effort going into it, the muscles starting out under his shirt and the sweat running down his face. But Norman's relaxed, plots his way from

Norman climbing Via Media

hold to hold, from rest to rest, occasionally commenting on the way the knee-pads disconcertingly twist, sometimes whooping with delight as he gets a foot on to a substantial hold. It is a very impressive piece of climbing—calm, strong and deliberate. Foot by foot, inch by inch, move by move, I see the accumulated force and strength of character which hauled those thin-air summits—Aconcagua, Muztagh Ata, Huascaran—into view. He looks up: 'I'm getting there,' he nods, and adds, 'the rubber in these knee-pads is great.'

Every move is an achievement. Why does he do it? Why does this inspirational man demand so much travail from his damaged body? I look down the rope into his face. There's a smile on his lips and a battle-gleam in his eyes. The Old English poem, *The Battle of Maldon*, drifts into my mind. The old warrior Byrhtwold, grasping his shield and spear, exhorts his men to fight on: 'Thought shall be the harder, heart the keener, courage the greater as our strength grows less . . . may he lament forever who thinks now to turn from this war-play.'

Climber, 1991

Bird Artist of Ynys Enlli

White-gabled amongst green fields, facing south and west down St George's Channel, from its windows on a clear day the Tusker Rock and Ramsey Island are clearly visible. Pass between these two and the next land mass is South America. Raise your eyes a degree or two from the house, and all around the horizon belongs to the levelling sea. Thus the view from this house on Ynys Enlli, Island of the Currents—Bardsey in English—a mile-and-a-half-long-by-three-quarters-of-a-mile-wide speck of an island off the westernmost tip of north Wales.

Weather conditions permitting, a small boat makes the two-hour crossing each Saturday from Pwllheli harbour. This magical brief voyage—dolphins weaving their ecstatic symmetries around the open vessel, a shimmer of hills beyond the folded cliffs and waves surging rough and urgent through the sound—takes you to a place that, despite its eighty-crow's-miles proximity to the west of Liverpool, feels to be one of the most remote in the British Isles.

The island's abrupt whale-bulk swims two miles offshore from Braich y Pwll—Land's End of the Llŷn peninsula. It is not as it seems. One of the great sites of medieval pilgrimage, behind its hill it conceals a seaward garden where the mainland is forgotten, an

SPIRITS OF PLACE

Ynys Enlli

irrelevance, and where modern pilgrims can find their desired *tabulae rasae* of wide sea and sky. Whether as ornithologists or in religious retreat, those who come here do so in essential reverence—to turn their backs on the world of synthetic normality, to be absorbed briefly into older patterns and rhythms, to be surrounded by the shifting, lovely plainness of the sea. The great outdoors takes on a proper meaning here. Every day you walk—on the crest of Mynydd Enlli, perhaps. Or round the jagged, Precambrian shore. If at night you set foot beyond candlelit indoors, tormented-soul-screaming of shearwaters and rush of their wings fill the proper blackness. This is a holy place.

There is a permanent population of five people. Jane and Arthur Strick have farmed here for twenty years, run 400 ewes on the land and breed long-maned Connemara ponies. Sister Helen Mary belongs to a contemplative order. Tell of your delight in little owls' rail-necked, twilight inquisitions from rabbit-burrow-mouths, or the *frisson* as you walk out in the inky night to feel it lacerated by those shearwater cries, and her brown, lined face communes in glowing enthusiasm: 'It is the nights which are illuminated here, full of spiritual matter. Those sounds are the sounds of Nature.' Her rising stress on the last word is thrilling. In exchange for fruits that are your gift to her, her grace confronts you with the unconsidered benediction of the everyday.

The two last residents occupy the white-gabled house of the first paragraph. Gwydion Morley has been on Enlli for seven years, farming in winter, an estate worker for Ymddiriedolaeth Ynys Enlli—the island trust—in the summer. With him in the wind-battered house, evening light streaming golden and low through its firm-battened windows, lives 30-year-old artist Kim Atkinson. Of all the population, she is most nearly a native of the place. A few months before the week I spent on Enlli, in a friend's house I saw a painting of hers entitled 'Young Crows in the Nest'. Its bleak power, starkness of line, monochromatic subject-presence disturbed and impressed me. The possibility of talking to the artist herself became a central part of the island's fascination.

Kim was born in Bath in 1962. The following year her father, looking for a farm, came to Enlli. The boatman, fearing wind and tide, allowed him an hour to see the farm and get back aboard. It was enough. With his wife and young family he moved to the island. They stayed for seven years, Kim and her brother Angus being schooled by their mother: 'My early memories are fragmentary. They centre on play. We did nature study mostly. My parents weren't very experienced, and they missed so much because they were busy. I find that now—I'm involved doing other things and don't *notice* the important things around me at times. But my mother and father had a strong intellectual interest in the environment. Mother did lovely, simple line drawings. She was always so busy washing nappies, feeding the pigs. But we were encouraged, and we always had art materials.'

Kim speaks in the distant, surprised pitch of one grown away from the habits of conversation. Images from infancy stream out in excited reverie, all of them drawn from the natural order: little flocks of snow-buntings on Mynydd Enlli; her father calling her when teal and shoveller ducks alighted on Nant Pond; a boat-trip to Ynysoedd Gwylan to see the puffin colonies; *encountering* (she uses the word unaffectedly, but its precision pulls you up short) trees, bluebells, an adder on the mainland at Rhiw; the particular and individual gleam of cliff-configurations, clusters of bushy vegetation, kingcups in the withies, all pulsing their presence through the remembered texture of her island childhood world.

Parental concern saw the shortcomings of what, viewed as

Kim Atkinson

SPIRITS OF PLACE

isolated images, could be taken for an idyll. Worrying about the children's lack of social interaction and a peer-group, the parents decided to move to the Tamar valley in Cornwall. The fortuitous and eventual outcome of this change was that Kim took the art foundation year at Falmouth College: 'It was a most heavenly place to learn about art. Most of my time I spent on the beach. I studied etching, spent time print-making, but wanted to go on to paint. At the time I worked on very detailed landscapes from drawings done in Greece and Spain. I was influenced by Anthony Gross, did minutely detailed paintings of olive trees . . .'

She moved on from Falmouth to Cheltenham College of Art to concentrate on her painting; laughs now about what she terms her obsession at that time with lushness, but the laughter modulates back into reverie as she talks of the orchard that became her favourite subject: 'I got really involved with it, painted it in all its changes—from first budding to full spring. My interest in oil painting really began with that orchard. I drew energy from its energy. It was full of birds. There were sparrowhawks and long-tailed tits. It was sold for building Wimpey Homes. I did what I could, but me against Wimpey—it was hopeless! One day a woman came in who used to play there as a girl. She started to cry . . .'

You sense from Kim's voice that this was a crucial point in her career. She tells of her change in direction, after three years at Cheltenham. She became one of the six students a year to take the natural history illustration course under John Norris-Ward at the Royal College of Art: 'The structure of the course meant that you

Shags; charcoal drawing

were free to do your own thing, even go to the zoo if you wanted to. I didn't get beyond the birds. Ravens with wings outstretched touching the wire on either side! Caged ravens! I didn't go again. Didn't need reminding what crows looked like when the plane tree outside where I lived filled up with rooks each night.'

Throughout all this time Kim often returned to Enlli, sketching, learning about birds, studying them. I asked her, crassly, if she considered herself to be a natural history illustrator? In her musing, distant voice, she opened out the term: 'Illustration's only a word. I used to do flower paintings, very exact and literal, but not now. You see, I came to see what I wanted to do . . .'

Curlew; charcoal drawing

She paused, looked around all the depicted presences in her studio—the charcoal sketches of curlews, shags, oystercatchers, by turns intimate, fearless, aloof. And then, more deliberately and insistently, began again: 'I want to show birds as they are and as I feel them to be. It becomes a battle against fuss, an attempt to simplify and strengthen. Living on Enlli helps. You can't help but try for that when you see the patterning of this immediate world—abstract shapes in the rocks, the spiralling of the tide-race. I'm attracted to these basics, want to show the birds within this environment in a unified way, rather than dominant over or stuck on to it. And birds which transcend the usual separations fascinate me—the way they dive underwater, become swirls of light . . .'

In the studio room with the flooding, lyrical light she talks on, directs me into sketches made in the last few days of young shags, holds up for my inspection a dead oystercatcher she found in the fields and has brought back to draw. 'Yes, it is getting a bit niffy,' she agrees, laughing as I wrinkle my nose. Putting it on to her cluttered table, she stands back, forgetting me, studying it with acuteness, detachment, loving and bright-eyed attentiveness. Her preoccupation, her immersed apartness, speak volumes. She reaches back into the conversation with mention of a book she's written, drawn from an Inuit legend: 'Did you know that to the Inuit the raven was the creator? He taught man how to live, eat, revere, enter into his creative spirit . . . I'm trying hard not to anthropomorphise,' she adds, with a wry, mischievous smile.

We walk out into her garden. She picks a sprig of lush parsley and hands it to me: 'The old herbalists reckoned that only women could grow parsley, you know,' and as she tells me, her round, ruddy face is lit by a lovely, mild smile. 'I suppose it's always a question of your own personal resonance with things.' She looks round the garden, sheltered behind its lichen-mottled walls, vivid with colour: 'It was superb last year, but I didn't feel like drawing it . . .'

A razorbill in whirring flight careers past the gable of the house. She locks her gaze on to it, the unspoken reason made apparent. We talk on: of the seal-cave on the east side of the island; of murals drawn in Carreg Fawr by a previous woman artist, Brenda Chamberlain, who lived here for fourteen years. It is Kim's birthday, so I give her a book I have been reading—*The Wise Wound*. In return she lends me *Nine-headed Dragon River*—Peter Matthiessen's book about Buddhism. We talk and drink wine late into the night, myself in thrall to her gentleness of expression and sureness of artistic purpose.

As I wait at Cafn next day for the boat to take me, regretful at parting, back to the mainland, two choughs conduct an idling courtship conversation from a gabion: 'tsee-oo-wee' goes their chuckling whistle, their play all red legs and tumbling wings. Seals bask on beds of khaki seaweed, stretching their flippers or raising their heads in soft, howling song. Across the water and back in our man's world, the television brings images of oiled shags crawling up beaches fouled by war. From my mind, Kim's shags, alert, companionable, in imperious, vulnerable pose, look on.

The Great Outdoors, 1991

Piper Errant

From the moment I first knew him, I do not recall exchanging a word of agreement or a disagreeable word with Ronnie Wathen. If it's possible for perfect good humour to exist alongside truculence, abrasiveness and scathing directness of comment, then Ronnie was its proof. Simon Clark, in his book *The Puma's Claw*—the account of seven undergraduates' trip to the Andes in 1957 to attempt a 20,000-foot peak, Pumasillo, which was far too difficult and serious for them but which they all nonetheless managed to climb—wrote the following about a member of the expedition: 'One of our party has a motto. He says: "I only argue with my friends." Among ourselves we were friends on such terms: we knew each other well enough to argue heartily and never to quarrel. We had the most enormous fun together . . .'

It didn't take much acquaintance with Ronnie to pick up on the distinctive trait and hence identify the character to whom Clark was referring. Clark's book is permeated by the sardonic humour, eccentricities and vast energy of a man who, despite a fall of several hundred feet whilst descending from the first summit bid, made the ascent of this technical and dangerous mountain.

'FOR ALL THESE, AND FOR ALL THESE, PEACE'

Not that you can circumscribe Ronnie Wathen's character within the narrow confines of mountaineering. His attachment to that pastime was romantic rather than diligent. It began from the influence of two meshing images—extracurricular study of Icelandic saga literature during his Marlborough schooldays in the early 1950s, and the presence in that establishment of the 'thirties Everester Edwin Kempson, under whose tutelage Ronnie's climbing began.

Ronnie came from a wealthy background of Scots and Welsh descent, was a good scholar, and—it was thought—should have gone up from Marlborough to Oxbridge. Instead, he deliberately screwed up his interviews, projecting the impression, as he later told, of a twisted mind. With a hearty 'Bugger You!' directed against Establishment values, and an Olympia Press edition of *The Ginger Man* in his hand, he escaped laughing to Trinity College, Dublin, and the honorary Irishness which was the pride of his whole life.

He flourished in Ireland, that country having the tolerance, intelligence, humour and overt narrowness his critical and idiosyncratic outlook on life needed. He had a book of poems, *Brick*, published by the prestigious Dolmen Press. He pioneered rock-climbs of some difficulty in Wicklow and Donegal. And—an activity for which he had a peculiar genius—he made friends. When he left with a degree in English and German to take up a British Council appointment in Karachi (which he resigned after three weeks) it was to go into an exile from which he always longed to return.

Of independent—though not lavish—means, he embarked on a phase of travelling, shedding an American wife he'd met in Dublin on the way. Whilst working on a banana plantation and living in a kibbutz he met an Icelandic woman, Asta, followed her to Copenhagen when she went back to her studies there, and remained wedded to her from then on. But if there was constancy in his emotional life, it had no spatial reflection: Iceland, India, Nepal, Uganda, Biafra, Morocco, Turkey, Greece (where a daughter was born), Spain (a son born here). He liked Spain. The Greeks in Crete, where he'd lived amongst the White Mountains, wanted to tell him how to live. In Spain he could do what he wanted without interference. So this vagrant family came to Deya in Majorca, built a house near to Robert Graves, settled into a life of Spanish winters and London visits, always with Ireland somewhere between, always with the writing going on. He wrote a verse history in two parts of Deya—too late for the dementing old shaman Graves to read but scanning over the aboriginals, bit-part-players and

Ronnie Wathen in the reed-makers' workshop at Milltown Malbay during the annual Tommy Clancey Week.
Photo courtesy Asta Wathen.

sycophants of the place with a sharp eye, deft prosodic ear and an acidulous wit.

Apart from the poetry—nine collections in his lifetime, often privately printed, never critically noticed, for the Skeltonic tumble of his verse, its verbal inventiveness, its exhibitionist array of stanzaic form and incessant flicker from iamb to anapaest and back again steadfastly and utterly refused to take itself seriously—there were the pipes, 'the Uillean Pipes of Ireland' as his letterhead proudly proclaimed. Dan O'Dowd of Malahide sold him his first set in 1969. He laboured as never in his life to gain empathy with and expression from them. And he succeeded. This man whose circle of close friendship was diverse enough to include Graves, R.D. Laing, Don Whillans and Paddy Maloney was most at home sitting in on a music session beyond hours in a bar in Lettermullen or An Cheathra Rua of the farthest west.

The last month of his life he spent on Achill Island and in Iceland, writing continually, tying all the threads of a promiscuous life together as though he knew the end was imminent. At the month's close a brain tumour was diagnosed. In ten days he was dead, this shambling, funny, savage man whose 'fierce mind fully knew/Which way his spleen should expend itself', and who was at the same time committed to the profound generosity and kindness of honest dialogue. He was buried on a bright September afternoon in an out-of-the-way graveyard amongst the Wicklow mountains. On the way there from Dun Laoghaire my taxi driver stopped to ask directions and buy us an ice-cream:

'They say your Ronnie was a grand fellow,' he told me, coming back.

He was. I still see him, stalking round my house, pipes under his elbow, fingers fast on the chanter, blessing each room with music. I still play the tapes he sent me from his own repertoire, the last one ending brutally, cut off mid-reel.

The Guardian, 1993

Foot on the Heath

Early-morning sky baleful over Hampstead, streets aswirl with dirndl skirts, swing of broad hips, purposeful green-wellingtoned stride oppressing dogs which plod alongside. From long, white deal posts, Glenda Jackson posters mutter in the breeze over winter-sparse hedges briefly illuminated by Jew's mallow and forsythia. Labradors raise indolent legs against peeling blue-pastel gateposts.

A rightful wind hustles half a Tory election poster into the gutter. I arrive at the basement entrance to an imposing, plain Victorian villa, knock. High yap of a terrier shrills within. Feet shuffle along a tiled floor. The door opens. A figure in shabby trousers, worn check shirt, red tatterdemalion sweater, shakes my hand with a vigorous, dry grasp. An unanticipated invitation to enter ('Don't expect to be asked in—he never does with journalists!' the secretary had warned). I'm ushered into a hall the walls of which are stacked to the ceiling with books.

Michael Foot, retiring Member of Parliament for Blaenau Gwent, former leader of the Labour Party and a man whose vilification-by-headline in the Tory tabloids made Neil Kinnock's later treatment at the same hands seem like fanzine gush, will be 79 in July. At his breakfast table I take in the features so familiar from two-dimensional images of page and screen. The pucker between the brows; the flyaway white hair; the eyes curious and alert behind myopic spectacles: all these I recognize. Images don't reveal presence. He's bigger, less frail than I'd imagined, and though he moves with the asynchronous, slightly swaying walk of the old, there's still a forceful, extravagant eloquence of gesture. The shoulders are narrow and his skull small, receding above eyes lit with mild humour. A livid purple mark like a coalminer's scar jags across his temple to the hairline, through traces of the eczema for which, along with asthma, he was treated throughout childhood. He seems every moment to be in a state of intellectual excitation: full lips purse, jaws work furiously, ideas spill out in exquisite, declamatory phrasing.

His wife, the feminist film-maker Jill Craigie, sits calmly meanwhile before a fireplace decorated in alabaster squares containing stylised, bas-relief astrological symbols. She looks up from reading Ian Aitken in *The Guardian*, rolls a fond eye around her leonine husband's bursting conversational impatience, his lack of social niceties, and pushes croissants and strong black coffee across the table towards me. Daffodils crowd a neat garden beyond the window, the dog barks and bounces ever more urgent and high, and I am moved to ponder Michael's nose.

To explain, a third party had better be introduced. I share with Michael Foot a passion for William Hazlitt, in one of whose essays you'll find the following description of the poet Coleridge's nose: '. . . his nose, the rudder of his face, the index of the will, was small, feeble, nothing—like what he has done.' Michael's nose being small—a barely adequate perch for his spectacles—and slightly retrousse, these words kept echoing through my mind: rudely, unfairly, insistently. The internal debate was forcing me either to laugh in the face of a living cultural hero or disagree with a dead one. Fortune bustled me out of the house without having to share the inappropriate joke.

We shambled along the pavement in a raw eight-o'clock wind. In attempting to pursue conversation I discovered two objective dangers. The first was temporary, for as soon as we reached Hampstead Heath, Dizzie, the Tibetan Terrier who had been progressing in a series of bark-accompanied waist-high bounds between us, was let off the leash to rush promiscuously about:

'Why Dizzie . . .?'

'Ah! Disraeli—the Good Tory. They have existed, you know!'

The second danger was more grave. Michael, who is a little deaf, had brought with him a stout ash-plant, a sort of knobkerry or shillelagh that he whirls violently about to underline the points in his oratory. Our discourse assumed a pattern. I await an opening in the flailing revolutions of the stick to dart in and address question or comment to him, then retreat to a safe distance to witness—for his gesture and expression are as eloquent as his words—the response.

Before the talk could begin, though, it had to be established whether or not I was worth engaging in it. A test! We had been progressing in a bizarre sequence of lurches, excited shuffles and violent meanders, each marking the introduction of a new line of possible conversational enquiry. Suddenly Michael danced two steps in front of me, wheeled round, and in the stance of Chaplinesque saint caught in the divine afflatus, raised his stick aloft and—eyes blazing—thundered the following at me:

'So where do you stand on William Hazlitt?'

I strung together what I hoped was an adequate response: a first acquaintance with 'My First Acquaintance with Poets'; disagreement with Michael's written opinion on that essay as 'the finest . . . in the English language'—my preference being for 'The Indian Jugglers'; celebration of Hazlitt the radical. I made clear my adoration of the man who could write—and hold to the judgement—about the underpinning ideals of the French Revolution, that 'These bargains are for life!'

As I finished, Michael lowered the stick and leant on it, considering. A drake drove noisily at a rival on the surface of the pond behind us. He turned to watch, rather dreamily, then looked me up and down again and with a nod like a don's at a *viva*, swished aside a windmill or two with the knobkerry and resumed his erratic progress up the hill, bellowing after Dizzie the while in terms of lavish endearment to follow.

'Ah, Hazlitt, yes, yes! "The Indian Jugglers", you say? H'm! I must read it again. My father brought me to Hazlitt, you know. "If you're going to be a Socialist," he told me, "you had better read Hazlitt." His preference was for Montaigne, in order to read whom in the original he taught himself French. Now what do you want to talk about? I know nothing of birds and bees and such things. If you want to hear about those, Hillaby's your man. D'you know Hillaby . . .?'

By way of response, since I didn't, I told him I'd enjoyed *Journey Through Britain*, and recounted the passage where Hillaby finds garnets in Glen Dessary, shows them to a shepherd, who appears to dismiss them as 'foul slewy'. Hillaby later discovers this to be Gaelic, '*fuil nan sluagh*'—blood of the hosts. Michael, patiently attentive, heard me out before hurrying into his desired theme.

'Interesting man, Hillaby. I see him most mornings. Perhaps we might this morning, but we're a little late. The other day I saw him just over there . . .'

The stick prods vaguely towards the other side of the pond.

'. . . and he shouted over to me, "Michael, who's the Sorrel Nag?" And that's a most interesting question. I presume you're fond of Swift . . .?'

'Yes, apart from *A Tale of a Tub*, which I could never square with Swift's own assessment of it. But the Drapier's Letters, the poems, Gulliver . . .'

'Quite, yes, marvellous . . .'

The stick was whirring perilously close as it described figure-of-eight formations between us. I retreated outside its orbit. Tumbling and rushing out in an excited spate of words came a peroration on the attitude to humanity in the 'Voyage to the Houyhnhnms', on 'Cadenus and Vanessa' as a love poem, on the names of Michael's last two dogs, his excitement at Hillaby's question, the mistaken attitude of some Swift scholars towards the writer's treatment of 'Vanessa', his belief that the Sorrel Nag—the only creature to show kindness and understanding of Gulliver's needs in the country of Houyhnhnms and Yahoos—is a composite based on 'Vanessa' and 'Stella'.

Michael by now breathless and the ash-plant having come temporarily to rest, I stole inside its trajectory and raised the issue of the Sorrel Nag's masculine gender, querying how this fitted in to the theory? The stick jerked upright, whistled remonstratively past my ears, carried its wielder off into a digression on the Drapier's Letters and the need for their modern counterpart which brought us to the brow of Parliament Hill.

He gestured expansively around, glowing with exertion and

A Foot on the Heath
(Photo: David Sillitoe, *The Guardian*)

pride, before launching into an account of the history of Hampstead Heath—the threats to it during successive Conservative administrations, its having been handed over to the ineffectual London Council, the staunch protection of it by the people of—the term put forth with smiling fondness—'Happy Hampstead': 'A good *Socialist* place,' he asserted, the shillelagh thumping the turf in emphasis, 'Hazlitt, Keats, Shelley (of whom my nephew Paul is very fond), the bookseller—what's he called—Hone, that's it. All good Socialists!'

This last dissertation in its turn, along with sundry separations of Dizzie from attempted liaisons with the Heath's female canine population, had led us into a pleasant, secluded area at the back of Kenwood House, on the history, associations and present management of which Michael briefly held forth. A pause. A bellow provoked by the absence of our companion:

'Dizzie—oh my lover, oh Dizzie, here, here my boy. Oh my love!'

And then a hand on my shoulder, the ash-plant extended to indicate a bush:

'Do you see that bush?'

I nodded.

'I first made love to Jill beneath that bush. Do you see that bench?'

'Yes . . .?'

'And its plaque?'

I kept silence, wondering what was coming next.

'It should have been to us, but it's not!' and with a delighted chuckle the stick cut great swathes through the air as we stumbled on our way.

The path skirted a copse of rhododendron, traversing a bank where their roots and stems writhed across slippery, bare earth. I positioned myself downhill from Michael as he careered across, conducting with his stick ardent praise of friendship in a man's life, extolling John Cripps, Frank Owen, Nye Bevan, Vicky—the century's best political cartoonist. Caught between anxiety and entrancement, I expected at any instant his foot to catch in a root, his body to come hurtling at me down the slope, but the Gods protect their own and he flung on without mishap until the stock of breath for this topic ran out and the baton gestured for my support. I mentioned my admiration for the Cripps era at the Countryside Commission, my despair at the political 'fixing' of that agency during the Thatcher years:

'Contemptible woman!' he roared, slashing the air, and then, more calmly, with a flicker of amusement crossing his face:

'Do you remember the coat?'

'The one you wore at the Cenotaph?'

'Just so! That one. They said it was a donkey jacket, and of course it wasn't. Now after the Cenotaph, you cross the road and go into the Foreign Office for drinks, and as I went in the Queen Mother came up to me and said, "Oh hello, Michael! That's a very smart, sensible coat you're wearing for a day like this." Which it was, and d'you know, I'd far rather take the Queen Mother's opinion than that dreadful woman Thatcher's. Though actually, it was from a member of the Labour Party that the complaint originally came, and of course the Press got hold of it and went to Thatcher for a dose of her characteristic spite.'

Our path was running downhill now towards the Vale of Health and the talk was all of Hazlitt—until now an onlooker to the conversation. I was teasing Michael about his favourite quotation from 'Mind and Motive', intoning it as we walked:

'Happy are they who live in the dream of their own existence, and see all things in the light of their own minds; who walk by faith and hope; to whom the guiding star of their youth still shines from afar, and into whom the spirit of the world has not entered! They have not been "hurt by the archers", nor has the iron entered their souls. The world has no hand on them.'

Perhaps, I suggested, there was both explanation and epitaph in that for his own career. Did it not stand at odds with his statement at the outset of his life in politics that 'I want the real world!'

He rested on his stick, one hand atop the other and elbows out, head to one side, eyes quietly intent as any cricketer's waiting for ball to come on to bat. Then he spoke:

'You assume, as many others have done, the quotation to imply that its author had no appreciation of the necessity and value of political expediency. But if you know your Hazlitt, you will know that not to be the case. Now listen to this: "To use means to ends, to set causes in motion, to wield the machine of society, to subject the wills of others to your own, to manage abler men than yourself by means of that which is stronger in them than their wisdom, viz, their weakness and their folly, to calculate the resistance of ignorance and prejudice to your designs, and by obviating to turn them to account, to foresee a long, obscure and complicated train of events, of chances and openings of success, to unwind the web of others' policy, and weave your own out of it, to judge the effects of things not in the abstract but with reference to all their bearings, ramifications and impediments, to understand character thoroughly, to see latent talent and lurking treachery, to know mankind for what they are, and use them as they deserve, to have a purpose steadily in view and to effect it after removing every obstacle, to master others and be true to yourself, asks power and knowledge, both nerves and brain." Was that written by an *ingenu*, by a man unacquainted with those arts? No! The man who wrote those words knew politics through and through!'

There were people passing us by: a woman with two Afghan hounds; a sturdy jogger. I caught the fondness of eye they cast upon my companion. This was no vain performance put on for my benefit, but the natural, unforced, eloquent expression of a 'close reasoner and a loose dresser', of a man to whom 'ideas, from their sinewy texture, have been . . . in the nature of realities.' How many people in public life, I mused, could retain to perfection in their memory argument of that degree of sophisticated complexity? Yet this is the quality of mind the electorate traded for Mrs. Thatcher's cliched and vituperative posturings in 1983. Striving to keep the focus on politics, I asked if for him it was still, in Nye Bevan's phrase, 'the Labour Party or nothing'. He rounded on me again, the stick flashing, Dizzie standing close, head cocked, puzzling at the intensity in his master's voice:

'Do you know the context in which he voiced that belief? It's more relevant now than ever. He was attempting to dissuade Jennie Lee from leaving the Labour Party after MacDonald's policies had split it in two:

> I will tell you what the epitaph on you Scottish dissenters will be: pure, but impotent. You will not influence the course of politics by as much as a hair's-breadth. Why don't you get into a nunnery and be done with it? I tell you it is the Labour Party or nothing. I know all its faults, all its dangers. But it is the party we have taught millions of people to look to and regard as their own. We can't undo what they have done. And I'm by no means convinced that something cannot be made of it yet.'

'Still so,' I quizzed, 'despite its impotence against the mauling given by the trash press to any Labour leader? Despite that press's glorification of self-interest and greed and its canonisation of the philistine, the corrupt and the fifth-rate?'

'Still so!' he thundered at me, chest heaving with the passion of Bevan's speech.

Presumably, I suggested, that meant he would have no truck with proportional representation? He pondered for a moment, then rather tentatively told me that, though a system with certain advantages, it broke what for him was the absolutely crucial relationship between a member of parliament and his or her constituents. And it was that relationship, he added, which gave him most cause to regret his retirement from parliament. His voice was faltering over the thought. He talked of his own No. 10—a terraced house in Nelson Street, Tredegar—and of the friends around him there. It was, he stressed, his real home.

We returned to the less threatened passion for Hazlitt, chatting amiably as we descended past the ponds in the Vale of Health about the painful honesty of *Liber Amoris*. I chaffed him for his own recollections of being made a fool for love. Had Beaverbrook's mistress Lili Ernst, when they'd shared a cottage, reduced him to that state? Or the red-headed fury of leftist politics in the 'thirties, Barbara Betts (later Barbara Castle)?

'Yes, I suppose I was besotted by Barbara for a while, but fortunately for me it didn't last, and it would never have done. She's far too bossy. I don't see much of her these days. She was terribly patronising and rather rude to Jill in our early years together. You know, of course, that Stendhal, with whom Hazlitt was on the friendliest terms, wrote his own version of *Liber Amoris* and gave a copy to Hazlitt? I often wonder what his response must have been to it.'

We walked on down the Vale of Health, the stick swinging to point out the house where Leigh Hunt lived and Mary Shelley stayed, the place where Keats came across Shelley sailing paper boats and recited to him the sonnet 'On First Reading Chapman's Homer'. Byron swept into the conversation, and the relationship between him and Hazlitt was explored: 'Would he, had he lived, ever have forgiven Hazlitt the jibe against "English Bards and Scotch Reviewers" that "It is the satire of a lord, who is accustomed to have all his whims or dislikes taken for gospel, and who cannot be at the pains to do more than signify his contempt or displeasure"?'

Away Michael galloped again, stick beating at the flanks of his ideas, geniality and intellectual excitement lighting up his face. The headings flashed by. Did not Eliot measure his own limitations in suggesting of Hazlitt that 'Of all our great critics, he has the least interesting mind'? Why did people seek to discredit the proper place of sentimentality when, after all, the genius of Charlie Chaplin was based on it? How dare Johnson refer to Swift as 'a driveller and a show'?

Bridling at the dismissal of Johnson, I asked him how he regarded the *Life of Savage*, drew a blank response, stressed that for me it was one of the great radical texts of its century.

'How do you mean, radical?'

There was no competitive dimension to the look on his face. It was a disarming expression of curiosity about a word used in what was for him an unexpected application. The intent, myopic gaze

Michael and Dizzie
(Photo: David Sillitoe, *The Guardian*)

fastened upon me, awaiting satisfaction. I talked about the levelling tendency of the writing, asked him to go back and consider the apostrophe to the reader after Savage has shared his last guinea with the whore on whose testimony he was convicted of murder, argued that it constituted one of the most direct challenges to the way we perceive our relationship to society and fellow humanity in the literature of its century. He nodded my explanation along, and at the end, in kindly manner, told me that he would read it with the greatest interest.

We returned to his house. Whilst he went through a mutually devoted ritual of drying and feeding Dizzie, I went to the downstairs lavatory. The walls were covered with cartoons by Vicky. Their tart, understanding love of cartoonist for politician was heart-warming. The caricature-Michael they put forth was not the figure of fun. That was rather the values of the society which attempted crudely to mock him. When I rejoined Michael in his study, he was looking down into the road, praising the inhabitants of Hampstead for their love of dogs. I reminded him of Rousseau's chiding Boswell that a love of dogs betrayed a servile nature, whereas a love of cats showed a free and democratic spirit. He laughed aloud, delighting in the thrust and parry of quotation, in the not being treated reverentially, and fondled Dizzie the more pointedly before departing upstairs to change for his day at the office. I was left to look round. A large portrait of Oliver Cromwell that had belonged to his father ('a very warm and solicitous man. As good a father as anyone could have had') was propped against a table. On the mantelpiece were photographs of his last dog, Vanessa ('How like Dizzie she looks, don't you think?'); of his wife, exceptionally beautiful in her twenties. And a copy of Haydon's sketch of Hazlitt.

He asked for a lift to his new office on Gray's Inn Road. He was going in to work on a book about H.G. Wells, about which, as well as Jill's forthcoming book on the Suffragettes, he talked as we drove through the London traffic.

As I dropped him off, I realised with a shock that the talk had rattled along for the greater part of four hours. Driving away, I caught a glimpse of him in the rear-view mirror, the cudgel replaced by a light, wafting stick, white hair waving as he stepped—Hazlitt *redivivus*, celebrant of the wisdom and vital dignity of humankind— head aloft and glancing excitedly around, through the gel-haired boys, the hustlers, the number-crunchers to whom figures hold more value than words. Seeing him there, uniquely of himself and vibrant amongst them, a surge of loving respect went through me for the example he so fiercely, vulnerably and eloquently upholds.

The Guardian, 1992

'A man who used to notice such things'

It is February, and already in the mountains the tiny buds of the saxifrage swell towards their flowering. On fleshy leaves, themselves only an eighth of an inch long, white specks show how lime-rich is their habitat, and I think always when I see them of Evan Roberts, who was, in Hardy's phrase, 'a man who used to notice such things'. These last few years, since Evan's death, the mountain flowers of Snowdonia that bloom in spring and early summer have been more gloriously abundant than I have ever known them, as though to commemorate the passing of a man who made them his life's study.

There is a term in Welsh, '*cymeriad*', which translates into English as 'a character', but which means far more than that. '*Cymeriadau*' were the necessary jesters, the sports, the ones possessed of the divine attentiveness of true religion in a chapel-straitened society. Evan Roberts—'Ifan Gelli', to give him his bardic name—was perhaps the last of the lineage, the great character within the Welsh community of Gwynedd over the last few decades.

I knew him a little, and knew far more about him than that fleeting personal acquaintance might allow. You could not notice the moss campion, the roseroot, the alpine chickweed, the *Lloydia* or the purple saxifrage without his name—who knew where they all grew—springing to mind. He was accepted without dissent as the pre-eminent field botanist of his time, and as an ecologist of international significance. Both of those schools of study have a formidable academic bias, yet this was a man who ceased full-time education at fourteen, and who spent the first thirty-three years of his working life in a north Wales slate quarry.

Evan was born in Capel Curig in 1906. He was blind in one eye. His family was very poor. He used to recall how, as a boy of twelve, he would earn a few pence by cycling the fifteen- or twenty-mile return trip to deliver telegrams to the mountaineers Mr Winthrop Young and Mr Mallory at Pen y Pass, or Mr Carr in Beddgelert. He could not then have mingled freely as an equal with these men from the English universities, but in the end his contribution to the knowledge and history of the Welsh mountains would exceed theirs. But this was far in the future in 1920, when he took his first job in the quarry at Rhos, on the shoulder of Moel Siabod.

It was hard, dangerous outdoor work that, by rockfall or dust, killed most of the men employed in it before their retirement age,

Evan Roberts

SPIRITS OF PLACE

Clogwyn Du'r Arddu—one of the finest arctic-alpine botanical sites in the British Isles

and left Evan with the gasping lungs of the silicosis-sufferer. The bleakness, though, was not the whole story. There were the extempore intellectual and debating societies of the *caban*; the quarrymen's subscribed pennies that set up the University College of North Wales. These argue a tradition of self-improvement, a stock of characters straight out of the pages of Dickens or Mrs Gaskell.

Not that Evan was like that in his youth. His early infatuation was with motor bikes. It was only after the financial stringencies of marriage and child-rearing caused these to be set aside that the cultural tradition asserted itself. When it did so, it was to remarkable effect.

The story Evan loved to tell was of a minor domestic row, his wife Mabel scolding him out of the house and from under her feet one bright May Saturday afternoon in the late 1920s. He wandered up on to Moel Siabod above his home, where his eyes lit on a clump of purple flowers—*Saxifraga oppositifolia*, the purple saxifrage—amongst the grey rocks of the mountain. He didn't know what they were, determined to find out, and so began one of the great sagas of passionate self-instruction.

This chance encounter with an unknown flower was the gate by which he entered on to the path leading ultimately to his acceptance as *the* authority on the distribution of arctic-alpine flora in Britain. I've often wondered about the origin of Evan's encyclopaedic botanical knowledge. It obviously didn't come from academic sources—he had neither the means nor the time for access to those. I think its tap-root reached into a reservoir of native lore that the science of botany had relied on too for its foundation, passed down locally through the oral tradition and strongly present in Evan's family.

When his biography came to be published in 1987, it was called *Llyfr Rhedyn ei Daid*—his grandfather's fern book. I expect that volume, with all its rarities, still exists, along with the similar ones Evan himself kept. I know he did that from a story John Ellis Roberts, Head Warden of the National Park, told me of a lightning trip to the Alps with him after his retirement to photograph *Eritrichium nanum*, the king of the alps. On the return journey they had to navigate by instinct, the road atlas being out of commission, filled by Evan with the pressed flower heads of more common species.

But this is to run ahead. I've not touched on his qualifying as a British Mountain Guide, or teaching the Commandos and Lovat Scouts to climb during the war. Nor have I mentioned the closure—a godsend in the matter of Evan's health as well as his career—of Rhos quarry in 1953, shortly after which he was taken on as the first National Nature Reserve Warden of the Nature Conservancy Council.

His special preserve was Cwm Idwal, and to be shown round this magnificent place by the old quarryman-botanist, with his strong hands and gentle, expressive voice, was a memorable experience. The students and their professors all came to consult and be instructed by him. The honours came too: Honorary M.Sc., MBE, and proudest of all, member of the Gorsedd of Bards in 1975.

He wasn't much changed by any of them, still tore about the life in a quietly madcap way. At 75 he was off to the south-west of Ireland on the back of his son Eon's motor bike, to find the Killarney fern that was supposed long since to have disappeared from its single recorded site in Wales on the flank of Moel Hebog.* He continued to lecture and lead students to his favourite locations in the mountains even into his eighties, by which time he was stone-blind. He had a child-like enjoyment of new equipment and gadgetry, would often be found camping out in his front garden in the latest tent and sleeping bag. Or you might come across him pushing a pram filled with camping gear, with maybe a grandson straggling alongside, on some remote road through Eigiau, Abergeirw or Pennant Lliw. He seemed to know every inch of his home hills, and was known in his turn wherever he went. He liked, even in his blindness, the sun and the soft wind in his face. After his death, a month before his 85th birthday in 1991, the local paper carried a simple headline in Welsh:

*In fact it hasn't. Dewi Jones of Pen-y-groes showed me a specimen here in 1993.

Mae Taid wedi mynd!—Grandfather's gone!

That was the measure of the affection and esteem in which he was held.

Radio Wales, 1995

Dignity

Heroism can as truly be embodied in attitude as in action, and though Sir Charles Evans, who has died in a Deganwy nursing home at the age of 77, may best be remembered by posterity as one of the major figures from a golden age of British Himalayan exploration, those who knew him will testify to the strength of spirit he brought to bear on half a lifetime marred by wasting illness, and the courage of his refusal to countenance defeat by this latter.

Robert Charles Evans was born in Liverpool to Welsh parents a fortnight before Armistice Day, 1918. His father had been killed—shot by a German prisoner as he crossed a river—in the last months of the Great War and Charles was brought up by his mother at her family home in Dyffryn Clwyd. As a child, he rode to school on a shire horse and spoke no English—a language he did not learn until he encountered boys from England on a holiday beach at the age of six, and found them unable to understand what he said. By the time he was eight he was writing Latin verse, and displaying the exceptional aptitude that was to take him on scholarships to Shrewsbury School and then to University College, Oxford, where he switched from Classics to medicine. It was during his time at Shrewsbury that he first began to visit the hills everywhere visible westwards from his childhood valley. A master, Patrick Childs, and a society called 'The Rovers' effected the introductions, and the boy was immediately entranced: 'It was a time when I lived for my Berwyn holidays, and when every spare moment of exile at school was spent in some kind of preparation for the real life in the hills. When not tying trout-flies instead of eating my breakfast, or making a new fly-sheet instead of watching a cricket match, I was reading uncritically, but from cover to cover, every book I could lay hands on about mountains and the wild, and about the adventures that were possible there. It mattered little whether it was Earl Grey's *Fly-fishing,* or Shackleton's *South*—I swallowed the lot. But one did make a particular impression. Somehow Finch's *Making of a Mountaineer*, with its exhilarating stories of two boys finding their feet in the Alps, had found its way into the school science library, where it stood rather incongruously . . .'

He went up to Oxford in 1939—the year in which he took his first alpine season—by which time he had walked and climbed extensively throughout Wales, Ireland and Scotland: 'In those days the Berwyn, the Cairngorms, or McGillycuddy's Reeks in far-off Ireland, seemed as vast and unexplored as the greater ranges do now, and the thrill of starting for them, and the satisfaction of completing a journey through them, was, if anything, greater than it is now when I go to bigger mountains. I should have missed a great deal if I had been taken at once, by experts, to the rocks and to the glaciers.'

His bent for exploration was early apparent—there is a fine clutch of climbs on the remote and beautiful cliff of Gist Ddu hatched by him in 1941. So too was his talent for rock-climbing, in which the powerful build, graceful economy of movement and stamina of his Welsh farming forebears were advantageous. He was selfless too—in going to the aid of an injured climber in Tryfan's North Gully in 1942 he was hit by a stone on the head which severely fractured his skull and which he confided to me in later life he believed to be connected to the onset of multiple sclerosis that confined him to a wheelchair for over thirty years.

His time at Oxford was curtailed by the war. Qualifying as a doctor in 1943, he was called up into the Royal Army Medical Corps, posted to India and the Burmese front, where he served as medical officer to an infantry battalion and was mentioned in

Sir Charles Evans
(Photo courtesy Denise, Lady Evans)

SPIRITS OF PLACE

On the way to Kanchenjunga

dispatches. In periods away from the fighting, he learnt Hindi, visited the Himalaya, and climbed Mount Kinabalu in Borneo. When he came home he qualified as a surgeon, being elected FRCS in 1949, and worked as Surgical Registrar in hospitals in Liverpool (in order to be near the Welsh mountains that were his first and last love) between 1947 and 1957. His professional competence must have been highly regarded, given that he spent as much time in that decade in remotest Nepal as he did in the operating theatres of Merseyside.

His first full-scale Himalayan expedition was with the legendary H.W. Tilman, on an expedition to Annapurna in 1950, in the course of which Evans reached an altitude of 24,000ft on Annapurna 4. The attempt failed because of bad weather, as did subsequent ones in Kulu in 1951 and to Cho Oyu with Eric Shipton the following year—an expedition which was regarded as training for the projected 1953 attempt on Everest. Shipton was appointed leader for this latter, but was deposed by what Evans, in a later review, referred to as 'an unworthy device'—a criticism which gained weight from its author's habitual reticence. In a recent interview, he expanded on this episode by telling that 'it was said that Shipton lacked the killer instinct'. He let the words hang for a moment and then, very softly and with a mocking smile, added, 'Not a bad thing to lack, in my view.'

Evans had been chosen as Shipton's deputy, and immediately and loyally offered his resignation, but the new leader, John Hunt, succeeded in gaining his confidence, Shipton added his voice to those persuading him to remain, and Evans played a pivotal role in the successful ascent of Everest. With Tom Bourdillon, on the 26th May, he reached the South Peak, at 28,750ft the highest summit then attained. Because of faulty equipment, which delayed departure from the South Col by an hour in the morning and provided Evans with only a trickle of oxygen on his climb, they were too late to push on and had to retreat. A frozen valve had saved Evans from becoming the most celebrated figure in mountain history. Their altitude record stood for three days, the main summit, 300ft higher, being climbed by Hillary and Tenzing Norgay on 29th May.

Evans may have avoided the pitfalls of popular celebrity—and he did so even more effectively by staying in Nepal to explore remote valleys rather than return to Britain with the rest of the expedition—but he had established himself as an exemplar of selfless competence and determination within the mountaineering community. His companions on subsequent trips all testify to his qualities of character. Norman Hardie, with whom he climbed in

Nepal in 1954, wrote that: 'We all felt humbled by this man's quiet authority, his wit and his tremendous prestige among the Sherpas.' For Joe Brown, then a young Manchester builder whom Evans had with foresight and egalitarian instinct invited on his supposed reconnaissance to the World's third highest peak, Kanchenjunga, in 1955, 'In Charles Evans we could not have had a better leader. He never told you what to do; in the nicest possible way he always asked if you would like to do something, and in consequence all of us would have done anything for him.' In Brown's case this included, in company with George Band, reaching the summit ('less five vertical feet', as Evans said in his victory telegram—the peak was a holy one and he had made this promise to the ruler of Sikkim) of the then highest unclimbed mountain, and a more difficult one than Everest. This was achieved by a small and relatively low-profile reconnaissance trip very much in the tradition established by Shipton and Tilman.

All this mountain activity had led to loss of professional seniority. Evans ceased in the mid-1950s to practise as a neurosurgeon (he had been Hunterian Professor at the Royal College of Surgeons in 1953), and returned to general surgery. The only year between 1950 and 1957 when he was not in the Himalaya was 1956, and he marked it by the publication of two books, *On Climbing* and *Kangchenjunga: the Untrodden Peak*, both of which transcend the merely competent and enrich the literature of the sport. The first is an instructional book the technical sections of which—as with Kirkus's *Let's Go Climbing*—may have dated, but its anecdotes from personal experience are told in plain, lucid style perfectly evoking the atmospheres of their settings. On a personal note, and to mirror his own story above, it was this book, along with Kirkus's, in my Manchester school library, which set me on the path to the hills. The Kanchenjunga book is an extremely well-written and exciting account of perhaps the finest British mountaineering achievement of its decade. He also published a book of sketches—*Eye on Everest*—that is now a collector's item, commanding high prices, and left on his death the typescript of a volume of memoirs of his wartime experiences in Burma and early visits to the Himalaya, which there are plans to publish.

His last expedition was a two-man trip in 1957 with Dennis Davies to Annapurna 4, the summit of which they reached. Their ambitious plan to traverse the long and difficult ridge along to Annapurna 2 was foiled by poor weather, but what he and Davies did achieve stands as an ideological landmark in the ethical history of mountaineering. He was married on his return to Britain to

Denise Morin, daughter of the great woman mountaineer Nea Morin (née Barnard), and herself a fine climber and future President of the Alpine Club. They had three sons. Their climbing partnership was tragically short. In the late 1950s Evans began suffering the symptoms of an illness that in 1959 was diagnosed as multiple sclerosis. In that year he found himself unable to ski. Within five years he could no longer walk, and though he continued to sail—up to the western seaboard of Scotland to visit the Longstaffs at Achiltibuie, for example—and to fish for salmon whilst wheelchair-bound, even these activities eventually proved beyond his physical capacities.

His career had fortunately changed direction with his appointment in 1958 as Principal of the University College of North Wales in Bangor. Though his tenure of that post was fraught, particularly in his later years, with political difficulty, his achievements through the Robbins era and after were significant. He presided over a threefold increase in the college's size, and in the establishment of international reputations in oceanography, marine biology, electronics and forestry. One former professor of linguistics at Bangor remembers being nonplussed in his interview at a line of questioning that required him to display knowledge in these areas as well as his own. Evans would allow of no exclusivity between the 'Two Cultures'. Nor would he countenance any discrimination for birth-language over the pursuit of excellence in the matter of academic appointments. In this he fell foul of the rising sense of Welsh nationhood, by whose most committed spokespersons he was perhaps unfairly demonised.

He bore these affronts, as he bore everything else in his life, with patience and restraint, and kept to his course. He kept in contact, too, in spite of his disability, with the mountaineering community, remaining on terms of close friendship with Eric Shipton (whom he succeeded as President of the Alpine Club in 1968), and with H.W. Tilman until their deaths in 1977. He was an Honorary Member of the Climbers' Club, and at his house in Capel Curig was always pleased to be visited by climbers of any generation. His own son Peter's growing expertise in rock-climbing gave him particular satisfaction.

I was too young to experience Charles as a mountaineer, or to see him in his physical prime. But even though I only ever knew him in his wheelchair—joking as easily in Welsh with the porters of his college as he managed its in-fighting professors—I never thought of him as an invalid. The times I spent in conversation with him at his house in the mountains, looking up to Tryfan and Snowdon, were in their way as memorable, and as instructive, as any I have spent with companions in the hills. The dignity of his acceptance, the calm depth and recall of his mind, the beautiful animation of his face even when every limb had ceased to function, alerted you to the presence of wisdom, and made you glad for once to be part of the human race.

The Guardian, 1995

Angry Laughter

He was complaining about the sheep, and not without an element of justice either, because the evidence of their presence was hard to ignore. Nor that only—the animals themselves jostled you as you dainty-footed your way through it, they crowded in on you as you opened your car door, they nuzzled at your pockets as you slipped through his gate.

'What sort of sheep are they, anyway?' I asked him.

'Mongrels,' he roared. 'Why didn't you bring your dog? It could have chased them.'

The sheep raised their mule-like heads, adopted pained expressions, whinnied in pure-bred protest.

'Why don't you put in some cattle-grids?'

'Listen, the sheep round here would drag planks up and walk across them,' he snorted.

He wasn't in a good mood. Comedians seldom are. I don't know if it's the strain of being funny all the time, or because of all modes of human expression comedy is the most critical and serious, but comedians are not a happy bunch. I mean, look at Max Wall, look at Lenny Bruce. And can you imagine anything more frustrating than comedy? You build up this rage against the world as it is, refine it into delicate deflation of its pomp and self-importance, and does your audience do anything to change it? No—it just laughs at you.

We were to go for a walk, but scanning through the options it appeared that in most places there would be something—some autocracy of the planners or inanity of the developers—which would reduce him, in his present state, to rage or tears or both. So instead we delayed matters, sat in the garden with a pot of tea between us in a little paradise-place looking out over Dentdale, removed from the prying eyes of humans and the prying snouts of sheep, and we talked. Which Mike can do, when the mood takes him, as persuasively as almost anyone I know. We didn't need to go

Mike Harding

for a walk just yet anyway. He was getting quite exercised enough about a word recently applied to him.

'Do you know what they called me?'

Behind the thick, familiar glasses his eyes gleamed and rolled.

'They called me an eccentric. Do you know what that means?'

'Well,' I responded, 'I suppose it's the same register as "extremist". It's intended to signify that people need no longer take what you say seriously. Key concepts in the smear-vocabulary, both of them, and used by charming, plausible people to twist the knife between your ribs. The defence is to turn it back on them—touch a sound values-base and query whether their stance is eccentric or extreme in relation to that.'

He was semi-placated by this, and we raced away into a state-of-the-nation discussion, a lament for the demoralisation of the left, and a heated disagreement with the recent strictures of another journalist against the Ramblers' Association's calls for more trespasses. Mike, as a past RA president and current vice-president, happened to agree with this policy of confrontation. He was sceptical of the value of negotiation with a government that consistently failed to honour its access, conservation and environmental promises. He admitted that the television programme that had led to these strictures had been open to criticism, but suggested that the journalist in question—a Scot—might have reached different conclusions had he been writing from a south-of-the-border perspective.

So that was the way the day started, and if you have any illusions that Mike Harding is 'just a northern comedian' and a bit of a folk-singer too, then get rid—he's a dedicated political animal, a campaigner, and as you'll be well aware if you've read his *Walking the Dales* or *Footloose in the Himalayas*, a lover of the outdoors above all things. He's 48 now, lives in an eighteenth-century former farmhouse on a quiet—apart from the sheep—hillside near the village of Dent, in the Yorkshire Dales National Park. A stocky, barrel-chested man with a bristling moustache, jutting chin, and endlessly surprised eyebrows, he grew up in Lower Crumpsall, north Manchester, in the years after the war. His father died on a bombing raid in 1944—a fact with which he attempted to come to terms in one of his most poignant songs, 'Bombers' Moon', and he was brought up by an Irish mother and Polish stepfather. He remembers a childhood home filled with vigorous debate, with intense political awareness:

'When I used to go to other kids' houses, I'd ask what was wrong, have your mam and dad been arguing, because their parents were so quiet compared to mine. And when kids came back to my house to watch this little Baird telly with a ten-inch screen, they'd ask what all the green streaks were, running down it. I didn't tell them, but my grandmother, who was an O'Shaughnessy and an amazing, tough old woman, used to spit at the screen—"Take that, yer murtherin' bastard!"—when Churchill was on.'

The memory seemed to put him in better humour. At last we were ready to venture on a walk. As we climbed the path from his house, he discoursed on names: Rottenbutts, Gawthrop, Foulsyke—did I know that the latter was probably so named because it was the site of the latrines of a Roman camp? Tofts up here—the whole history of the place was recounted, right down to the two last owners, a pair of ageing brothers who wouldn't retire because if they did they'd 'nobbut dee', and who wouldn't sell the beautiful medieval house on their land because if they did, 'summ'un 'ud ony do summat wi'it'. As he talked, the breadth and richness of his interest in the land came out, and his ambivalence towards those who own it.

Beyond the old house we rocked back on our heels for a while and rested against a wall. From the wooded crag above came the raucous calls of peregrine eyasses, demanding to be fed. He told how the nest had been robbed last year, the eggs recovered in a police raid from a collector's fridge in Rochdale. The fine was £1,000, but the thief had said quite blatantly afterwards that he'd be back for them again next year. It was worth it to him.

We carried on, chastened by yet another aspect of rural business practice, underneath the escarpment and round into Barbondale, talking as we went of the survival of old lore into the urban situations in which we'd both grown up, two or three miles apart in the Manchester slums of the 'forties and 'fifties. He told me of his grandmother collecting scraps of lead and on Hallowe'en melting them over a flame in a spoon, pouring the molten metal into water and reading the signs in it as it set. We exchanged reminiscences of folk-beliefs our grandparents—his from Ireland, mine from the Welsh borders—had retained, displaced into their new settings in the mean streets of the industrial north.

The path we were following reached Barbondale, a dull valley running south-west that we descended a little way to reach the Occupation Road hugging the contours along the southern slopes of Dentdale and Deepdale. The lumpy outline of Casterton Fell in front of us prompted Mike to launch into a tirade against the attitude of cavers to access, and their only recently having become aware of the complexity of the issues involved: 'They're like so many people—they imagine that just because they negotiate an agreement for themselves on an informal basis, it will last for the rest of time or the duration of their interest with no further

To exorcise the shadows of the mind

problems. But it's not that simple. Ownership changes, agreements don't have to be renewed. The Scots are the worst, in my view.'

I asked him how was that. He told of an occasion when he was still president of the RA. He'd been on tour with his audio-visual show in Dundee. A deputation from the local mountain rescue had come to talk to him afterwards and had warned him not to rock the boat in Scotland.

'They were telling me they had a perfectly workable situation there—local *ad hoc* agreements, access more or less when they wanted it. I just asked them what assurances they had that the situation would go on like that? You can't rely on temporary goodwill for the continuation of vital national amenity. You've got to have assured agreements and proper legislation to safeguard free public access to wild country. Otherwise we're just going to go back to some sort of neanderthal forelock-tugging.'

The track underfoot was rough, the hill-shapes round about undramatic and the vegetation sparse. I heard Mike praising the verdant nature and difference of Dentdale, but after my home-country it seemed dour, plain land. We turned down a path alongside Flinter Gill. I asked what had brought him to the Dales. He described his first teenage escape from Manchester into the country, that brought him cycling and walking to the Dales. And he described another of those moments of vision that dictate the course of future life:

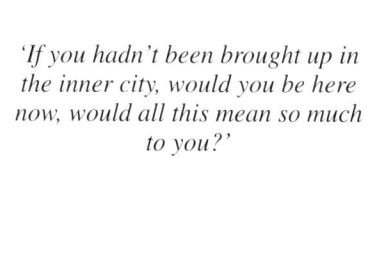

'If you hadn't been brought up in the inner city, would you be here now, would all this mean so much to you?'

'After school, one of the jobs I did was de-scaling industrial boilers. It was absolutely filthy work, desperately hot because the firebricks retain the heat for weeks after the fires are out. All you could bear to wear were rags to cover up your genitals. I can remember coming out of one of these boilers on a beautiful summer's morning and sitting outside. I think it was at a mill in Accrington. It was quite early still, all the people were going to work, and I knew then that I didn't want to be part of that—I wanted to live somewhere like out here.'

We drifted down Flinter Gill, talking about catholic childhoods and the brief consideration of priestly vocations, about priests who taught us to love language and the way in which our educators' remorseless logic ultimately proved the instrument with which we undermined our own faith. Shared experience is a powerful bond, a still reservoir of understanding between you. It brought us to the neat streets of Dent, where we idled over lunch and where Mike made a round of calls—to buy darning wool ('No, it's not for my wife—I'll be doing it myself'), to view new paintings in a gallery, to visit Ben Lyon, the local industrialist. Afterwards we made our way back along the river bank, Mike assiduously naming and noting every bird and flower, expatiating upon the history and society of the dale.

'If you hadn't been brought up in the inner city, would you be here now, would all this mean so much to you?' I asked.

There was a sort of sadness across his face, and he fell quiet.

'Nor to me either,' I said, taking my answer from it, and we walked on homewards together in companionable silence.

The Great Outdoors, 1993

No Home but the Struggle

Dave Cook died in St Thomas's Hospital of pneumonia at the age of 51 on Thursday afternoon. He had been unconscious for a fortnight after being knocked off his bicycle by a lorry whilst cycling through Turkey on a round-the-Mediterranean bike ride. After his accident, the injuries he received in which were not initially thought grave, he was taken to hospital in Turkey. Alison Fell—his lover for the past eighteen months, and his two sons Henry and Lester flew out to him immediately and arranged for him to be flown back to London by air ambulance. All of us who heard, and who kept in touch daily with his progress, thought that this strong man of leonine constitution would pull through. But the infection that was to kill him had already set in, and the end was as rapid as it was unexpected.

The fact of his death leaves me numb, struggling to relate it to a character as full of life and as gracious as anyone I have ever known. He was a big, handsome man with a teddy boy's quiff, greying sideburns, strong features, laughter lines, and the most humorous brown eyes that ever led suggestible humanity into dancing glee.

The two main loves of his life were rock-climbing and the now-defunct Communist Party of this country. I was fortunate enough to be his sometime comrade in both spheres of activity for nearly thirty years. His climbing began whilst he was a pupil at Solihull School in 1958 (his father, a water engineer, had settled in nearby Knowle after a peripatetic early life). In early days it was pursued chiefly in the company of fellow Brummies Ken Wilson and Dave Potts. He had a fund of fond anecdotes about the former, perceptive about character yet without an ounce of spite or malice in their re-telling. Human foibles were Dave's speciality; as to human vices, I don't think he so much as countenanced their existence. He went up to St Katherine's College, Cambridge, to read History in 1959, and his enthusiasm and talent developed rapidly upon joining a talented group of climbers in the University Mountaineering Club: Nick Estcourt (killed on K2 in 1978), Mike Kosterlitz, Dick Isherwood, Rupert Roschnik, Unity Stack. In the vacations he was one of a circle—for the most part weird or gifted or both—operating out of Cwm Wrach at Nant Peris: Barry Webb, Al Harris, Van Dave, Black Ron, Crew, Ingle and Boysen amongst them.

He was immediately active in the Young Communist League at Cambridge, and when he left with a 2.1. in 1962 to take a postgraduate education certificate in Leeds, he found himself in an amenable environment for the development of both these interests. He became Yorkshire District Secretary for the YCL, and an initiate into and devotee of the mysteries of gritstone climbing. This blunt and abrasive sub-species of the greater sport, that takes place on smoke-blackened, moor-rimming Pennine outcrops and demands a disproportionate outlay of sweat and blood for success, he seemed to relish almost as objective correlative to the class struggle to which his early politics were committed. He was one of the significant figures from the last really vital phase of the YCL, when a working-class and in the main non-university-educated group of people—Pete Carter, Barney Davies, Dougie Bain amongst them—created an extraordinarily attractive, modern and politically creative milieu of anarchic attitudes, irreverence, resourcefulness and highly-charged sexual energy within it. It and climbing went well together then. They were the same kind of societies.

Dave himself had started out from a very orthodox Marxist position, but moved with this group to a more radical stance and into the Movement Politics of the late 'sixties. His work here brought him to the notice of the then National Organiser of the Communist Party of Great Britain, Gordon MacLennan, who contrived his appointment in 1971 as National Student Organiser, in which role Dave's organisational powers really began to take effect.

The Student Organisation had been under the prevalent and baleful influence of Stalinists in the CPGB for many years at the time of Dave's appointment, but shifts in the climate and emphasis of student politics in the late 'sixties and early 'seventies—leftism was losing the momentum given by '68, and student organisations countrywide were beginning to look favourably at the CP again—allied to Dave's endearing and persuasive character brought about a renaissance which was ultimately to work itself out in the splits and controversies of the late 'seventies and 'eighties.

The position of Student Organiser was largely autonomous, one which Dave enjoyed enormously and where his political brain, his Bonapartism and his warm personal qualities found free expression. In 1974 he changed roles to become National Election Agent, and in 1975 succeeded Gordon MacLennan as National Organiser. In this role he acted as catalyst to a great release of political energy, and his promotion of events like the 'Ally Pally Rallies'—with acts like Scritti Politti and Shakin' Stevens performing—proved his capacity to attract young, vibrant people into the Party.

But he came to the job at an inauspicious moment. It was a time of heightening debate within the Party on Women's and Gay Rights—both of which he staunchly espoused without perhaps clearly understanding the detailed issues involved—and on the drafting and re-drafting of the policy document *The British Road to Socialism*. Dave also worked wholeheartedly on the Commission on Inner Party Democracy, the minority report from which prepared by Dave and Pat Devine sought to bring about abolition of the Recommended List and more democratic and accountable functioning of the Party. He also played a significant role in the Campaign Against Racist Laws (CARL).

In his work on the Commission, he crucially declared war on the majority position within the Party and became identified as a reformer—a dangerous stance to hold—whilst CARL, along with other initiatives like the People's March for Jobs and the Big Red

Bike Rides, brought him widely in touch with the Party's grassroots, which was perhaps the main contributory factor towards the enormous affection in which he was held at that level.

A conservative realignment, given the Stalinist nature of the Party's old guard, was perhaps inevitable in the face of his calls for a more open and pluralistic Party. Dave was made to pay. From 1977 he found himself increasingly squeezed. His allies were booted off the Executive and Political Committees. He himself was treated with scant honesty, his job restricted to menial tasks of card issue and collection of *Morning Star* subscriptions.

His close ally from the time and editor of *Marxism Today*, Martin Jacques, recalls that '. . . conservatives believed that the Party had gone too far over towards accommodating new social movements, and no longer sufficiently concerned itself with the traditional obsessions of class and friendship with the USSR. These were bad times. Dave had one of the key jobs, so became focus for their animus. He was anti-Stalinist, Eurocommunist, very principled, utterly brave and never deterred. When he had his own base from which to operate in the student organisation he was very effective. As National Student Organiser he was responsible for the Communist Universities which ran in central London each summer, and which in their heyday were brilliant and potent exercises in promiscuous heresy. But within an ossified national apparatus he found himself between a rock and a hard place. He wasn't an operator—with Dave, what you saw was what you got—and they treated him dreadfully. He left in '81 to work in a Support Unit for difficult children, which he was very good at, but came back as National Campaigns Organiser in '83 after the *Morning Star* split, but the ruling faction still distrusted him. Right to the end, though, he kept his romantic attitude towards the Party, even when it was clear to me and others that it was a bust flush.'

For all this activity over a quarter of a century or more, I have the record in his full-tilt, slant-scrawl hand hastily and warmly urging the latest political venture whilst always ending with a climbing postscript—usually on the latest gem from the gritstone *bijouterie*: 'Ramshaw Rocks—*The Press*—maybe the best ten feet of climbing in the world!'

The romantic Socialist attitude was still obvious, as was his total lack of cynicism about the state of leftist politics, even after the collapse of the Eastern Bloc and the Moscow Gold revelations. His continuing optimism led him to set up, with Pat Devine and others, the Red/Green Study Group—a natural direction for his energies. As late as the autumn of 1991 he was explaining in the columns of the *New Statesman* why he was still a communist and how the democratic nature of that quasi-religious belief still held its force for him. But his Party had gone, had become *Democratic Left*. His home demolished, he looked to other struggles.

There were always plenty of those in his personal life. Bea Campbell describes him as a man who was '. . . robustly candid about his commitment to sexual pleasure, and completely comfortable with his masculinity. He was one of a group of men for whom issues of sexual and personal politics had never been part of their political project. The debate on them didn't come naturally to him, but he put himself out to make himself an ally in the way feminism was attempting to navigate a life for itself within the CP. He was a person with whom you could do business.'

Partners, as opposed to political colleagues, could find him less amenable. His long-term and loving relationship with the journalist Sarah Benton foundered on what was for Dave the vexed issue of sexual fidelity. The very rewarding relationship current at his death with the novelist and poet Alison Fell went through periods of anguished debate around the same question. Both relationships were of remarkable quality. His acknowledgement of the intellectual superiority of Sarah and the creative precedence of Alison was grateful and unconstrained. But principled promiscuity makes for tempestuous bed-fellows.

It is, I suppose, as a companion in the hills that I shall chiefly remember him. Of all the people I climbed with in my brief zenith as a rock-climber twenty or more years ago, Dave was the most reassuring and encouraging to have hold of your rope on a difficult route. He seemed to will you into climbing better than you ever thought you could. His own climbing was earnest and dogged, but seldom less than effective and always taken with joyful and voluble enthusiasm. He was an inveterate seeker-out of appalling new routes. He once talked me into climbing a new line with him on the Far East Buttress of Clogwyn Du'r Arddu. The state of the rock on it can be judged from the fact that at one point, with a hundred feet of rope out and no worthwhile protection, a twenty-foot-high pinnacle weighing several tons on which I was standing slid slowly down for eighteen inches before coming to rest again. Had it not done so, he would have written my obituary twenty years before this goes to press. As it was, he just laughed, and so did I. You could forgive Dave almost anything for the innocence of his commitment.

Not only for that, though. His political creed was expressed in a complete readiness to share everything and anything he had. He was the most exemplary man I ever met, and as good company as I ever met with too, whether sitting in his Brixton home with a carry-

'He was the most exemplary man I ever met'

SPIRITS OF PLACE

out from Momma Redstripe's to keep us arguing till the small hours, or at some bleak and ill-attended political rally on a November Sheffield night, or on a dusty summer's Sunday at Harrison's Rocks, or an occasion the year before last when he and I drove down to Pembroke for a criminal trespass on the military ranges in order to extend climbing's purlieu there. I was on crutches after breaking my heel the previous week, and eager for some squaddie to issue forth and ask us what we were doing, but there were none about—they'd all gone to the Gulf—so Dave led me up the last new route we were to climb together. 'No Peace for the Wicked' he called it—conventional by comparison to the messages he'd built into his route names in the past: 'Soledad Brother', 'Sandinista', or—this from a past President of the East Finchley Rock Preservation Society!—'Hank Williams Will Live Forever in People's Hearts'.

Dave Cook trespassing on the Castlemartin military ranges, Pembroke, 1991

His sporting and political interests coalesced admirably in his writing about climbing, which is widely admired by the activity's devotees, and cuts a swathe through the bigotry, sexism, willy-waving, ignorance and exclusivity that still bedevil attitudes within it. At the time of his death, a book about his bicycle ride to Australia is being typeset by the Ernest Press and will be published early next year.* His life, after the political depression suffered by all of us on the Left in the early 'nineties, was opening up again. He was enjoying his grandchildren (Dave's three children, Henry, Lester and Alberta, had all lived with him in Brixton). There would have been another book about his Mediterranean ride.

He was fun to be with, but there was a sharper edge to him than just that. He wrote once, reviewing a book in the *New Statesman*, that it 'forces the reader to think of a world where the story might have ended differently'. Dave's sights were clearly set on that world, and he communicated it by precept and example to everyone he met. If only, for our sakes who knew and loved him and for the principles for which he worked lifelong, his own story could have gone on longer, could have ended differently too. He was one of the great characters from post-war climbing, and one of the two or three major influences on my life. For the pleasure of his company and the force of his example, I shall always be in his debt.

The Guardian, 1993

* *Breaking Loose* (Ernest Press, 1994)

3: 'NEVADAS OF RAPTURE'

Bog Trot

New Year; I roll back in from pub and party at 2 a.m. to find a message from Beatty on my answering machine: 'I'll be in the greasy caff on Victoria Station approach at 8.15, having a pint of tea and a bacon butty before getting the 8.55 train to Marsden. Don't expect you'll want to come, but if you do, that'll be great . . .'

The Marsden-Edale! I last did it with Len Chadwick 33 years ago, at this hour of night have forgotten about the experience sufficiently to be tempted by it now. I pack my rucksack, scavenge round the fridge for Christmas relics, set the alarm for a quarter to six. Three hours' sleep later I fall out of bed, dress, make a pot of coffee, pour the last remnants of the whiskey bottle into a flask and the coffee on top of it (imagining the while what my Scottish friends would say about this waste of Glenmorangie), call my diminutive and psychopathic Jack Russell, The Flea, to heel, collapse out of the door and into the car for the two-hour drive to Manchester.

All the way along the north Wales coast it rains, it sleets, gusting sheets of hail slap the screen. A vile day's in prospect, and the radio forecast confirms it. I don't have the moral force to say, 'No, this is stupid', and turn back, so I carry on, let things take their course. As I pull into the car-park by Victoria, there's Beatty, peering through a misted cafe window with intense, raptor's glare, scanning the tarmac for any poor rodent to be pinioned in the talons of his day's designing.

His eyes fix on me. A sadistic, joyful light comes into them. I slouch into the cafe. Before he can seize on me I'm rescued by a worn, pretty woman with guarded smile and pained waitress eyes. She calls me 'love', pours balm on my morning-sick soul and a cup of tea before she's called away to a table of weekend needy workmen with toast and bacon and beans in front of them. I slide into a booth opposite Beatty, who's all exclamatory gleam and inane grin. I refuse to be drawn in, watch the waitress, spin Raymond Carver fantasies around her as she goes back behind the counter, rubs her belly and talks women's talk in muttered tones and a flat north Manchester accent familiar as old memory to a buxom cook in grease-stained blue-check apron.

We run across the station concourse for the train with Beatty breezy as a chaplain on the walk to the execution chamber. The line of The Flea's mouth is unusually phlegmatic. His inappropriate cheeriness is getting on her wick too. She's marking him down for an admonitory nip when the chance presents. Cloudy diamonds of rain spill across grimed windows. At Stalybridge (what's in a

Mudpit Mires

name?) Alistair MacDonald springs aboard, disgustingly cheerful. Do they know we're bound for Black Hill, Bleaklow, Mudpit Mires? I begin to suspect something else is amiss:

'You're dressed for running . . .'

They both are. We're setting off for a twenty-five mile traverse of the worst slop and gloop in the Dark Peak in a January south-westerly gale, and they come on like they're out for a Sale Harriers' summer evening fun-run through Dunham Park. I sense that the pace will be—shall we say rigorous? Since I'm here now, and committed, I strap on boots, gaiters, waterproofs, bestow compass and antiquated O.S. 1:63,360 Sheet 102 (Huddersfield) map about my person, glance at grim-walled mills sidling past, console myself that if I get left behind I'll make Edale at my own stolid pace, ruminating that it's my own fault for getting lured in to the Rucksack Club's annual New Year Marsden-Edale meet.

But do you know about the Marsden-Edale and the Rucksack Club? Here's what Eric Byne and Geoff Sutton had to say about 'the most famous moorland traverse of them all' in *High Peak*, their 1966 memoir of Derbyshire walking and climbing: 'This expedition, which in wintry conditions is probably the best twenty-five-mile bogtrot in the Peak, is meritorious for leading straight across the tops of Black Hill, Bleaklow and Kinder Scout, without roads or easy options for miles.' It was developed in the years before the First World War by Cecil Dawson, a Manchester cotton merchant and early member of that city's Rucksack Club. Dawson was known, for reasons slightly obscure, as 'the Colonel of the 94th': 'A big, upright man, light of body but long of leg, he was taciturn to those he did not know, and his gruff voice startled many a stranger. His determined features were adorned with a great flowing moustache, and altogether his appearance was that of a Prussian officer in mufti. It is said that his map-and-compass work was faultless. He appeared never to alter speed or stride, continuing at the same pace uphill or on the flat.'

In the years before the Great War and even as late as the 1940s, this walk was a radical venture, traversing some of the most strictly-keepered grouse-moors in the Peak District: 'The Marsden-Edale became every strong walker's yardstick, and few winter's weekends went by without some group making the long crossing. Nor was this always for the walking alone. There was also the adventure of wondering whether one would negotiate Wild Boar Clough on Bleaklow without encountering the notorious keeper who sometimes waved a revolver in people's faces.'

As for Dawson's relations with these custodial thugs, '. . . he was known, hated and hunted by all the Bleaklow and Kinder Scout

John Beatty

keepers, but was never caught, although on one occasion after a day on Bleaklow [he was] followed to the Miller's Arms near Hazlehead and only managed to escape by climbing through the window while the keepers were waiting in the passage.' Strange, the social mores by which it would have been acceptable for a respectable Manchester cotton merchant to be set upon by a gang of vicious, forelock-tugging louts . . .

We heave out of the train on to a drenched and windswept platform in Marsden. Beatty and MacDonald race up the steps, turn left over the bridge, and discuss the likelihood of reaching Edale before dark at 4 o'clock. It's 9.30 already. Allowing for a rest or two, that's four miles an hour for six hours of ascent, descent, sucking knee-deep mire. The world's wearing a grey cap. You can't even see Shooter's Nab quarry, with its majestic face-crack, the name of which escapes me though I remember its crisp solo moves from a bright spring evening years ago, and the woman beneath and our looking at each other for the first time in a particular way. It would be misery there today, I reflect. That's why we're doing this. At least this is mobile misery.

Beyond a packhorse bridge, its gritstone winter-black and soot-stained, they decide on the easy start up Wessenden Clough, a sinister valley with a sequence of reservoirs leading to mist-shrouded moors. A car coasts up the track alongside us. Its occupant lets out a large dog. The Flea flies at it in a rage, venting on it her feelings about the day. Ten times bigger than her, it leaps back into the car. I know how it feels. The prospect of this walk is having the same effect on me. But I tag along as we get into the rough going, the blond-quiffed tussocks and the orange moor-grass that you think in its October reds cannot get brighter but its glow intensifies winter-long. We cross Wessenden Head Moor where Brady and Hindley buried their victims, and where some still lie, knowledge of what was done to them hanging heavy about the place.

Across the Isle of Skye road a line of flagstones and setts wavers towards Black Hill. We run down it, whingeing the while about its intrusive incongruity. Beatty turns aside where a little stream jags through, explaining that it's a short-cut of his father-in-law's. An arctic hare starts from the heather. We follow it on to the blasted, dismal landscape of Black Hill—a waste of frozen, black peat-flats, the O.S. pillar standing proud of its eroded surface. We skate and pole across them. I think I have never been in such a starkly desolate place—charred earth and cold smoke like the Nordic version of Hell. There are other vague figures stumbling around half-lost in the gloom. Beatty says to let it swallow them up so they can't follow us. A quick check of the compass—every reading today is between 160 and 200 degrees, south all the way—and we're off again into the mist, into the wind and rain over White Low and Hey Moss and down into Longdendale, where we huddle behind a wall to eat lunch, see straggling figures from earlier trains making their way on to Bleaklow by the Rollick Stones Ridge.

Soon we're after them, grinding up to the plateau which is the crux of the walk: 'In bad weather it is easier to go wrong on the section between Wild Boar Clough and the Snake road than anywhere else, and the consequences are more serious.' They would be today—the cold's bitter, and we're thoroughly soaked by a drenching small rain on the wind. All across the plateau, visibility's down to 20 or 30 yards as we lurch through sucking groughs, slithering on ice, seeking out the easiest line over interlinking gravelly flats. The four-mile crossing takes an hour-and-a-half. I don't care any more about keeping to dry ground, splash down the stream in Hern Clough below Bleaklow Head wondering at the stupidity of environmental consultants in planting flagstones and alien Eurograss along it. Whenever Beatty comes across a marker stone or other foreign form, he rants and gesticulates, eyes fixing you with his Ancient Mariner glitter, doing his gimlet-hypnotic, passionate-proselytising number. I save my energy, too numb to care. Parasite worms expelled from warm gut to cold moor win a glimmer of fellow feeling from me in their slow, dying writhe on the white-tipped khaki cylinders of grouse droppings. We stop at the Snake Inn for whiskey and beer, finish our own supply of the former in the plantation below the road as the light fades. I scold a passing mountain rescuer for the noise pollution from his radio. Slightly drunk, we weave up Seal Flats in the dark to make the short crossing of the Kinder plateau, questing, stumbling about with one failing light between us by Nether Tor and Ringing Roger for the steep descent by The Nab. Down on the road a sweet old fellow of seventy or so from the Rucksack Club who's done the walk more times than he cares to remember counts us in.

By six, we're in the Nag's Head in Edale, dripping liquid peat, drinking pots of tea, waiting for the train, musing on mountaineering's winter varieties. Stragglers falter in. Talk rattles along. The Flea, who has scrabbled heroically through the mire and been dyed black in the process, sleeps soundly on my knee, does not even rouse herself to give Beatty the bite he so soundly deserves when he reaches across, benign now, to pat her. We share disconsonant warm memories of cold mist-miles and the characters young and old, living and dead, who've known them before we too, in our turn, disperse on the long ways home.

Climber, 1995

The Flea

Eating Bear Meat

There is an afterword to the paperback edition of Primo Levi's two attempts—*If This is a Man* and *The Truce*—factually to record the experience of Auschwitz and its aftermath. It's entitled 'The Author's Answers to his Reader's Questions'. In it, Levi asks himself the question, 'To what factors do you attribute your survival?' Part of his response runs thus:

'The fact that I survived and returned unharmed is due, in my opinion, chiefly to good luck. Pre-existing factors played only a small part: for instance, my training as a mountaineer . . .'

I like that invocation of chance, that proper perspective on the hubristic self-belief of the mountaineer. 'A small part'! That's all, I think, that mountaineering has to play in the sagas of human adventure. Yet continually, increasingly, it's referred to as an 'adventure sport'. The point to be made about this unthinking collocation concerns its inherent contradiction. Sport and Adventure are not the same thing at all, at some level may well be mutually irreconcileable. Their active principles are poles apart: sport and adventure—rules and chance.

But then, what do we mean by adventure anyway? It seems to me one of those debased words, like freedom or God—originally coined to *comprehend* an area of human experience—which have become loose tags ever more divergent from the concept they once bodied forth.

I have on my shelves at least two books by mountaineers on the subject of adventure. One concludes that adventurers have big hands and a faraway look in their eyes. The other ends with the ultimate—and ultimately farcical—willy-waving fable about a man who grew and grew until finally he surpassed so hugely the mountain he'd initially stood beneath that he burst, and out of him came another man who also grows and explodes and then another, and the author '. . . knew somehow that, after the next explosion, my man would be just that much bigger again. And again.'

Between all this veiled tumescence and parturition-envy there's a good deal about crops, onions, cabbages, gardening and the like. My response to the whole idea as an adequate image by which to understand adventure is derision. Beyond that, it's to ask why there is this failure of imagination on the part of mountaineers to understand what adventure is about?

I suspect that the answer to what the non-mountaineering public would consider an absurd conundrum lies in the depths of that vast gulf which stretches between adventure and achievement. Can a

SPIRITS OF PLACE

successful mountaineer truly be called an adventurer? Perhaps that depends on what it took for him to become a successful mountaineer. If the answer is a solar-powered lap-top computer (if you think that's some notional red herring introduced to prop up my argument, I recommend an attentive reading of Chris Bonington's *The Everest Years*), then for a very simple reason the answer has to be 'No!'

That reason is the fundamental one of calculation, for once that quality intrudes, adventure goes out the window. Human resourcefulness, not material or technological resources, is what's called forth by adventure. Spontaneous adequacy, not planning and conquest, is its linch-pin. The word earns two columns of definition in the Oxford English Dictionary. The keynotes are 'that which happens without design . . . chance . . . hap . . . luck . . . a chance occurrence . . . a trial of one's chance . . . chance of danger or loss . . . risk . . . jeopardy.'

All the things, in fact, that so much of modern climbing has set its face against. Which is not to stigmatize modern climbing. To watch Ben Moon on Hubble is to witness exquisite gymnastic complexity. But it's not adventure, and climbing once gravitated to that. Which brings me back to Primo Levi and the title of this piece.

Levi's best book is the enthralling mix of memoir, fact and fiction called *The Periodic Table*. Its chapters are all given names of elements, and treat of characters who, for Levi, possess like qualities. The one on Iron focuses on Sandro Delmastro: 'He spoke grudgingly about his exploits. He did not belong to that species of persons who do things in order to talk about them (like me) . . . It appeared that in speaking, as in mountain climbing, he had never received lessons; he spoke as no one speaks, saying only the core of things . . . To see Sandro in the mountains reconciled you to the world and made you forget the nightmare weighing on Europe . . . We would come out at dawn, rubbing our eyes, through the small door of the Martinotti bivouac, and there, all around us, barely touched by the sun, stood the white and brown mountains, new as if created during the night that had just ended and at the same time innumerably ancient. They were an island, an elsewhere.'

One February day (the period described in the book is the early 1940s), Levi and Sandro

'The taste of being strong and free'

set out 'for the winter climb of the Tooth of M., which for some weeks had been one of our projects'. Here's Levi's account: 'We slept in an inn and left the next day, not too early, at some undetermined hour (Sandro did not like watches: he felt their quiet continuous admonishment to be an arbitrary intrusion). We plunged boldly into the mist and came out of it at one o'clock, in gleaming sunlight and on the big crest of a peak which was not the right one.'

They discuss the matter. Levi suggests that they carry on and 'be satisfied with the wrong peak, which in any case was only forty metres lower than the right one'.

'Sandro, with splendid bad faith, said in a few dense syllables that my last proposal was fine, but from there "by way of the easy north-west ridge" (this was a sarcastic quotation from the . . . Alpine Club guidebook) we could also reach the Tooth of M. in half an hour; and what was the point of being twenty if you couldn't permit yourself the luxury of taking the wrong route.'

The ridge turns out to be disconcertingly difficult, covered on the one side with melting snow, on the other with verglas:

'We reached the top at five; I dragged myself along so pitifully that it was painful, while Sandro was seized by a sinister hilarity that I found very annoying.

"And how do we get down?"

"As for getting down, we shall see," he replied, and added mysteriously, "The worst that can happen is to have to taste bear-meat."'

They survive the night, in the morning return to the inn: 'This was it, the bear meat; and now that many years have passed, I regret that I ate so little of it, for nothing has had, even distantly, the taste of that meat, which is the taste of being strong and free, free also to make mistakes and be the master of one's own destiny. That is why I am grateful to Sandro for having led me consciously into trouble, on that trip and other undertakings *which were only apparently foolish . . .*'

Sandro's end runs thus: a resistance fighter, in trying to escape from captivity with the Fascists he '. . . was killed by a tommy-gun burst to the back of the neck by a monstrous child-executioner, one of those wretched murderers of fifteen . . . recruited in the reformatories. His body was abandoned in the road for a long time, because the Fascists had forbidden the population to bury him.'

I wonder if there's an image of the degradation of mountaineering in his fate? I know that unless you understand *viscerally* what it is to 'eat bear meat', you contribute to its death.

Address to Karrimor Adventure Symposium, 1992

Adventuring on Llŷn

Hold your hand up to the white light above the dentist's chair and muscle fades to shadow, dark brittle sticks of bone show through. I noticed this the morning after our small Sunday afternoon adventure down on Llŷn. Its intimation of mortality seemed more than usually apposite. My dentist is a climber. It's the way of things in north Wales. All the professional people are from the climbing ghetto: doctors, solicitors, accountants—even Ian Lowe, the climber's dentist:

'Fantan B, Ian—have you done it?'

'Yes—twenty-three years ago. It was quite popular at one time, wasn't it? Freda and I did it when she was six months pregnant. She found those top overhangs rather hard going. Dreadful descent to it, as I remember . . .'

You can rely on Ian for an orderly account of things. I pressed him with another leading question:

'What is a Fantan B?'

'It's a drug. Pete Crew apparently found a discarded pharmaceutical container in the rubbish dump near where you start the route, and liked the name. I think it's an anti-depressant. Let's look it up.'

He picked up his formulary and thumbed through:

'Here we are—Fentan—that'll be it. Typical of Pete to get the spelling wrong. It's obsolete now, which would fit. When was the route done? About 1966 . . .?'

'Exactly then. He did it with MacNaught-Davies. I remember him raving about it. So everybody went down to do it and most of us ended up not being able to find it. Anyway, I did it yesterday. It was terrifying.'

Ian smiled his detached dentist's smile at this:

'Yes, I remember feeling a little apprehensive here and there . . .'

I held up my hand to the light again, old mortality imaging forth, and comforted, relaxed back to await the drill.

Cold December morning on the streets of Llanberis. I skulk into The Newt's house on Goodman Street, let hot coffee and a warm fire take the chill from my fingers.

'Any bright ideas, Andy?'

'Have you done Fantan B?'

This stirred memories, but they were as vague and unsatisfying as December daylight, and all to do with horrid descents. In the course of the day they resolved themselves into having been to look for it once, and having gone to the wrong crag—Trwyn y Gorlech rather than Craig y Llam. This had given me a jaundiced view of climbing on the north coast of Llŷn: 'Guano, shattered granite, vegetable decay—frightful to get at, worse to get off!'

'So you've done it?'

'Not sure—I remember doing something on Yr Eifl, but I've no idea what.'

'Paul's guide raves about it—let's give it a try. He also gives it a very long description, which usually means that he's had a gripper on it.'

'Show me . . .'

One of many things that Paul Williams' *Rock Climbing in Snowdonia* guide is good for is getting you enthused. I read the Llŷn preamble: '. . . the Lleyn holds a certain fascination for a discerning clientele: the climber in search of adventure, the connoisseur of the esoteric, the seeker after solitude . . . to see another party is a rarity.' So far so good—glimmerings of interest were aroused. But what did he have to say about the route?

'A thrilling sea-cliff expedition with impressive situations which has been compared with A Dream of White Horses as an experience, though Fantan B is much steeper and more isolated . . . difficulties increase with height . . . rock sometimes suspect . . . belays and runners are often difficult to locate . . .'

'Alright—I'll go for that. HVS 4c—that means terror-terrain, doesn't it?'

'You get that impression from the rest of the description, don't you.' We dawdled around, drank more coffee, and towards mid-day sauntered out of the house. This may have been a mistake. We were setting off on a miserable December day to drive for the best part of an hour to do a 600-foot route with a complex and frightening approach, difficult route-finding, seven or eight pitches, poor belays. All this, as you know intuitively at the time, adds up to the trap closing behind you. But you carry on because to commit yourself to it brings into play a primal reliance on your own resources that's close to the essence of why we climb.

Turning off the road beyond the grey-terraced chaos of Llithfaen, a track winds forever down plunging hillsides. Steep. Rough. Wet. Will the car get back up it? Already, questions-that-will-have-to-be-answered are being set. We park in a mouldering quarry. On its farther side a rusting hawser runs through a gap. We cross to it and look down on the sea, shockingly far beneath, the grey winter grass steepening out of view. We consider the matter, go back to the car, decide to carry a sack each and to descend in our trainers rather than rock shoes. Clearly we're not bound for some sunny, brief rock-outing.

SPIRITS OF PLACE

High on Fantan B

When we return to the hawser, the sacks bulge more than might be expected if they contained only a pair of rock-shoes apiece. This leisurely approach and inspection has taken us beyond one o'clock. Three hours of daylight left! I remember a December day at Cheddar twenty years ago when Sue Whaling and myself had started Coronation Street at three o'clock, finished the top pitch in darkness, been faced with finding the descent in pitch-black night. Looking around at the old quarry workings between the car and where the route must finish, it occurs to me that there may be similar excitement in store.

The hawser is knotted loosely round a granite block, the gap in the rock wall polished by passage of anxious bums. Andy heads off down. After 60 feet and a small rock step, the hawser ends. Damp grass heels over in convex plunge towards sullen water. We falter down, zig-zagging, fearful, questing for the route. A few sheep watch, then flounce purposefully away to gentler pastures:

'This is worse than the descent to Easter Island Gully!'

'. . . And I always put a rope down for that!'

We don't have a spare rope, and anyhow it wouldn't be long enough, so we carry on with our nervous crawl downwards. I remember Harris walking unconcernedly across the steep grass above Cilan, and think what wimps he would consider us. Eventually, matters ease. We reach rock terraces running out west 60 feet above the sea, and traverse across sluices and dripping slabs to ledges where the cliff rises vertically from the sea. Beyond them an arête rears at an eighty-degree angle for several hundred feet. Above, fronds of grass like hanks of soiled and rotting fleece are caught in the mesh of this fractured granite. We belay on a Friend. Andy takes a bunch of pegs and a hammer from his sack.

'Psychological props,' he explains, placing a Leeper next to the Friend. Beneath us a seal the size of a small whale rolls and gawps.

Andy has left Paul's guide at the car—sensibly, since it weighs over a pound and our sacks already are mysteriously over-full. Instead, he has brought an old interim guide with an inexact description. The first feature is obvious—a pink ledge out on the arête. He ties on and leads across to it, belays, and I follow after hammering out the Leeper. The climbing is easy enough but everything is covered in birdlime and the holds creak and shift as you use them. On the ledge I pick at his huge rack, adding to my own burden, reassure myself about his belay and set off to traverse steeper rock to a further rib. Nothing is hard, but nothing reassures either. Cracks are all parallel-sided and poor for nuts, or behind detached blocks. Holds are latticed-about with fracture lines. Instead of simple, solid structures, the definition of the rock splinters, and with it your ease of mind. Beyond a step up on to the rib that's given 4a in Paul's description but would be straightforward on sound rock, a scooped and blocky area leads up to overhangs. At a ledge beneath them I tie on to a rusted blade peg and drape a long sling carefully over a flat spike to back it up. There is no obvious way ahead.

My vote, when Andy joins me, goes to the left arête, which looks polished. But the guide gestures right. He traverses to an arête, disappears round it, the rope runs up, he reappears briefly on the edge, is gone from sight again, then stillness, silence. I wait. The rope snails out a foot or two more over the arête, then stills. It is very cold, the water very far beneath, Ireland somewhere over there in the haze, brighter in that quarter, reminding of time passing. I intone Buck Mulligan's address: 'Grey, sweet mother. The snotgreen sea. The scrotumtightening sea.' A seal wallows, a cormorant hustles past with a low, complaining croak. Lichens which would glow orange in the sun are muddy-hued. Tide withdraws in little, gasping sighs from a shingle strand across the headland. Our life and ambition are a presumption to the place. From somewhere above comes the 'ting, ting, ting' of a driven peg. I cannot recall when I last heard the sound. The halfway marker on our 180-foot ropes slips through my fingers. There is more movement, no sound. I shiver a little as a wind brushes the ledge where I sit. Time passes. The rope's taken in. I untie from the belays, stamp, shake warm blood into cold limbs, move stiffly to the arête.

The view is suddenly heart-stopping. The ropes run up and across into the centre of a huge, scooped face. Andy's perched, a tiny figure, on a ledge beneath tier upon tier of spiring, dark overhangs. Streaks of birdlime are the only light relief to the dark, gathered power of the place. I hurry to join him. The climbing is nowhere technical, just naggingly insecure. A hundred feet on fissile holds, and he's teased in three runners. I climb past him up an awkward ramp without daring to look at his belay, and in my turn tie on to two poor nuts, and a Friend in an expanding crack. The rock above is oppressively steep. When he arrives, we piece together the line from the description. The next stance, sixty feet away, is a jutting, ridiculous block between sets of overhangs, a falcon's perch, a wild trip. Simultaneously we look at my belay, then at each other. No words are spoken. I drag a jacket and scarf out of my sack:

'My psychological props,' I explain, and take a look at my watch. It is a quarter to four.

He climbs a wall for 30 feet without runners into the base of a groove, then places three of them with an audible sigh of relief. To his right are guano-streaked prows and roofs. He sidles across into them, flicks a chock up into a notch above him, launches out with the brief injunction to 'Watch me!' With a gasp he flops on to a ledge. Out of his sight a falcon flashes by. 'Out there!' he yelps, in fearful delight. Paul's guide gives this pitch 4b, and technically it's no more than that. But the sea is hundreds of feet beneath, rock poor, protection scant. As you pull on to the ledge a nest of gorse-sticks, fur and bones greets you. You are in the fortress of the Roc. There is no retreat.

Chance or bad management has given me the crux pitch. It climbs two overhangs. The first of them is straight above and the light's failing fast. I reach up for what look like holds and, fearful of delay, when they come to hand pull on them. They bring me to a ledge. I fiddle a nut insecurely into a fractured area of rock and heave up a smooth slab to the next roof. There is a flaking peg beneath it that I clip, fiddling the tape round a nubbin of rock alongside as I do. It looks like the last barrier. I step up on friction and grope for holds. There are none, so I layback an edge in strange exultation at its technicality, angle my right foot carefully into a poor nick, and grasp a flat block above in glad ferocity. A great sweep of slab soars black against the sky. I sidestep to a ledge, place a nut that might be good if I could see, and a worse one, and bring up Andy. He scrabbles round the top roof and surges past. Rope creeps out, darkness falls. He runs out the full length. Across the gloom of Caernarfon Bay, South Stack lighthouse flashes, the lights of Brynsiencyn and Newborough glimmer. I follow blindly, fingers an obscure, thin-muscled gleam, not knowing if he's belayed, climbing by touch. At the top, he fishes two headtorches out of his sack:

'More psychological props?' I ask.

'Alpine scale, alpine gear—I thought this might happen!'

We creep along quarry ledges, throw stones to gauge drops, reach the car; chastened laughter from prisoners on parole who know they must go back, are unsure which is captivity, which is release.

Climber, 1991

(Beinn a'Chaoruinn and) The Vision of Glory

Three dreary months round Christmas, sunless, short-dayed, my mood dull as the season. Trudging between dark squads of regimented conifers up the forestry track into Coire na h-Uamha, above Loch Moy, there was no expectation in my mind beyond that of dogged exercise. The northernmost of the mountain's trio of east ridges bulked sullen into dank cloud above. There was not even relief in the particular. Everything crystalline and light-reflecting was subdued, stilled. I shuffled through soft snow to the foot of the ridge's first buttress and embarked on the climb.

There is something to be said for creating interest in your choice of line for the ascent. Technicality puts an edge on the way mind apprehends the immediate world. The focus closes down: to the ash-petalled lichen on the blocky face before you; to fronded heather moustaching the ledge into which you have swung the pick of your axe; to a fine balance in the configuration of your limbs across this airy crest. You are entering the dimension of approach; a lightness is beginning to hover in hitherto-leaden air. You're heading into the white world, cloud and the void beneath.

Which is how it was on Beinn a'Chaoruinn. I picked my way up the buttress—easy enough in summer but treacherous terrain now: powdery snow, rock greasy underfoot—and on to the snow slope above that curved up to the summit.

Let's introduce an element of misadventure. I took my crampons out of my sack at a ledge above the buttress, for the slope beyond was iron-hard *névé*, and steep. In my carelessness, my hurry to get out that morning from the chalet at Roy Bridge, I'd forgotten that they were adjustable, had last been worn by a friend with bigger feet. When I stood up, they rolled off my boots. In amused disgust, I pushed them back in the sack.

Amused? Oh yes—and you would be right to question by what token I found it thus. A few hundred feet of hard snow ahead, the potential for a fall of a thousand feet, bumping and sliding into the corrie below. But I still went at it, smashing the axe into the snow with murderous intent, belting at it with my boots so that three or four ferocious kicks would produce half an inch of precarious purchase, getting a rhythm into the work, resting after a hundred feet or so with one leg down a little crevasse the melt-and-freeze had produced against a small outcrop of rock.

Then it came. I was slumped contortionate against the rock, panting from exertion, head lolling backwards over my left shoulder, when the hovering brightness intensified. Suddenly the mist was scoured with utmost speed from the face of the mountain, shreds of blue sky tore across, shafts of brilliant light pierced into the corrie. From the ridge opposite diamond whirlwinds danced along the cornice edge, all glitter and coruscation, shapes of the Mamores beyond a phantasmal ivory gleam.

I do not know how you can adequately describe these moments and their effect on our lives. I write this eight months after the glance over my shoulder away from the dangerous world of the particular in which I had been engrossed. Yet what I saw in that moment is imprinted on my consciousness, is a part of the heart-life.

Our essential life, the joy-life, is a sequence of these moments. How many of us could count even sixty such? I recollect: the

Above the cloud sea, Sgurr nan Gillean, dusk

badger that passed three or four feet upwind of me one moonlit night, and I was so still it knew nothing of my presence there; the descent one evening down the Foxes' Path on Cadair Idris at sunset, and the sun caught ice-rimmed melt-holes where rocks pierced through, making each a flaring rosette sharp against the mauves and blues of gathering night; morning light in a room above the sea in west Cork, hair of spun gold on the shared pillow and her eyes a clearest blue flickering into wakefulness; or on Brandon Mountain, a glory round each of our spectral reflections on the mist . . .

SPIRITS OF PLACE

There is a common element in all this. It is beauty, and I am continually astonished how little is said about it in our modern world, and in our specific outdoor world where it is surely the prime and common factor in all our activity.

Once, years ago, I was out walking in Derbyshire. It was an October half-term, I was twelve or thirteen and had caught the train from Manchester to Hayfield, intending to walk up on to Kinder Scout by way of Kinder Low and descend Grindsbrook to Edale. I knew next to nothing about mountains and to me this was a mountain. The day was fine, the bracken golden on the lower slopes. I dawdled along, started to climb the hill's shoulder towards a prominent group of rocks. On an instant the sky darkened. From the moor above streamers of mist poured down in front and behind. The gritstone outcrop ahead writhed, its nebs and boulders shape-shifting amongst the vapours. I was suddenly cut off from all the world of normality, nature animate all around me, and I was intensely scared. I fled. I ran terrified down out of the mist to the top of Jacob's Ladder, stopped there, chest heaving, watching all the frightful mystery down out of which I'd come. And it transfigured itself before my eyes. There and then it became not a thing of fear but a vision of vital and resonant loveliness.

'The occasional going through into the white world'

The valley-greens flared with fierce intensity, bracken seemed on fire, mist was gilded with the sun. What had been terror was now beauty. As I sat and watched it there was a stillness within me beyond anything I'd known. I was annihilated, had no existence, simply looked out at the inconceivable beauty of the world that had detached me from any concept of self in order that I might *see*.

Does not everyone who comes to the mountains know something of this experience? It is at the root of a thousand hero-myths; it is Wordsworth's 'Fair seed-time had my soul/Fostered alike by beauty and by fear'; it is Simone Weil's 'Everything has to pass through the fire. But those who have become flame are at home in the fire. But in order to become fire it is necessary to have passed through hell.'

The moments seem to come more easily in the mountains. Their literature—beyond the ego-fixated narratives of achievement—is permeated by accounts of them. Here's Eric Shipton—greatest mountaineer-explorer of the century—groping towards its definition as he falls asleep in the Karakoram: 'We settled down on a comfortable bed of sand, and watched the approach of night transform the wild desert mountains into phantoms of soft unreality. How satisfying it was to be travelling with such simplicity. I lay awaiting the approach of sleep, watching the constellations swing across the sky. Did I sleep that night—or was I caught up for a moment into the ceaseless rhythm of space.' *(Blank on the Map)*

Once, on the High Street of a busy Welsh town, I stopped to talk to a good, resentful, careworn woman who told me this or that ugly thing about her husband, knowing he and I shared a passion for the hills. Behind her I saw light travelling across the cliffs and gullies of Ysgolion Duon, and wished her the moments that being there might bring, that her anger might be purged, affronts to her sense of self cleaned away by them. What you go through on the mountains is not the nagging, passive fear of abandonment and loss; it is not the burdening responsibility; it is the occasional going through into the white world, into the world of light.

Whatever our stated reasons for coming to them, it is the vague sense, the half-understood glimpse of this that draws us back time and again to go beyond fear, effort and discomfort into quietude and appreciation. We should not plan to conquer our hills, but rather to abandon ourselves to them. I remember so thinking as I pulled my foot from its crevasse on Beinn a'Chaoruinn and set back into the slope, into the sting of spindrift that obliterated the summit, my movements a joy and imprinted in my mind the vision of glory harvested there.

The Great Outdoors, 1993

Small Climbs in Germany

Like civilisation itself, I got lost somewhere in the region of Dachau. Maybe it was the ordinariness—the grey skies, the flat plains, the traffic jams—but somehow, circumnavigating Munich, my attention wandered and instead of the *autobahn* to Stuttgart I found myself in deepest Swabia. We were retreating from a rain-sodden Kaisergebirge. The weather-map in the international edition of *The Guardian*, which we'd studied and debated the length of a wet and desultory afternoon in a Salzburg cafe, told us to head north. Andy Newton and Kath Griffiths had gone ahead. I was to meet them at the Bethof camp-site in Rheinland Pfalz. But I was well lost. I went into a bright Greek cafe on a large square with lime trees and solid, careful sculptures in a modest, anonymous town. The waitress was dark and fine-featured. I'd anointed her with an olive complexion from the Sporiades, but when she began to talk she was a serious girl from downtown Stuttgart. I asked for the menu:

'We have bean soup,' she confided. pre-empting further questions.

'Sounds like a fair synthesis,' I replied, in acceptance.

She grasped eagerly at the abstraction:

'So—you know Hegel was a Swabian, then?'

I didn't, but was about to find out. Two hours later my mind and slender stock of conversational German were exhausted. Customers waited in silent patience at the bar as she pressed on into an analysis of Kant's influence on Hegel. There were two empty bottles of Retsina on the table. I didn't remember drinking any. I paid and left:

'Why is it so urgent that you see your friend? Are you homosexual? Do you not want to talk philosophy?'

Beyond the Rhein I got lost again on the way to Landau and stopped in the station bar in Bad Bergzabern to ask for the road to Vorderwiedenthal and a glass of beer. The barman's name was Dietmar. He was from the Pfalz. Did I know the Pfalz? No. Where was I from? Wales. He spoke back to me in perfect Welsh, held forth for the next hour-and-a-half on the origins of Celtic languages. Periodically a tumbler of Schnapps materialised on the bar, in appearance harmless as water. Much later, I arrived happily in Bethof. I enjoy travel. Meetings like these don't happen every day in Lutterworth or Carshalton.

With regard to this prologue, there's an interesting thing about Schnapps. It appears not to produce hangovers. Andy and Kath studied me carefully next morning for the tell-tale sounds and signs—the groans and sighs, the slumped posture. I didn't give them the satisfaction. Andy was anxious to do things and Kath, who is conscientious, was going to sun herself in the camp-site glade and—being a teacher—prepare what she termed 'all this National Curriculum bullshit'. So Andy and I consulted the guide. It's a thick red volume to the Sud Pfalz and opens with a sixty-page essay on geology, complete with diagrams. The route descriptions are less expansive, and instead of stars there's a system of symbols. A flower denotes a three-star route, a cross something well worthy of your attention, and two fingers giving what looks like a well-known gesture means it's death. The other thing you notice in the guide is that almost every route was done by Hans Laub and Fred Frey in 1933, apart from ones done by Fred Frey in 1943. We speculated endlessly on how he'd got the time off. After that, Wolfy Gullich added a few routes in 1980, then Hans took over again—he's apparently still doing new routes sixty years on. We wondered who he was and if we'd bump into him. The more of his and Fred's routes we did, the more impressed we became. The gritstone saga of Joe and Don pales into insignificance alongside their output.

My memory of this first morning in the Pfalz is hazy. Maybe I was overwhelmed by the beauty of the scene—round hills, red rock towers poking out of pine forests, small attractive villages with small attractive bars and large attractive waitresses. Andy, who is a man who notices such things, hustled me past all these to a piece of rock called, if I caught the name accurately, the Piffelfels, where he'd recently seen a young woman clad entirely in Lycra ascend a route with ten bolts on it. I'm not sure which he enthused about most warmly, but the bolts at least were still there and he led up it with only a little whimpering and backsliding and I followed with a lot of both, and grievous complaints about how one's arms hurt. The route finished on top of a pinnacle, from which it was a 100-foot abseil to the ground. Back at the bottom, it was my turn to lead.

Since I was standing at the bottom of a pleasant little slab with two shiny bolts, I opted for that. He looked it up and it appeared to be something called the Kieselweg or Kieselwand. If my schoolboy German doesn't deceive me that means either the gravelly path or little pebbles wall. I soon found out why. Also, he told me it was 7+, which was a couple of grades harder than the route I'd just been in desperate straits following, but my head was clearing and I had a new pair of sticky boots, so I thought to try it anyway, not having any idea of grades on the continent and liking the look of the thing.

'Untergriff . . . loch . . . ja?'

I'll tell you something about the Pfalz. The rock is sublime—it's like Helsby in appearance and like Stanage in friction and reliability. But it has these pebbles that were rattled down some mountain stream and dumped on the gravelly bed of the ocean aeons ago and are slippery as glass. You have to stand on them, which is fine when they're the size of duck eggs but less so when they're that of mouse droppings. On this Kieselwand route you have to pull on them as well and they're the size of pigmy shrew droppings—6b moves to clip the first bolt, and I had to come down and change into my old boots, whose margins of friction I know, before I dared make the move and even then I did something wrong—clipped in the wrong karabiner because I didn't know, being incompetent, that these bent things were for ropes not for bolts. Andy, who is scrupulous, soon put me right. I sometimes wonder why he doesn't charge me for climbing with him, since he has to spend half his time on systematic eradication of errors in my technique.

After the second bolt the little pebbles wall definitely became the gravelly path. There was a smooth slab and the last bolt runner receded far beneath. I moaned terribly but Andy just laughed and told me not to fall off because the bolts only went in half an inch. This, added to the fact that every tree round about displayed notices about rabid foxes, disenamoured me of the place so we went for coffee to Dahn, and ate cakes until we felt sick. Dahn has the best cakeshops I've ever seen. There are chocolate-coated croissants filled with apple, and Matterhorn replicas entirely of chocolate, and truffle-and-custard-dripping conch-shells. I could go on. Above the cafe was a 200-foot pinnacle with a crucifix on top called the Jungfernsprung, with a flowered route winding its way heavenwards. It was Andy's lead. He coasted up one side, then down and across the front to the other. I followed, cowering, to find him belayed to a bolt beneath a ten-foot roof cleft by a vile off-width crack. He was grinning and so was the crack, but I soon wasn't. These bolts in the Pfalz are massive affairs with welded rings through them. The crack had one on its left wall, the ring hanging out at a crazy angle.

'Should make it easier to clip if you're feeling bullish,' he told me. Afterwards he complained that it was the only overhanging crack he'd ever encountered that was more strenuous for the second than the leader, and that was before he'd even touched rock. I knew what he meant, but unfortunately there came a point where the runners were below and within and the crack had to be jammed. Imagine a wider version of Brown's Crack on Ramshaw and you'll have an idea what the fist jams were like. Also, getting at them demanded the most extraordinary contortions. It was gritstone 6a and I could feel the muscle fibres in my left arm ripping apart as I lay horizontally beneath it. In situations like this you understand why Baron von Munchausen was German. There was a ledge above the roof that nobody had visited or wiped for years, and the route book further on confirmed that impression. I draw a veil over our subsequent antics on this climb, except to add that they were very public. The whole town seemed to have a view on which way to go and a stance on how to do it. They were very friendly too. Imagine people who live above Lamorna or Wintour's Leap giving you amiable advice on how to do routes on their local crags, and you get an idea of how different is the atmosphere of the Pfalz.

Preliminaries over, Andy decided to placate me for his sadism in the matter of the crack by introducing me next day to Bärenbrunnerhof. If you were to find yourself in a valley clearing with great towers of perfect, characterful rock rearing up from the woods all around, and a sunlit terrace cafe with friendly people, beer, gorgeous cakes, beautiful waitresses, might you not have to pinch yourself to find out whether you'd just died and gone to heaven? If, afterwards, you went into the woods, found yourself beneath a crack that sidled over a roof to run up 120 feet of perfect vertical red rock and finish at a line of bolt runners leading across a slabby, delicate wall; if you climbed it at a blissful grade of E3, 5c, what would you think then? When we got to the top we were ecstatic, and fortunately unable to write anything in the route book because someone had stolen the inside from the pen.

This route was called the *Jubiläumsriss* on the Nonnenfels—Bärenbrunnerhof has a religious history, hence the Nuns' Rock and its neighbouring Cloister Rock on which we did a fine, wandering HVS called the Klosterwand later. We did some more things elsewhere too, but I'll leave those and tell you a couple of singular things to finish: of how, for example, we met a little fellow wearing a cloth cap on the Rödelstein one day. We listened carefully to hear if his wife called him Hans or Fred. He was five feet two, rather fat, in his sixties at least and cruised up the classic hard routes on the crag—5c's, 6a's. One I liked the look of he told me how to do in two words and a mime:

'*Untergriff . . . loch . . . ja?*'

The undercling, then the hole. When I came to do it, I could grasp the holds but not the problem of how he, at his height, could reach between the two when I could not. Nor could I understand why the first bolt was beyond its ground-fall-potential crux. But it was a great little climb. And he, like every other climber we met on the crag or in the Bärenbrunnerhof cafe where we sat on the terrace

Klosterwand

SPIRITS OF PLACE

Kieselwand—Mr Newton, grasping the holds but not the problem, contends with gravity

drinking beer, eating our rye bread, *bratwürst* and sauerkraut and watching the glowing buttresses merge down into dark pines each twilight, was as welcoming, outgoing and supportive as I remember the climbing communities of my youth to have been before commerce and competition spoiled them.

All this made the more sad something I saw on our last day there. We'd done a classic long 6+ on one of the buttresses around Bärenbrunnerhof. Half way up there was a route book with the guidebook diagram and route descriptions carefully pasted into it, and some uplifting quotations too in Gothic script. There were respectful entries from maybe a dozen nationalities, and there was one from the Brits that read like this: 'Fuck the Krauts—pile of shite!'

All the names driving back—Mons and Lens and Le Cateau, Ypres and Poitiers and the Somme—and it still goes on. I coasted sadly through France, following an inclination to catch the Cork ferry and thence back to Holyhead and home, not wishing to encounter that version of civilisation I'd have met between Dover and Shrewsbury. Sometimes you just feel ashamed . . .

Climber, 1993

Contumely of the Conquistadors

Re-reading *The Ascent of Everest* forty years after its first publication, I'm struck on the one hand by how decent and worthy, indeed gracious a book it is, and on the other by how entirely alien it now appears to the consciousness and mores of the last decade of the twentieth century. Its very first sentence sets the tone: 'This is the story of how, on 29th May, 1953, two men, both endowed with outstanding stamina and skill, inspired by an unflinching resolve, reached the top of Everest and came back unscathed to rejoin their comrades.'

My post-modernist perception struggles to set that language in context. As Yeats wrote, 'We traffic in mockery.' There is a problem in those words' register that haunts and strives to undermine them. They no longer conjure up images of joyful achievement and aspiring, of innocent mountain ambition, but darker ones, satirical shades. It's the speech of Newbolt and Kitchener; it frames the poster from which the recruiting sergeant's finger points out to underline the message that 'your country needs you'; it's the imperial afflatus that Wilfred Owen undercuts with the grim reality of 'sacrifice' ('What passing bells for these who died as cattle?'); it's the same nightmare or farcical rhetoric spoken by the court martial in Joseph Losey's *King and Country* or the General underneath whom the boards burn in the closing sequences of Lindsay Anderson's *If* . . . We can no longer take it seriously, mutter to ourselves in sardonic accompaniment a chorus of 'Play up, play up, and play the game!', view it from a cosmically different perspective where martial celebration is beyond the pale. The standpoint of 1953—that Everest had to be climbed—has become the philosophical scapegoat to an era where what's chosen for celebration is mountaineering bad faith.

But this, without substantiation, is perhaps to assert too much: 'martial celebration'? 'Everest had to be climbed'? Our current bad faith? Are those charges true?

The first is easy enough. If you read through the whole history of human involvement with Everest, it interlinks inextricably with that of the Great Game, is riddled with militarism. Consider only the ranks of those centrally involved in its exploration: Colonel Younghusband, Captain Noel, General Bruce, Major Tilman, Brigadier John Hunt—the list goes on. The military presence throughout sets up a fascinating tension with a more individualistic parallel tradition that reaches its most succinct expression in an anecdote recounted to me by Jack Longland to explain the failure, twenty years before the successful expedition, of Ruttledge's trip in 1933:

'. . . the crucial point was when the two soldiers, Bousted and Birnie, took it on themselves to say that conditions were too cold to establish Camp Five on May 20th. Wyn Harris, who was an infinitely more experienced mountaineer, thought this an absolute nonsense. I remember I was at Camp Four at the time and Wyn Harris came down in a complete fury, saying "The fucking soldiery!" And he was right, because on the 20th for the next three days not only was the weather good but it was before the upper slabs were covered with new snow.'

It's a tantalising prospect, that had it not been for the inexperienced autocracy of 'the fucking soldiery', with a fit, capable and competitive team of Shipton and Smythe, Longland and Wyn Harris well positioned on the mountain, Everest *might* have been climbed during the dark years of the depression instead of synchronously with the 'glad confident morn' of the Coronation. The military, after that fiasco, needed to redeem itself and how *gloriously*, in 1953, it did so—with knighthoods and honours all round as just and due reward.

All of which tends to obscure the fact that the 1953 venture was less expedition than expeditionary force. Its planning was meticulous, disciplined, exemplary; the terrain was studied from every angle (one of the most telling passages has Hunt poring over aerial photographs of the South Peak and summit ridge); lines of supply and command are firmly drawn up. There are ways in which

The Ascent of Everest reads like a textbook of classic warfare. I open it at random and read thus:

'First we must stock our Camp IV with stores sufficient to enable us to await an opportunity offered by the weather; we were already planning to besiege Everest for a fortnight. If the mountain held out for longer than this, then we should be forced to replenish from Base Camp. At the same time we must place the stores required for the Assault—all those to be carried above the head of the Cwm—at Camp V, which would thus, in effect, be a depot of the Assault stores. The exact amounts and their weights were already known, and consequently the number of High Altitude Sherpas required . . .'

The message is relentlessly hammered home: Everest had to be climbed. This was why Eric Shipton, the original choice of leader, was removed by—in the deputy leader Charles Evans's phrase—'an unworthy device'. Shipton was compromised and forced into resignation by the Himalayan Committee's designation, against Shipton's will, of John Hunt in increasingly senior roles on the expedition. If I have one criticism of Hunt's book, it is that in it this saga was glossed over in a single, and possibly disingenuous, sentence:

'Eric Shipton himself had already started to lay down the foundations for planning and was available to give advice from his immense fund of Himalayan experience.'

Nearly forty years after this was written, when I interviewed John Hunt for my biography of Shipton, I had a feeling that this omission still rankled in his conscience, urging him 'wherever possible to pass much of the credit back where it belonged, with Eric Shipton'. I don't wish to delve into psychological theorising, but there seems to me an element here of an honourable man (and forget MacNaught Davis's cheap sneers about 'Sir Isaac Hoont' that Ken Wilson chose to publish in *Mountain* some years ago, for as his record of public service alone shows, Hunt is exceptionally principled and altruistic) having been placed in an invidious position by the perceived necessity for Everest to be climbed. With Shipton, they were taking too much of a chance; with Hunt, as far as it ever can be in the mountains, chance was to be eliminated. The Good Soldier had been put in charge. His team was hand-picked and assembled round its leader, every member vetted: 'There was the need to be sure that each one of the party really wanted to get to the top.' The thing was becoming competitive, the Swiss had already 'entered the lists', Everest had to be climbed.

And climbed it was, through exemplary planning and magnificent teamwork and no small personal example on Hunt's part. Everyone under his care came back alive. The success was celebrated in appropriate style: 'In our light-hearted mood, we remembered our two-inch mortar. It had not been called upon to clear a path up the mountain for us, but it would carry out a no less appropriate function now. A salute should be fired, a *feu de joie*. We had twelve bombs, a gift from the Indian Army. With each of us taking turns, these were duly loosed off, to the delight both of ourselves and of the whole of our numerous retinue. This was followed by some practice with our equally neglected .22 rifles, the targets being some spare mortar-bomb detonators . . .'

Yet however much John Hunt's book strives for magnanimity of gesture and stately appropriateness of language, there is a subtext to all this that cannot entirely be concealed. It's the same one picked up by Tilman after his ascent of Nanda Devi in 1936: '. . . after the first joy in victory came a feeling of sadness that the mountain had succumbed, that the proud head of the goddess had been bowed.' Victory necessarily implies defeat, and conquest subjection, and invasion loss, and the treading of peaks can be the crossing of watersheds of the spirit. I believe John Hunt recognised this in his concluding chapter:

'Ultimately, the justification for climbing Everest, if any justification is needed, will lie in the seeking of their "Everests" by others, stimulated by this event as we were inspired by others before us.'

The words (witness that qualifying 'if any justification is needed') are uneasy. Hunt is too intelligent a man not to be aware subliminally of the implicit problem they raise.

Which is this: there are other 'Everests', but there is no other Everest. The mountain climbed 'because it was there' has done a disappearing act, is no longer there. History has absorbed it, feet have trodden it, words have described it. We do not know what it is like to stand on the summit of Kanchenjunga or Machapuchare, but we do know—personally in increasing numbers and vicariously by the tens of thousands—how it feels to raise the flags over Everest. The ultimate has become the everyday.

We're made the more aware of how momentous was the ascent of Everest by studying the directions taken by mountaineering thereafter: emulation or regression—you could take your pick but one or other it had to be. In a spirit of emulation, there was for a time the increasingly desolate and dispiriting movable caravanserai of Second Lieutenant Christian Bonington, camping out under the latest last great problem with its corporate sponsorship, contracts, career structure and increasing death toll. There were the crack regiments of the army moving in to clean up on the conquests he'd not made. And thankfully, apart from that tradition-robbed-of-its-focus, there were the regressives, those who looked back to Shipton, Tilman and Longstaff for their examples and from whom, for the last fifteen or twenty years, mountaineering has derived its stimulus and drive. They cut in early, their banner raised by Charles Evans's brilliant, under-rated and reverent reconnaissance expedition to Kanchenjunga in 1955, when Joe Brown and George Band climbed up to, but not on to, the summit. The 'more individualistic parallel tradition' I mentioned above later re-asserted itself under the banner of 'alpine-style': not pulling together but personal responsibility, not management but living-on-your-wits inspiration and self-sufficiency, not emblems but the unknown, not the world's acclaim but authentic experience.

Which is how—reactively—mountaineering came to be embroiled in issues of authenticity and bad faith. Take that sentence I quoted at the outset and our ironic mockery of it. There is no doubt about its authenticity. This, without false modesty, is what John Hunt believes, and is perhaps what we still aspire—robbed of our ultimate symbol and aspiration—to believe about ourselves. But our characteristic mode now, post-modernists all, is irony, wherein, according to Sartre, '. . . a man annihilates what he posits within one and the same act: he leads us to believe in order not to be believed; he affirms to deny and denies to affirm.' Belief requires a focus, and the focus has gone, the ultimate despatched. Experience alone, keynote of the regressive tradition, is left: 'If man is what he is, bad faith is forever impossible and candour ceases to be his ideal and becomes instead his being.' But man is defined by his aspiring, in Nietzsche's phrase is 'a bridge and a going across'. Once over the abyss, astride the peak, it is no longer emblem but commodity, attainable, measured, and the style in which we record our response to it modulates inevitably into bad faith. I look back on the innocence of that opening sentence of John Hunt's and realise with shocked clarity that in the success of that climb was the Fall. Whither, or wither, mountaineering now . . .?

Mountain Review, 1993

'In the success of that climb was The Fall'

Three Cornish Climbs

The Atlantic Ocean Wall (E5, 6a, 6b, 6a): I am forty-five years old, unfit, overweight. I spend most of my time behind a desk. The rest gets divided out between too many responsibilities. Of time for climbing I get not nearly enough. Also, I am incompetent, my rock-gear palaeolithic, my body showing the strains of having climbed for too long from too young—arthritis, tennis elbow, tendons, shoulders. I last led a route of this grade in the year Atlantic Ocean Wall was put up. I'm apprehensive before I even see it, and when I do it looks huge. Patiently Rowland Edwards, who is to take photographs, explains the line. It's in the back of a square zawn, towers above as you view it from the top of Longships Wall. The angle of the section level with us is cruelly apparent—ten degrees over the vertical for perhaps forty feet. Rowland's son Mark, who is to lead me up it, is entirely calm and composed. I ask if he has qualms about going on to it with an inept geriatric.

'None at all,' he replies, so I ask how often the route gets done.

'Five or six ascents to date, to our knowledge. Not that you can ever tell. Mick Fowler failed on it . . .'

I look down at the incoming tide, study ominous black streaks of water at the wall's base, and then, farting with fear, launch on to the abseil down Longships Wall and scrabble across awkward moves to the stance at the wall's foot with waves slapping at my heels. Mark prepares to climb. I note the height to which water's rising in the zawn corners, the lacey foam, the continous low-frequency roar, and hope he races up the first pitch. He's elected to start up Astrodome, which leads to the same stance beneath the second pitch of A.O.W. It's streaming with water, a black glisten of ooze down the initial wall. Mark despatches it in about five minutes, most of which is taken up in arranging protection for me. The ropes signal my reprieve from the encroaching tide. I start to climb. There's a difficult move on small, wet footholds to reach a bulging, diagonal crack. The jams in this are good but widely spaced, so you have to turn on the power to move up it, but that relaxes me and frees my stiff, fearful movements. I reach the arête and stand in balance, breathing hard. The groove ahead is easy but you have to leave it, balance across a steep wall with hands and toes on widely spaced breaks, then mantel on to the sloping stance. Mark clips me in, doles out extravagant praise, sorts out ropes and gear whilst I look around. There is a good peg crack at head height with a broken leeper in it weeping an ugly brown stain down the pale granite. To its left a crack takes a poor medium-sized nut. Beneath

'NEVADAS OF RAPTURE'

Starting the Atlantic Ocean Wall

it, two bolts have been drilled into the rock—small bronze bolts without hangers, to which we're attached by wires from which the nuts have been pushed down.

'Why these, Mark?'

'We thought that, rather than have the crack battered apart by peg placements—and remember that ordinary steel pegs last no time here—the bolts would prevent degradation of the rock. But no

145

one wants to listen. They just rant on about bolts in Cornish granite—people who couldn't get to a place like this to save their lives dictating to us what to do . . .'

He moves past me on to the rock. I sense fierce will and covert anger. Above is a roof giving into a diagonal, leaning crack. He crouches beneath it, makes the positional adjustments, then swings round to relax into jamming his way up the crack. The rope crawls and stutters out, I crane my neck to watch his unflurried progress, envy the lightness and stamina. Soon he's belayed. The swinging loops from beneath my ledge disappear upwards. It's my turn to climb. I make the crack, get insecure jams, place my feet carefully on a green vein intruded across the prow where I squat. The top surface of rock flakes away, leaving me dangling from a jam. I flail back in contact, grab for a runner. Blood trickles down the back of my hand. Panting, struggling to retrieve Friends from the crack, I wrestle to an area of crumbling holds and almost-balance. In front is a peg runner, above me an overlap. I rest haplessly on the peg, peering into illegible rock above. Mark decodes it for me—a side-pull, a better hold above and right, little footholds, the flake above. It overhangs gently, but somehow, in a failing rush, I make it to the latter, where all feels better. There are good jams, small footholds, the possibility of rest even in a layback, and the position is exhilarating. A little, easy traverse from the end of the flake and I'm at the stance. It's a good foothold in an overhanging groove. There are two small bronze bolts in the wall. Looking down at the sea 140 feet below, and then into the crumbling back of the groove, I don't feel like criticising them. Mark climbs the groove with finesse, tip-toeing and pirouetting. I just back-and-foot. After what's gone before it's a cinch. There are various bits of rotting iron driven into the mud at the back, sharp and flakey in their decay. A clump of royal fern sprouts sturdily. As I near the top, ledges are covered with rock sea-spurrey, star-petalled, long-sepalled, flowering from a thick, delicate succulence of tiny leaves. It brings me back to level earth. We scamper through a rock-arch into strangeness of peopled land. The route is one of the best I've ever done. Like its flowers, it should be five-starred.

Demolition (E6, 6a/b): Of an argument, perhaps? The route's at Sennen, takes a blank wall just left of Demo Route. Soon after its first ascent, a Cornish climber had written in to one of the domestic magazines complaining about a 'craftily erected foothold', about the route being a 'cunning example of the chipping art'. Well, I've seen chipping on routes in my time: the first ascent of Linden on Curbar, of Downhill Racer on Froggatt, of Razzle Dazzle and The Gadfly on Crystal Slabs. I've seen the effect of retro-chipping of routes like Rusty Wall, Pedlar's Slab and Long John's Slab. I don't like it. I wondered what I'd find here. Mark led up the route. It was a gusty October evening with a spit of rain on the wind. He did it without faltering, took the rope in and I tied on. There's a hard, reachy move, like the crux of Beatnik on Helsby, for the first break and the last runners. Above is a 25-foot slab at an 80-degree angle with a thin flake at bottom right and a vague, incipient crack at top left. Between the two and level with the first are two scooped indentations, toe-sized. You step into the second with your right toe and are faced with the crux. Above is a minute rounded boss of crystals and just to its left a fingerhold. It is two centimetres long and two millimetres deep, slightly sloping, and the tips of two fingers can rest on it and gain enough purchase to keep your balance as you lash a foot way out left not on to a hold but on to a vague, rough rib. If you fell off from this position leading, you would hit the ground. If anything hereabouts has been chipped, it has weathered back into the appearance of naturalness. But there is nothing here anyway. A fingernail balance hold! 'The chipping art'? I cannot square the rhetoric with the reality. What's been said had its origins not in honest comment but in animus. The smallest example from any route listed above would appear far worse than anything that could conceivably be seen as having been chipped here.

Rock Dancer (E1, 5a): They decide to give me a route—or rather, I can choose the route to do before I set off home. In the morning we've been informally discussing a memorandum from the National Trust with the Chief Warden for Penwith. It states that '. . . climbing is damaging nature conservation interests in the area, and . . . ways and means of allowing recovery and preventing any further damage need to be considered.' Afterwards we go to Kenidjack, where I want to ease my aching frame on something straightforward. They—Mark and Rowland—point me at Rock Dancer, a slab climb. Despite the low technical grade, it's sustained, the protection very widely spaced and the holds fragile. But it's also beautifully direct in its line, the climbing bold and intricate, and a much better route than Saxon, which I'd done before and which wanders around and across the face, seeking the easiest way up, its climbing undistinguished. I bring up an Edwards on each rope, which must be a unique experience, and then scan the new guide. Rock Dancer gets one star, is described as 'challenging and direct'. Saxon has three, 'one of West Penwith's great lines—classical and exhilarating'. Odd how bias against climbers can extend even to their routes.

Climber, 1992

Day Trip to Dalkey

So why was I running through the security barrier at Holyhead in the early hours of an April morning, wearing three jackets with pockets bulging, and with my rock-boots in a camera-case? Here's the scam—Sealink do a day return offer (their publicity people choose to call it a pleasure cruise) from Holyhead to Dun Laoghaire for £7. You can catch the boat at four in the morning from Holyhead, snatch a few hours' sleep, disembark in Dun Laoghaire before eight, take the Dart from the station right by the harbour for three stops south to Dalkey, have breakfast in the Country Bake cafe on the main street, read Fintan O'Toole in the *Irish Times*, soak in the atmosphere of cosmopolitan Ireland whilst you're re-caffeinating, and then the quarry's half a mile up Ardbrugh Road. So you climb all day, get the Dart back into Dublin when you're knackered, take in the pubs, the films and the music (Dublin has the best of all these) and be back in Dun Laoghaire in time for the 11'o'clock boat. How's that sound?

Naturally, there's a problem. It's called 'Conditions of Special Offer', and it tells you unequivocally that no hand luggage is allowed beyond a 'small camera case for gentlemen and a small handbag for ladies'. 'Curious concepts at work here,' I thought, and plotted how to get round it. Hence three jackets (no restrictions on the number of clothes you wear) with pockets bulging. As soon as I was on the boat and past all the checks, I took a rolled-up rucksack out of one pocket, filled it with the contents of the others, made a pillow with two of the jackets, a blanket from the third, and joined the rest of the ship's complement at that ungodly hour in billowy slumbers.

This is where the instructional bit ends. If you had a rope and a rack to carry, you'd have to devise your own means of bestowing them about your person, but from now on I cheat. A friend arrives as I walk down from passenger arrivals in Dun Laoghaire, whisks me off on a brisk constitutional to study the climbing potential of that most traditional of Irish Mountaineering Club stamping grounds, Bray Head. It appears to be either non-existent or to consist of a railway cutting. A man comes out of a shed in the latter with a shiny tin kettle and disappears. I mention this fact to my companion, who has not seen him, is pragmatic in these things, and would never have made the cast of 'The Egg Man and the Fairies'.

'Nonsense!' comes the response, 'Where is he?'

'Down there,' I point.

We crane over the wall. No sound but the sea, and a faint rustling of thrift flowers in the breeze:

'Admit it—you made it up.'

'I did not—I'll bet you the money in my pocket.'

'Which pocket?' A sceptical eye is cast over the three jackets, and then more conclusively, having found one that jingles, 'You're on.'

We look back over the wall. A man disengages from shadow and walks to the door of the hut.

'There you are! I win!'

'What d'you mean?' I protest.

With all the aplomb of the scion of a betting nation, before she rifles through my pockets my companion points out that he has no kettle. We repair to the bakery cafe. A sulky-faced waitress of sixteen or so slams cups of strong coffee down in front of us, spilling half the contents in the process. A teacherly woman in the queue at the counter asks one of her charges, 'Shall you be bold today, Ursula, or shall you be good?' We finish our croissants—Dalkey's that sort of town—and head up to the crag.

In *The Dalkey Archive*, which is by a good way Flann O'Brien's worst book, James Joyce is alive and well and experiencing a late vocation. I was feeling much the same way myself, but not for the Jesuits (of whom I had enough at school, for Christ's sake). It was the quarry that was calling. Here was a place of which I'd been aware for the whole of my climbing life, and the only time I'd set foot in it was on a day of tippling rain ten years ago when my old climbing companion Emmett Goulding (who was, as a matter of historical interest, widely regarded during his sojourn in Britain in 1964-5 as being the most gifted technical climber of his time in Britain or Ireland) showed me round. He'd made a particular point of taking me to the top of a waterfall with a slab rippling beneath its surface before the stream flowing down it leapt over an undercut wall at its base.

'That,' he'd told me, 'is The Ghost, and it's one of the great outcrop routes.'

'Here?' I'd asked.

'Anywhere!'

This exchange I mentioned as we walked in from the car-park on Killiney Hill. I had no idea of its grade. It could have been anything from Diff. to E6, but I wanted to do it.

'Sure, we'll do a route or two first to get you used to the place. You'll be grand.'

Dalkey's extensive, its ground plan resolved around two bays with a dividing ridge, a plateau area above, and beyond that the Upper Walls beneath the summit of Killiney Hill. The rock is granite, and was quarried from 1817 onwards for the building of

SPIRITS OF PLACE

Dun Laoghaire Harbour. Apart from a brief re-opening during the Great War, quarrying finished here in the 1850s, since when it's been going back to nature. Now it's a sunny, friendly belvedere above Dublin Bay: local people chat to you; ragged small eejits try to outdo the climbers and in the attempt frighten the latter more than themselves, especially on the higher walls, which reach 100 feet in places.

Mid-morning, the sun's shining, ropes uncoiled beneath a forty-foot wall of imposing steepness.

'My leader . . . adjusts gracefully and effortlessly up the ensuing wall and groove'

'What's this? Just looking at it makes my neck ache . . .'
'Will you stop your complaining and hold these ropes.'

My leader sets foot purposefully on rock, climbs to a little roof, pulls over it—all eager confidence—places protection and adjusts gracefully and effortlessly up the ensuing wall and groove. I follow in due course. It's intricate VS climbing, the holds sharp and well-spaced, the moves not immediately obvious.

'What's that called?'

'Jameson's Ten. We'll do another route and when you've got the feel of the place, then you can look at The Ghost.'

Next choice is a thin crack, finger jams and friction, up a slab, and good VS. The leader skips up it, pony-tail bobbing assertively, and gives me a tight rope on the first moves. I don't quite catch the name, but it sounds like Mahjongg. When I ask for clarification I'm told to look it up in the guidebook. For several weeks now an extended discussion's gone on between us as to whether climbing has a better dimension when you dispense with the guide, so this wins points in the debate. My progress up the crack is considered and judgement deferred on whether I'm yet ready for The Ghost, but we wander across to the top of it anyway and peer over. A rope stretches down, with Calvin Torrans coming up it neatly using a shunt. We hail him—you meet everyone on the Irish scene in Dalkey apparently. I haven't seen him for ten years. He comes over, exchanges friendly words, slopes off. We in our turn wander shamelessly off down to the pub for lunch.

When we get back, the slab of The Ghost is covered with abseilers—another joint Irish/British curse—so I'm dragged over to a sunlit wall in the East Valley and led up another of the quarry's classic VS's, Street Fighter. It's dispensed with in short order, and when I follow there are awkward steep moves to start, then strange crabbing movements up a slippery ramp before you pull out up a steep, fingery crack. At the top it's pointed out that I haven't done much leading so far, to which proposition I happily assent until the rider that it's about time I did is insisted upon. I've been eyeing up the neighbouring route—a flake crack to the right like a thinner and steeper Right Unconquerable that the guide I now avidly, and to my companion's great sarcastic glee, find myself consulting calls 'a classic battle', and 'probably the most fallen-off route in the quarry': The Shield, E2, 5c.

'But it's jamming—perhaps you don't like that?' I whimper, trying to off-load.

'That's alright—I'll manage.' (Attempt recognized and straight-batted.) I tie on. There are some intricate moves out of a niche, steep and on awkwardly placed finger jams, to gain a foothold on

The first pitch leading to Scimitar Crack at Glendalough

the right wall. Then comes the crucial sequence. It's not a simple crack—it overhangs, slants and cuts back in, and the jams are thin and awkwardly spaced. I use a poor left-hand jam and move on to worse ones above. They start to slide.

'I'm jumping off on to this runner, but it's not very good.'

'Shall you be bold today, or shall you be good?' is the teasing response. The runner holds. I retreat to the niche for a rest. The Shield was living up to its reputation. When I went back up, I made a mess of the moves on to the foothold and the jams felt worse than before, so I grew a mite angry and frustrated, got a Friend at the ready, started the sequence with a higher left toe-jam than before, found better jams in consequence above, jabbed in the Friend and suddenly thought, 'I remember this feeling!' as I carried on in a state of elated absorption to the ramp above. My erstwhile leader, needless to say, climbed it meticulously, with only a trifling complaint about the difficulty of removing runners on which overmuch reliance had been placed—and at the top emerged with hands, unlike mine, that were unmarked. The Ghost was still being abseiled and it began to rain. The boat sailed, I stayed: an Istvan Szabo film, cool Guinness, warm love in an unfamiliar bed—there are other boats in our lives.

It had become a point of honour to climb The Ghost. So I came back. I was led up a delectable HVS at Glendalough called Scimitar Crack to show that Ireland has other rock delights than Dalkey. It had two 150-foot pitches up a perfect line in the airiest situations on rough natural granite. The crag was covered in violets, heather still flourished on the ledges, and peregrines cried around us. But no other people. The valley below was as beautiful as any in Snowdonia. I wanted to stay for other routes, but The Ghost was now a voyage of necessity.

My first companion was working, so I recruited Paul Kiely, a friend from Wicklow with whom I'd climbed in Wales in the past. He drove at one hundred miles an hour to Dalkey, rapping on about the attitude and its demise. Afterwards, we soloed a few routes: Pilaster, a reachy bold buttress on good grips; Sham Gully, with its boulder problem start. But we'd come to lay The Ghost.

It's an eighty-foot slab, undercut at its foot. A thin, fractured flake slips between slab and lean. I tip-toe across, the ground falling away, and place an R.P. at foot-level. The ordinary path into the niche above is a lunge and scrabble at 5b on good hand-holds, but above on the slab is Dermot Somers' 5c variation—as bold (English meaning) and argumentative as its pioneer. So I take that instead, place an ill-fitting hex in a borehole at the niche, step up on slick granite and side-pulls and move out on friction that you

The Ghost

must trust and that will support you to shimmy over to a good foothold. At knee-level there's a rocky Rock Three to be placed and—barely half-way up—that's your ration of runners for the entire pitch. I step far out right, unsure and awkward in consequence, to move up on dimples and rounded handholds—slate E4 but without the bolts—for distant holds. Two onlookers exchange cordialities from the side. I tell them, half-amused, how afraid I am, coming to terms meanwhile with cat-padding moves round a tiny overlap, nervous of what's to come, fearful of the fall, but knowing that to sight-lead this pitch is a fine adventure, is more than a climb, is metaphor for the tentative spirit journey.

At the top I look down on the boat that will soon be taking me away and know as Paul follows and I belay that this day-tripper will soon be back:

> The dressed stone which rattled down the metals
> Is salt-bleached now in the quay of farewells,
> And gorse, nut-scented, brightens the shadows
> Above the harbour, where the quarry stows
> Its stock of migrant memory away,
> Turns its weathered face on our crass, light play.
> Schoolgirls judder breathless down fearful ropes
> Where quarrymen mined blocks to embark hopes
> On the passage to whatever new world—
> Toes on ripples supervene, fingers curled
> Round edges which support no other dream
> Than our ambiguous and escaping gleam
> That might, past all necessity, endure,
> Subsumed into the complete metaphor.

Climber, 1993

'In dreams begins responsibility'

Because of a certain anguish in my heart and mind I went out this evening with rock-shoes and a chalk bag to seek on the rock some clarity and peace. Not that I went far—just along the road to the Bus Stop quarries. I started by soloing the 5c pitch up the middle of the 50-foot slab on Blast Shelter crag, and did not feel good. Feet were shaky and the fingers felt weak, but there was a mental drive pushing me on. I forced myself up the slanting crack where fingers gouge into soft, repellent mud, then crossed the road into the Bus Stop itself.

There are times when you walk as if in a dream, drawn on. The Rippled Slab at the back of the quarry was gleaming, a glistening streak of damp here and there across its top from the morning's rain. As I flitted across the blocks jumbled beneath it, Stevie Haston's account of going up to identify Derek Hersey's body after his death-fall from the West Face of Sentinel a few weeks before was running through my mind: 'All we could say was, "Yes, those were the clothes he was wearing". There's not much left of a body after it's hit rock from 600 feet.'

Normally an image so morbid and powerful would register, but when part of your mind is a dead zone your will drives on and the rest of you, hapless, does not much care. I found myself at the foot of Massambula, and though I'd not soloed anything of that grade, at that height, for years, knew that I was locked in—that from the emotional morass a fierce head had arisen, muttering its need for icy simplicity.

So I tightened my shoes, rubbed the edges until the rubber squeaked, bouldered the most difficult moves I could find to the first ledge, wandered up to the flared crack where, if leading, you can place a nut, moved past to the hand-traversing flake, stepped up and—for luck or in grim amusement—flicked the loose bolt-hanger so that it rattled dully round on its axis.

For some reason, I found myself wishing that I'd brought a sling with me. I was maybe 60 feet up by this time and the landing looked bad from that height—sharp boulders, wicked crevices, a steep slope. I think you might not survive a fall from here. But I remembered too the time fifteen years ago on Coronation Street when I'd had slings with me, had clipped into the pegs after The Shield, had sat there and become terrorised by the situation. That memory reconciled me to their absence now, and I began to feel at the moves above. Understand that I am not a particularly good climber these days. Ragged tendons and arthritic finger joints—legacy of 34 years at the sport—make the training without which there is no strength and stamina a purgatory to me now. So instead I just climb when the opportunity arises, which is not as often as I could wish, for the partners of your own generation when you reach this stage have mostly desisted or died. And what is it you see or seek anyway from these mirrors in the cliffs?

> I look into my glass,
> And view my wasting skin,
> And say, 'Would God it came to pass
> My heart had shrunk as thin!'

Isn't the heart, though, in all phases of our life the last thing to shrink? As year mounts upon year and desire and illusion are stripped away, in the one direction, in the isolation of your warrior maleness maybe you're left only with the tragic exultancy of Byrhtwold's great rallying cry from *The Battle of Maldon*:

> Thought shall be the harder, heart the keener,
> Courage the greater as our strength grows less.

Not that my courage felt great by the bolt on Massambula, but in my mind I knew the crucial juncture. There is a sequence of moves—5b going on 5c, with the rock above difficult to read and the climbing of a type that would be precarious to reverse. The rain had washed the chalk from the holds so I was unsure, even though I'd done the route on two or three occasions, which way to go. I ran my fingers up and felt holds at the extremity of reach, body spreadeagled on the slab. They are small. They take maybe a third of the first joint of three fingers. And they flex and are flat rather than incut. I can tell myself rationally in situations like this that they'll suffice, but still, as I splay my foot across to an awkwardly placed and equivalently sized edge, why should I believe what I assert? And the sun has gone in, the slab's white gleam has become a dull, cloud-shadowed ivory, and by that gate what dreams come in?

If I thought hard enough I would imagine the drops of rain, heavy and slow as the last moments after release, upon my cheek. So instead I feel intensely at these holds, hear from within my chest a strange swishing of blood against echo-chambered rock, move up, move down, move up and am decided through a convulsive arching of the back and a clenching of fingertips on these flat smooth nicks, and a breathless, precise angling of toes on to chalked rock edges. After which comes a trembling and a great fear, because now I am 70 feet up and the involuntary shake of a leg on holds like this will cause my foot to slip, so by effort of will I still the movement, relax, and then—what comes?

Oh, I'll tell you—a great deep breath and I am calm, fiercely happy and I climb slowly on in deliberate control, skitter back laughing down slatey scree and make my way over to the foot of Scarlet Runner, which is two grades harder all round at E4, 6a, and while the moment lasts—for all this takes place in a suspended moment—I climb calmly and delightedly up that and find it easier than the first. If I fell from here, I tell myself—well, I could jump into that tree. This is less difficult, I tell myself, its reputation rests only on the distance you must climb as a leader before clipping the first of its four bolts. Its supposedly ferocious move high up feels no such thing. Soon I'm clattering back down the scree again, to complete the trio of quality routes on the slab by taking in Gnat Attack—at E1, 5c supposedly the easiest of the three.

Except that it doesn't turn out that way.

Soloing is a quirky activity, with a psychology all its own. Gnat Attack, for example, is a relatively straightforward pitch to lead. Like the other two routes, it's about 100 feet long and bolt-protected. But as you start the crux sequence on Gnat Attack the bolt is at head level. Also, you cannot quite make the move statically—to the soloist an important consideration—and the edge you're making for dynamically is thin and fragile. Finally the landing, if you were to fall, is worse than that from Massambula, and from as great a height. To add to these mental problems, my son arrived beneath as I was feeling at the move and proceeded to chatter about television programmes. A frame of my dear friend Peter Biven's death—at an age younger than I am now—at his son's feet in the Avon Gorge flashed through my mind. I switched off both it and my son's prattle, launched into the sequence before hard-won confidence ebbed away. It felt the hardest climbing of the afternoon, I had not expected it to be, and so was disappointed, needed something else, went over to Fool's Gold with its tenuous 6a move at 30 feet and thought to try that. Still William tagged along, talked away, exacerbated the feeling of guilt present anyway in this fool's game. So after exploring the moves and making up my mind that I could or should do them, I sent him home to feed the dog, and my sense of responsibility aside from action with him.

The thing I like about soloing is that you have to climb so cautiously and well. On Fool's Gold a thin crack runs down and divides. You move into it from an easy groove on the left. There is a good finger-lock, greasy with rain tonight, low down, from which you cannot quite span to the crucial objective of an incut hold above. The footholds are verging on non-existent—a polished pyrites excrescence for the right toe, a shallow vertical groove for the left. There is a higher but poorer finger-jam. To climb the route statically, you use the lower jam to position your feet, work the fingers of your left hand into the higher lock, straighten, transfer confidence and weight on to it, then breathlessly let go and reach for the hold.

If either foot slipped, the jam wouldn't hold but you'd get away with broken ankles. I made the move. The crack above was anti-climactic. I came down, took off my boots, ambled across the depths—filled in, grassed over now—where Harris and I played our youthful, fearsome games, and down to the road where young Jack Longland, grandson of the great, berated me for the performance and I just laughed and evaded. A woman walked past

'NEVADAS OF RAPTURE'

with a baby in a pram. The sun had slipped under the clouds to shine like a searchlight. It was the most beautiful evening, colours glowing and adrenalin-dyed to an aching splendour. I went and sat in a place in the fragrant heather where I often go, looking out west over the Irish Sea, and because I was relaxed and a tension had dissipated, I promptly fell asleep and dreamed a vivid dream.

You know the way it is with dreams—all the unpurged images of day in weird conjunction? I was sitting in the Sligachan Hotel with Menlove Edwards and Norman Collie, who were discussing incubus boulders and broken pipes whilst I talked with Sandro Delmastro, the enigmatist, who looked—in my dream as in Primo Levi's description—like Dermot Somers. It was after mid-day, raining beyond the windows. A sturdy, vigorous woman came in whom I felt I should know but perhaps, in the way of dreams, did not. She announced that it was clearing and sure enough, Sgurr nan Gillean resolved from the vapours. Menlove and the Professor continued their conversation. Sandro gave me a sly, encouraging look as the woman and I set off towards the hill.

Cuillin Ridge from Sgurr nan Gillean

On Sgurr Banachdich

How we raced across that bog and up the spur that curves sensually round past the tiny lochan to the foot of Pinnacle Ridge, where the rock at times was so rough to touch it seemed the magma still burned. Spires eased past as we mounted them in a sweet flow. We found ourselves beneath the abseil from the third by a traverse, and were soon slipping through the hole to emerge on the summit of the Young Men's Peak, where public schoolboys brayed of bloodied knees and lit mincing cigarettes whilst we pressed on down the West Ridge, swarming down the exposed chimney as a party from an outdoor centre were roped and belayed down a parallel line. We ourselves at the Bhasteir Tooth took out the rope, dismayed at the sight of Patey and Tiso beneath us, the former laughing at the latter up-ended by his own sack in the snow. There was a peg—no back-up to it, and it flexed, but still I threaded the rope through and lowered on to it, conscious of the weight of self and sack. The rope was too short. A leap into a gulley. When my companion came down she threw me her sack, then leapt too, the drop beneath immense.

All afternoon we pounded along, over Bidean Druim nan Ramh, over Sgurr a'Mhadaidh and Sgurr a'Ghreadaidh and Sgurr Thormaid, along the fissile half-world of this shattered ridge where the feeling and the symbolically feminine were unassimilated. And yet, in discreet crannies the saxifrage bushed and bloomed; from smoother clefts fleshy roseroot hung down its golden flowers and violets were everywhere, shades darker than the clear blue of her eyes. I remember reaching down and taking her strong hand in a wrist-lock, my other on a sharp spike, and hundreds of feet of space beneath us; I remember following her across a traverse on slimy basalt round to a gap in the ridge, both of us in our walking boots with heavy sacks, the consequences of a slip inevitably fatal.

St Kilda was a glistening fang beyond the Butt of Lewis and a great bank of cloud was welling up over the Outer Isles. A gibbous, yellow moon was sailing out across the Hebridean Sea. In our apartness, we had kept pace all day, neither knowing the other. The switchback ridge jagged on into a luminous distance but light and faith were ebbing away. Sgurr Dearg rose ahead. The spell broke. We chose to descend. Not by her preferred ridge route, but down the fierce draining gulley into Coire na Banachdich. The downclimbing was difficult. One swing round on a good hold maybe a hundred feet above the gulley bed led to a friction move across a gabbro slab. I waited at its farther side, watching, giving encouragement, but always she moved on, absorbed in her dangerous task, accepting the responsibilities the route and I had thrust upon her.

'Light and faith were ebbing away. Sgurr Dearg rose ahead.'

Who was she? Was she lover, friend, even the feminine side of my own nature? I cared for her, feared for her, yet always as I watched her head was bowed to the task. She kept on, elegant, engrossed, expressing no fear. Was she my responsibility? Was I hers? How had we come to be together in that place? The images flickered on: racing down through boulder scree; phosphorescence on the sea; an owl's call from the trees by Glenbrittle House; stretching ourselves out side by side on the gravelly sediments of Glenbrittle shore to the sucking waves and slow-dancing mist, above which cooled magma of rock and unconscious alike; the final benediction of her stooping, loving, forgiving kiss that awoke me with a start on my bank of heather to a chill draught of coming night.

I don't know what any of this means, or if it need mean anything at all. The man who sang praise of eating bear meat leapt to his death down a stair well. And I, who had soloed two 6a pitches on the Friday, fell on a 5c whilst leading the next Monday. Perhaps it is as well that in our dreams begins responsibility; or perhaps, if this is a man who desires to survive the concentration camp of his own nature, it is proper to ponder that, and also to disregard it—each in its proper place and time. Who knows . . .?

Climber, 1993

Learning Curves

We disembark from the plane in Delhi in the night, walk down long tunnels with the last monsoon rain beating on the roof and moist, burnt air like a slow, clinging slap across the face—first indicator of the all-out assault on every sense, sixth included, which is India. Hoardings big as the promises they carry loom by: 'India's pride and the World's envy', in sardonic counterpoint to dogs asleep in the road, prone human forms beneath the downpour on traffic islands, taxi-drivers curled up by the roadside on sisal webbing stretched across wooden frames. 'With you always' proclaim the sides of police cars as they cruise along Janpath, where we disappear from this reality into a hotel.

Delhi breaks your heart, is the first stage in a dissociative process by which you enter in to the mysteries of Himalayan climbing. It bears no relationship to your life *back there*. The insistent dry scrape of a beggar girl's thin fingers at your wrist, the gesture with her other hand towards her mouth, the lolling head of the infant whose mother—a shrivelled breast drooping from her sari—jabbers at you unceasingly outside the Mercedes showroom that 'this baby will die': these are not of your own country's mindscape. You reel from them in weeping desperation into a maelstrom where all values are whirled from your grasp. *Here* is not a place you recognise. *Here* demands of you the readiness to see things, to look at them, entirely anew. Delhi, however much of an interlude, an annoyance, a frustration it may seem to the unready, is the proper gateway to what you will go through.

The black kites circle lazily overhead; hoopoes flit eccentrically across the grass; pigs root in a dungheap; men and women shit in companionable groups below the walls of the Red Fort, then waddle duck-like to puddles to wash themselves; above the official's head streamside willows wave through a broken window as he talks of water from the Ganga, with a permit to visit the source of which he may soon issue us: 'At holy times we put a drop on the tongue; we bathe in it before marriage and before death. This water has the property that it never corrupts. There are no germs in it. It is always pure. The scientists have tested it, but have not found what this property is.'

The Chief Minister of the Punjab is blown apart in a bomb-blast, 23 people are shot in a night in Srinagar, the hostage crisis continues, travel is difficult. We wait in the capital, increasingly restricted to the hotel in readiness for quick departure, watching translucent hippy girls glide by, nodding to white-knuckled trekkers from the north of England whose eyes semaphore panic, exchanging quick glances with mysterious long women whose Indian adornments and languid gestures glide across white pages on which they incessantly write.

Then we leave. The low-frequency ever-present noise of traffic and air-conditioning and distant voices gives way to Mother Ganga's song in Gangotri. I sit on the temple steps and listen. The high surface note is all rush and hiss, beneath it a deeper, percussive rumbling of stones and boulders pounding along the river bed that seizes on your imagination. In the river's voice I heard my own part in the scheme rehearsed; by the river's flow I felt the expansion of my own lungs: to be a *part*, to accept, to become absorbed into the rhythm of the place. In slow, steep turns the path climbs out of the temple at Gangotri into the Deodar woods, and the deep, deep breaths that impel you onwards are themselves an elation—that your breast could swell with so much of the living air.

You learn also from those at home in the place. The Garhwali porters, sinewy and slight, trudge past as you sit drinking *chai* in the *dhaba*. They walk unconcerned with their fifty-pound loads across the log over the torrent where you balanced tentatively. You watch more closely. These distant-eyed men in sacking and flip-flops move as you do not move. The placing of each foot is deliberate, the transfer of weight on to it instinctive and assured. Their walking is an art which, once you have noticed, you begin to practise—too consciously and too late perhaps, and without their natural grace, but nonetheless, you have begun to learn to walk. Also, you begin to learn to speak, balance words, listen to content and not talk merely for sound. You recognise its role of reassurance, but village gossip from back home grates. You avoid its pollution, listen instead to the simplicity of porters, *sadhus*, cooks.

Ed Douglas and myself sit in a damp twilight on the terrace of the Hotel Ganga Niketan in Gangotri. Four Korean climbers take a table by us, appraise our gear without approval except for Ed's Lowe mountain cap, which they ask to see, examine thoroughly, ask for how many dollars he would sell it? Ed, irritated, firmly reclaims it as they list their peaks as though other items of merchandise. To get away, I move next to a monk in saffron robes who's smoking Capstan cigarettes. Where does he live? Up there, beneath a rock, in the summer; Varanasi, where he reads Sanskrit and Indian medicine at the University of Benares in the winter. And his object in being here? To teach meditation and sexual healing, for which many students come to him.

He studies my ear-ring and asks if I am homosexual. Wrong ear for that sign, I respond. In Europe, he tells us, he has many friends who would buy him an air ticket but he will not leave India. I catch the eye of Sylvia, the trekker from Dresden who joins us for part of our expedition. She transmits a delicate scepticism, and I'm already aligning with that position. The monk is very beautiful, quite aware of it in the way he caresses his long, brown hair and practises expressions on us. He looks like the young Krishnamurti, and like Krishnamurti there is an element of mischief and showmanship about him, and just enough suspicion of charlatanry to free him from the taint of bland piety.

Next morning I go to the temple with Chander, our 17-year-old Liaison Officer, to make *Puja*. The priest views my awkwardness with patient amusement, goes to an ornate statue in the temple's dim interior to pray, returns with water in a tiny ladle which he pours into our hands for us to drink, and little balls of fine-ground sugar before marking our foreheads first with red and then with yellow paints. Clouds drift amongst craggy spires above the village, accentuating towers, arêtes, great clefts. A Lammergeier glides across, its shadow traversing the rock face. Two helicopters fly up the gorge, minute against the peaks, their engine note absorbed into the river's roar, and we start for the mountain.

This having cut loose, this being brought face to face with the new, is a liberation if you go unguardedly, if you look at what you are and lovingly at what you are amongst. I have come on this trip on false pretences. What mountaineering have I ever done? Two wet trips to Chamonix in the 'sixties, the misery of Snell's Field, the Pointe Albert and the Aiguille de l'M in the rain cured me of that desire. Yet now, eighteen months off my fiftieth birthday, having had a knee operation four days before flying out, unfit and derelict and against all advice I'm hobbling towards Shivling to be born, and wide-eyed with the wonder of every moment. I lose myself in the glacier on the way there. I've gone on ahead, because I feel so alive and untrammeled and energised in this place. I don't know where the path to the meadow of Tapovan leaves the glacier, so I wander off along gravelly flats, but in the sun's heat they're bombarded by boulders from the mud cliffs above. I tack inland. Glaciers! I thought they were white, gleaming places of snow and blue crevasses. This is a mile-wide motorway construction site with towering hills of spoil two or three hundred feet high. House-sized blocks rumble down them; rock-slides start at a touch; voids lipped with gravelly ice, the sound of rushing water deep within, block your path. Laurence Gouault, Stevie Haston's wife, ran down a gully in the mud cliffs to rescue me, laughing and shrugging at my incompetence.

People become your object of study in the base-camp life to which we settle in at Tapovan. On the days of acclimatisation or of rest our routine is almost monastic. We rise when the sun touches the tent, watch what court the clouds will pay to Shivling and the Bhagirathi peaks today. (Five people die on the latter in the course of our time at Tapovan.) We eat simple food—dhal, *paratha*, vegetables. Sometimes we boulder. Mostly we sit around and talk. I've never spent this length and intensity of time with a small group of people before in my life and for the most part am amazed by how much I like them. Stevie Haston, our lead-climber, is all animation and electric energy, incapable of stillness. He roams, paces, pounces, argues and expounds volubly and emphatically, bullies and exhorts, is consumed by noisy self-doubt, mocks and laughs. He examines the body which, as a mountaineer, is his livelihood obsessively each day. He dispenses practical advice like benedictions to the less competent amongst us: 'Look, fasten tape like this between the spikes of your crampons to stop them balling up.' Laurence, whom he met here at Tapovan five years ago, argues with him, chaffs him, looks on with a faintly sad and amused resignation at times, but guides him, supports him, instructs him like the needy and loveable child that in some ways he is. Also, she keeps up with him, operates in his sphere of competence, is his trusted companion.

Amongst the rest of us, I suspect only Martin Crook could share that position, for Martin, with his great reserves of physical strength, technical competence and good humour, is the perfect foil to Stevie's restlessness. Nothing ruffles Martin. Whatever comes along, he remains teasingly imperturbable, and self-contained too, independent, without need of anyone else against whom to define himself. What Martin does, he does because he enjoys doing, because he wants to do it—not because of any potential trading balance his achievement might bring in the World's currency. Martin in his turn has a foil with whom he gravitates into partnership in Nick Walton. Even in appearance he and Martin complement each other. Martin's stocky and solid, with a mischievous, open smile, whilst Nick's tall and lean, handsome in a keen-eyed, sharp-featured way, very graceful and fluent in the way he moves on mountains, and effortlessly competent. Of all of us,

With Haresh Thakur and a silly hat at Tapovan

Nick seems the one who grows most in stature through the expedition. He is endlessly willing and organised, with practical skills and resourcefulness that put the rest of us to shame. He looks after the sick, repairs the stoves, does the cooking in the high camps, constructs our majestic base-camp latrine. Best tribute to Nick's and Martin's openness is that the Indian friends and helpers we have with us adore them. Ed Douglas, by contrast, is the baby of our team, and gleefully adopts the concealment offered by that role. We're not fooled. In the parliament that assembles within the circle of our tents each day it's Ed who's the most vigorous and questing debater, who has the sharpest mind, the widest range of cultural reference and clearest tongue. He's endearingly greedy and proclaims himself to be entirely selfish, which is a manifest untruth and the only one in which we catch him out. What he means by it is that he's developed a hard-headed capacity to assess the risks and consequences of mountain undertakings, and the insight to balance those with self-reliance and the ultimate need for self-preservation. His humour, even temperament and joyful engagement with the project of climbing this mountain make the days I spend at the high camps on Shivling with him pleasurable as they are memorable. And then there is Tom Prentice, watchful and wry, considered in his every pronouncement, more than any of us driven by the urge to climb Shivling, which results in his overcoming apparent frailty and illness to make the summit alone in worsening weather at the very end of our time.

Other characters drift in and out of the plot: Zoe Brown, Chander Mohan, Alistair Hughes, Haresh Thakur, Silvo Karo, John Middendorf, Sylvia Meschke, our cooks Bardhu and Bihari. Each of them adds something considerable to the mix. In this setting—the high meadow of Tapovan, with Shivling soaring above and the strange birds, the tracks of bear and snow leopard in the mud each night and the herds of bharal—you become acutely alive and responsive to personality. The whole process of inter-relation becomes charged, love and forbearance and disaster wheeling round the circumference of your every word. And above you, always, the great presence of the mountain, phantasmal by moonlight, glistening in the morning sun, by turns repellent and inviting, fulfilling in its atmospheres of warm rock and furious blast, its concealments and splendours, its crystalline apartness, the notion we have that this is the World's most beautiful peak.

Somehow, I do not have an overwhelming desire to reach Shivling's summit. At times in base camp, looking up at its unworldly aspire, Menlove Edwards' words steal into my head: 'This climbing. Perhaps, really, one was never made for it. I have a

Shivling—the world's most beautiful mountain?

conceit that I was even made for more than that: more than to satisfy extremely one's own pride. It would be nice to feel that one could have possibilities of interacting in an expansile manner, contacting with life beyond and outside of ourselves. No, I do not particularly want to make things quail before me: the satisfaction of seeing them bow the head is charged too much with despondency...'

All of us, I suspect, have mixed emotions towards the peak, from aching, anxious desire to the psychological devastation of abject fear. Some of us look wisely at the serac barrier at 6,100 metres, below the final snow slope, and arrive at the detached conclusion that its threat is too great and unpredictable to put oneself beneath. Others accept the risk. Our climbing is anyhow disparate and promiscuous. Stevie and Laurence, their object of a free ascent of

SPIRITS OF PLACE

The ridge leading up to the rock steps and serac barrier

the 'Impossible Star' route—the Spanish Pillar of Bhagirathi 3—precluded by heavy snow and the lateness of the monsoon, climb Shivling in nine hours from base camp to summit and then find a beautiful 600-metre pillar of red granite rising straight from a meadow on the south side of Shivling, on which they climb pitches of E6 and E7 virtually to its top. Martin and Nick, in an incredible day from our base camp, climb an adjacent arête of similar length and stumble back along the glacier in the dark. Four times, by myself and with different partners, I'm drawn to Shivling's high camps and apartworld, load-carrying, feeling my way, becoming accustomed, nauseated by other expeditions' attitudes on the mountain, terrified by the sight of a Korean with cerebral oedema being dragged down, toes trailing, across the moraine of the Meru glacier in the twilight.

One morning in particular sears memory. Ed and I have spent a night of excruciating discomfort—my third sleepless one in a row—in the tiny tent at 5,800 metres, and set off exhausted at daybreak up the ridge above. In the blue shadow fingers and toes have no feeling. Avalanches and rock-falls are streaming down the sunlit face of Meru across the glacier. My usual reaction to our hill rations—puking and shitting, nauseous at the grease and meat that gluttony made me force down last night is in force. When everything's come up, the discomfort intensifies as fits of vomiting and coughing co-incide to ram bile into every cavity of the head before it sprays out of mouth and nostrils to marble the snow around me green and yellow—all this to a gasping refrain of laboured breath. I'm encountering the pain of Himalayan climbing, the unfamiliar gear, the weakening resolve, the stumbling incompetence.

The rock steps on the arête ahead rear up. By effort of will I relax, fight to establish rhythm and control, set to the climbing and become engrossed in its subtleties and technicality. There are two of these towers and the crux is on the second—a long, slim groove of red granite with festoons of old fixed rope hanging down its sides and a ribbon of hard ice in its back. The drops to hanging glaciers on either side are immense, the risks as we solo up grave, but suddenly I'm captivated by the process of climbing, enraptured by surroundings, revelling in the certain delicacy of crampon placement on tiny flakes and fractures, the smooth lean of the body in making for ease. In a half-hour's climbing at a grade of Scottish Four I find out for myself what the power and appeal of this game can be, and it is enough. I understand. I watch from the lateral ridge abutting the seracs as Ed—young, fit and acclimatised—climbs the short ice-wall which is the last technical barrier before the summit.

He hesitates, his feet slip in places. I cannot see the fixed rope up which he jumars, assume he's still soloing, watch him join the three Czechs who are ahead of us, look ruefully at my single walking axe and conclude that what's ahead isn't for me. It is ten o'clock on a bright, still morning. I go down with only a tinge of regret, knowing that I will be back now, that the lure of high places has hooked in to my resistant psyche and I'm embarked on the steepening, deadly curve by which they impart to you knowledge of their—and your—own nature.

Afterwards, by the stream through Tapovan, I rest. An avocet stalks past along the sand-flats on coppery-blue legs, upturned bill probing, pied plumage gleaming. R.D. Laing's acid illumination's my prayer to her: 'I have seen the bird of paradise. She has spread her wings before me and I shall never be the same again. There is nothing to be afraid of. Nothing. The Life that I am trying to grasp is the me that is trying to grasp it.' On the last night of my time in India, on an Agra hotel rooftop with Stevie and Laurence, the dome and minarets of the Taj Mahal glimmering above the haze under a bright full moon so that we ache with the evanescence of this most beautiful of human creations and finest of all monuments to human love, I have my own intuition: that there are ways of approaching mountains; that properly, if your own character is to grow through contact with them, it must be by appreciation of their beauty, by respect and a desire to establish between you and your desire's object the perfection of mutual rhythm—that it must be to do with love and not the assertion of power, must be a marriage and not a rape. Do those who come here know that? How many willed deaths of those who do not?

Climber, 1995

Camp at 18,500 feet, Shivling

Judas Climbers and the Trees

Years ago, in the era before the madwoman of Chelsea and the synthesized nonentity with the switch-on smile who succeeded her had destroyed any pretence this country had to being a democracy, there was a telling incident on a Welsh cliff. Two young hot-shots, fuelled more by ego and testosterone than respect, cut down an oak tree on a cliff in Snowdonia to gain access to ten feet of unclimbed rock. As news of their action spread amongst the climbing community, the reaction to it gathered into a wave of quiet rage that forced the malefactors to disclose their identities, apologise for their deed and confess their error in all the climbing magazines of the time. The internal disciplines of the sport had censured those who offended against its implicit creed.

If the tone of that sounds religious, then so, in a sense, it is. There is a basic and recurrent belief amongst the sect whose goals in life are travel amongst mountains and the attainment by diverse techniques of crag or mountain summits that reverence for natural environments is crucial. Some—romantic writers and educationalists for the most part—are even prepared to extend that article of faith and claim that there may even be a beneficial spin-off here in terms of our common humanity, that climbing may in some sense be character-improving. But as Flann O'Brien would have put it, I'm not sure about that.

One thing I am sure about is that when, at the recent DMM British Mountain Festival in Llandudno, an anti-award, the Downside Award, was given out to Richard Turner Ltd, a roped access company from Chesterfield, in the words of the citation 'for abusing climbing skills by employing them against environmental protesters and upholders of conservational values at Newbury and elsewhere', the disapproval of the largest gathering of climbers in Britain was palpable against our sport's techniques and training being used in officially-sanctioned and brutal attempts to defeat the valid and courageous protests of our natural allies. Andy MacNae, National Officer for the British Mountaineering Council, our representative body, added a further gloss: 'Climbers have an enviable environmental record, and the vast majority will be outraged at being associated with actions of this kind.'

The debate had, in fact, been pursued in the climbing press—particularly in its more radical organs, *The Thing* and *On the Edge*—for over a year, since it first became known that a group of well-known Sheffield climbers working for Richard Turner Ltd had been involved in the evictions of tree protesters at the M65 extension site near Blackburn. When stories—with photographs and videos to back them up—of violent and dangerous tactics (which, as an aside, were against the roped-access industry's codes of safe practice and could lead to the rescinding of the workers' certificates of competence) being used began to circulate, anger began to grow. And as it became apparent that the so-called 'crusties' were now viewing climbers as yet another threat to the environment, and one so vicious and amoral as to be willing, for Judas money, to enact the will of the dead-in-life who comprise the Tory Government, the desire to distance ourselves from these assaults and that perception grew, and with it a degree of radicalisation, of *pro-crustyanism*.

The Conservatives had achieved, through habitual obtuseness

and arrogance, one of the few things they've proved good at in recent years—providing common cause for the unlikeliest allies. We are, after all, as Andy MacNae said, proud of our environmental record. We operate well-publicised voluntary bans countrywide—the incidence of transgression against which is minute, and invariably through ignorance and lack of information rather than selfish intent—on sea-cliffs during nesting seasons. We do our best to respect, learn about and protect rare birds and flowers on the crags and mountains. Our guidebooks carry notes on them, our magazines incessantly debate ways to minimise the effect of our presence in terms of erosion and damage on the mountains. As a point of honour we listen to and try to work with those whose interests are located in places where ours lie too. These ideals are pursued with a passion that often surprises outsiders to the sport. They have, in the past, led to climbers' frequent involvement in high-profile environmental protests organised by Greenpeace and others.

So if for no better reason at the outset than to protect our previous good name, a dialogue opened up between the climbers and the crusties, and a sense of parallelism, of shared sympathies, of like lifestyles began to emerge. Did we not all as children start as tree-climbers? Were not the crusties' self-taught rope-techniques like our own rudimentary initial attempts? Was not their acceptance of threat, danger and discomfort in the pursuit of an objective, their fixed-rope walkways between the tree-tops, their dwelling in base-camps threatened by avalanches of bailiffs and police and the objective hazards of that cosmic bad joke and piece of spitefully self-interested malice which goes under the name of the Criminal Justice Act, their stoical willingness to sit it out in all weathers for weeks on end in ramshackle bivouacs—was not all this a reflection of the highest—literally and figuratively—practice of our own sport in the crystalline apartness of the great peaks? And was there not also a shared philosophy at some level? Were we not both communities of the margins, anti-authoritarian risk-takers at the altars of belief, resisters of the pervasive comforts and buy-offs of society, scorners of the collusions and masonic backhanders of so-called progress and development?

Talking led to action. Information took root and grew into response. This winter, regularly, climbers have been visiting the tree-camps of Newbury, and amongst them the foremost performers of the present day: Ben Moon, Jonny Dawes, Adam Wainwright. Training in techniques has been given. Companies run by climbers have been covertly supplying the protesters with ropes, karabiners, harnesses, nets and industrial safety equipment. The reputation of

Anti-authoritarian risk-takers at the altars of belief
(Photo: Ray Wood)

SPIRITS OF PLACE

Swans viewing with appropriate suspicion the vandals' assumption of virtue.
(Photo: Ray Wood)

the collaborators, meanwhile, has deteriorated even further, helped antithetically on its way by a glowing testimonial given them by feature coverage in the *Daily Mail*, and directly through the witness provided in recent days from Newbury by Ben Moon.

Moon's position in British climbing needs to be made clear. In his mid-twenties, and the finest British rock-climber of the 'nineties, his character is perceived as honest and simple beyond reproach. There's something of the wise child, the holy fool about him, that illuminates beautifully the divine idiocy of his craft. Quiet and slight, he has an iconic significance within our community. On Thursday, by some of his erstwhile climbing companions, he was manhandled, threatened, handcuffed and arrested:

'You run up the trees, the adrenalin's really flowing, you're seventy, eighty feet up not clipped in to anything, and they're grabbing your ankles. It's a miracle there haven't been fatalities. There was one Belgian guy Dick Turner's lot caught—I was just a few feet away—and he didn't have a harness for them to clip on to, so when they got him they just looped a couple of slings in lark's feet round his ankles, called up the cherry-picker, fastened the slings to it and then its hydraulics were used to drag him by the legs from the branch he was hanging on. He was in agony. I think they broke one of his legs in the process, because he was screaming as they lowered him swinging by his ankles down to the ground and bundled him off under arrest in an ambulance to the hospital. But these things don't get in the papers because the police won't let the press near, and the police themselves are taking videos of the protesters' camps to give to the bailiffs to study, which is not what they're supposed to do. As for the roped-access guys—I've been away on climbing trips with them in the past. O.K. I always thought they were hard, selfish characters and that we had nothing apart from climbing in common, but what they're up to now is just legalised GBH. They must know it's wrong, but they seem to be able to switch off and just think of the money—£50 an hour, guaranteed ten-hour days—nice work if you can stomach it . . .'

'If we don't do it, somebody else will', is their argument, and *bounded rationality* is the term which defines it—first used, I think, in Wilhelm Reich's *The Mass Psychology of Fascism*. But maybe nobody else would? The roped-access industry is staffed almost entirely from the community of climbing, the response from every other company from which I've taken soundings to the question of whether they'd accept this work is 'No way!' They feel, as Hardy felt in representing John South's death in *The Woodlanders*, that trees have totemic significance, are life-giving, their deaths to our discredit. They recognise the sacrilege of Richard Turner Ltd's

Networking, Newbury.
(Photo: Ray Wood)

employees having laid rough hands on the shaman, and shake their heads in disbelief. Like Arnold's Scholar Gipsy, dreaming through these same Berkshire woods and downs, they know value of place, and like Arnold himself, they sense how philistinism displaces culture and gives sway to anarchy.

As a climber and environmentalist, nothing that's going on now remotely surprises me. You need only cast your mind back ten years to the overweening arrogance of Nick Ridley's overthrow of parliamentary precedent (and holding a celebration party at public expense when he'd done so) in forcing through the more costly southern route across public amenity land for the Okehampton by-pass to realise that the New Conservatism of the last twenty years always acts thus. Its power has been absolute for so long that its political judgement has entirely gone, along with any honest consultative procedures. The new alliance of climbers and crusties may not seem significant on the macro-scale, but if I—heaven forbid!—had foregone humane considerations, intellectual questioning, morality, respect and appreciation for life to the extent where I could be a Tory MP, I would feel distinctly worried about what it represented.

A hitherto apolitical body of sportspeople has been radicalised, brought face to face with the realities of a tradition quite apart from that of the environmental pieties to which they were always willing

SPIRITS OF PLACE

Fair game?
(Photo: Ray Wood)

to assent, and which echoes back along chapters of women manacled whilst giving birth or at the funerals of their ten-day-old babies, of the unbridled savagery of state policing at Orgreave, of the unpunished state murder of Blair Peach. Those who find themselves drawn in—as the police have been for years—to act in return for pecuniary consideration as the agents of government oppression are now being savagely ostracised. Like Judas, they are hanging themselves by their own ropes.

At present they are on a roll, making plenty of money, backed by the full panoply of state power, and issuing threats. One of the climbers who was at Newbury working with Friends of the Earth last week received anonymous, untraceable telephone calls at his home during the weekend telling him that if he was seen on the rope-ways this week, 'they' would make sure he never climbed again. But the cowardice of anonymous yet identifiable threats needs to be put into the context of what awaits the roped-access bailiffs who learnt the skills of their demeaning trade within the climbing community. The traditional fate of the collaborator is already confronting them: vehement and rigorous denunciation, exclusion from social venues, continual haranguing, icy contempt—the same arctic contempt the majority of the population of this country with every justification now feels for its own government.

Beyond that, for the climbers who have betrayed the ideals and beliefs of their own community, the evidence of their actions is on record to sustain—come the day when there is no regime to hide behind—the criminal charges which must follow. More positively, what will ensue from the pro-crustyan alliance is surely an influx into the mountains and an espousal of their freedoms by adventurous rebels who've learnt about climbing as a result of our making this common cause. They will replace the Thatcher's-children apostates whose solipsistic stress on individual achievement at any cost corrupted the atmosphere of climbing in recent years, and from whose ranks the bailiffs are drawn. Already, in their fine, brave personal disregard for safety in pursuit of a cause the crusties align with the out-on-a-limb adventurers from every climbing epoch—the Shiptons and Tilmans, the Kirkuses, Streetlys and Browns —who represent the admired traditional values of the sport. For my own part, I await with gleeful anticipation and my membership application completed the formation of a British chapter of *The Monkey Wrench Gang*. So let bailiffs and government be warned, and let the deep play commence.

The Guardian, 1996

Kaleidoscope of the Senses

Shale—the word's only the hovering of rationality around the dip and slip of rock beneath my fingertips. There's an illusory friction in its patina of lichen that I rub away, a fine, grey-green dust adhering in the whorls of each finger. I cloud it with chalk, cough away the inhaled dryness, press on the shelving hold again and ease unwilling joints across to where, for balance, body must stay in a tensile arch. My runners in that shattered crack are fifteen feet away, the terrace twenty-five feet below. Looking down for footholds I catch Martin's eye, shake my head ruefully, he raises an eyebrow and smiles:

'I could make it to that streak of birdshit twenty feet up, but there's no gear, I'm pressed enough just hanging on here, it steepens above that and God knows how I'd get down.'

The raven swoops, air hissing through its pinions. There is metal in its blackness and sardonic cry. Giggling laughter and retreat. Later, above Martin's belay, just momentarily the instinct choreographs a dancing step or two; bridged across a strange groove with loose block at chest height, there comes the visual rush. A layered terracotta pillar leaps into vivid life, its grainy pastels imprinting into memory. On top, on a terrace of deep heather with the cuckoo's call drifting muted from the valley woods, we give best to Clogwyn Pot, name our exploratory route 'Ravens on Speed', and run away.

Of that action, I recall the stone I stepped on in the ragged wall coming down the scree—a slivery ochre piece which twisted under my foot. For a moment the rocks above it slid grudgingly, then a roaring and crashing and bounding, a sulphurous smell, I was gasping for breath twenty yards back, clinging to Martin, shrieking with laughter, stones pouring like lava down the slope.

Iwan's across the valley, a white dot endlessly moving up and down a slab on a buttress the name of which I don't know. From beneath the crack of Spectre, on the road below I see a mini-van with flower transfer pull in to the lay-by. Two figures emerge—a man's red hair, liquidity of a girl's movement accentuated by swirl of hair and skirt. By the wall they kiss. My son comes across the slab to join me. I fret at the belays, flay a shin as I struggle and flop into the crack above, and from its prickling soreness comes distant laughter of dead friends with whom I've shared this climb—Tim Lewis, Al Harris—dearest I ever had, and how different things might have been had they lived, who were a part of our collective sanity: the screams in the hospital night, the wet road on an autumn night—oblivions for graced lives.

SPIRITS OF PLACE

Charenton Crack

His pale face below me—at fifteen—was I his age when I first did this climb? With Bill Birch, more than thirty years ago. The feel of that afternoon. There was strength and ease in our bodies that day, an accord between us who'd never climbed together till then. I remember how elegantly you climbed, the good humour and the friends around us; also, the configuration of crystal in a particular hold, the way it cut off sensation and numbed a finger joint. It's here's again to bring it back. When the planes shift, this other William, my son, with his anxious face as I ease past the stacked blocks into the groove on The Grasper and him secured only to two pegs on that perch of a stance. What detail will cause him to recall? I did so little with my own father. Lightness and protruding bones as I carried him from bed to chair in his last illness, when I was William's age, in exorcising which waste I rage to record.

Weirdwood with the knotted branches and bearded rocks, my sly-sweet inquisitive friend after his forms of knowledge again. Ah, Martin, with your women and your rocks, I share your bent again today, recognise the thrill of curiosity, jostle with you even a little to be on with it, but it's properly your climb, your fingers probe the passage, your limbs comfort themselves along its curving ridge. We sit astride this jokey pinnacle your imagination searched out amongst the trees and on its quivering top conspire together in the appropriate symbol of release, leaping across the void to mainland mother earth. 'Priapic Worship', we call it, in order to mock. The Doric Column, Old Pan at play in the sacred groves, yet they passed by, all of them, on the road, bound for the heights against which to measure themselves, the numbers by which to assess, whilst it waited across the water, secret, discreet. Dust blew in our eyes and the husks of dry grass seeded our hair.

Twenty-four hours in another place, the sunset coastal road heading south speeds past, needle flicking time and again over the hundred pricks at every sense whilst Andy and Martin sleep. Irish friends in the Bosherston pub, good-humoured jockeying games played out around the table or in the cliff-top car-park, waves hushing under a sailing moon, sleep lacy with aspiration and good memory, morning sun on the dewy gorse, its nut scent mingling with the new-biscuity smell of morning piss, figures groaning from sleeping bags into clothes, ordering of strewn chaos, Mrs Weston's rolling south-Walian tones warming you with promise of coffee and eggs and toast that comes starred with yellow butter dripping clarified between your fingers where your lazy, delicate tongue reminds you you're alive and across on the ranges the death-dealers crump and crash and roar.

South Face of Mowing Word. We're here because military activity and the bird bans have occluded other possibilities, and now we're glad of it. Andy and Martin are on the ledge below Charenton Crack. When I first climbed it, twenty-three years ago, I named it after the Paris lunatic asylum in which the Marquis de Sade was incarcerated. It seemed appropriate. There was fear and the strength beyond panic as runners flicked out and made their stuttering descents of the rope. My fingers were lacerated from the calcite edge of the crack, smeared with clay dug from it, blood oozing from cuts and splashing in crimson drops on to the grey block around which I belayed. Out amongst the sculpturesque bosses at the edge of the tidal platform today I trail those same fingers in a salt pool as Martin fights his way up, know that this time it will be easy, I will be safe, and strong enough, and know what to do, and so I turn away and look down into the crystal pool.

The life that's here starts out and astounds me. Mussel shells lie open, showing a gentian blue; there are dusty pink corals and all manner of draining and crackling and popping shells of the names of all of which I am entirely ignorant, all manner of forms of which I want to sing in praise—encrustations and labia and fronds, threads and ribbons, castles, curves, with texture and colour glimmering across the spectrum. In and out between the closed anemones there are green worms winding, and they are so mossy and delicate I sit wide-eyed and stilled, and when I look up the waves are surging against the cliffs and time has ceased, I'm become a part of it all and there is only the urge all around of process, of which you on the sand over there were a part when you stepped so delicately from your orange bikini to run naked into the foam and hiss of the waves, and you too, dear late lover, were also a part, telling of your pleasure as we listened to these waves, of your release into delight, your blood shadowy in the moonlight across my hand, its metallic taste between our lips, so intimately were our sensations shared, and everything we have known through the full life of the senses is still present in this moment. How much of this do we all know? I solo up to the ledge and ask about the worms:

'Maybe they're six inches long, velvety, mossy, dark green and so lovely . . .'

You who decry or ignore have the dead albatross about your necks. You find peace when you bless the worms.

Climber, 1995

'Everything we have known through the full life of the senses is still present in this moment'

4: The Bereft Lunatic's Embrace

Sketches from a Journey through Wales

Following Borrow

Llangollen is a difficult place to leave behind: bookshops, cafes, music on the streets, bustle, its river-and-hill setting, and all the Borrovian association too. Time passes easily in a town like this, and I've been a devotee of George Borrow's eccentric personality and writing since my earliest teens, when I set out in 1960 with a copy of *Wild Wales,* bought from the bookshop on the Chester side of the bridge, in my rucksack. Throughout the next fortnight, by candle or streetlight, in the barns, telephone boxes and bus shelters in which I slept, I laughed at his prejudices, thrilled to his enthusiasms, thought his vividly-sketched characters and ranting perorations entirely wonderful. Over thirty years on, I still re-read him, though I prefer now the vigour and verbal portraiture of *The Bible in Spain*, or the gypsy lore and vagrant life in *Lavengro.* By the time he made his 1854 Welsh tour there'd been a severe hardening of the prejudicial arteries. But *Wild Wales*, for all its dogmatic authorial persona, is still the best regional British travel book ever written. The idea appealed of following a stretch of the route it describes, to see how things had fared in the years between.

At about eleven o'clock on the morning of the 21st October, 1854—a fine, cold morning with a rime frost on the ground—Borrow took leave of his wife, daughter and the church cat (the story of which latter I suspect is pure invention) and 'started on my journey for South Wales, intending that my first stage should be Llan Rhyadr'. At about eleven o'clock on the 11th November, 140 years and three weeks later—a morning so cloudy and dark it scarcely had the energy to rouse itself into daylight—I set off from the same place on the same route and with the same initial destination, twenty miles away, in mind. Llangollen's marginal embroidery of new bungalows and spruce cottages with lamp-posts, white-painted wagon-wheels and torrents of aubrieta down garden walls soon receded. The bed of the sunken lane I followed was stony, running with water between dams of fallen leaves. On the O.S. 1:25,000 map it's called Allt y Badi, and is clearly one and the same with Paddy's Dingle, which Borrow's Welsh guide John Jones feared to descend in the dark lest he be robbed of the money in his pocket as he passed the Irish tinkers' encampment.

There were no tinkers in camp today, nor have been, I suppose, for years. The sheaf of propertied prejudice which masquerades under the title of the Criminal Justice Act has outlawed anything resembling their (or Borrow's own early and late gypsy) lifestyle. The view as I climbed was blinkered, sodden and dull as our present Government. Mist hung thick amongst gorse and heather at the hill's summit, as it did when Borrow passed this way. He uses it in *Wild Wales* to foist on the reader the first of his long translations from Welsh poetry—a gabbling, exclamatory version of Dafydd ap Gwilym's *cywydd* on the mist. Borrow's translations from Welsh poetry are for the most part an embarrassment and this one's no exception:

> Pass off with speed, thou prowler pale,
> Holding along o'er hill and dale,
> Spilling a noxious spittle around,
> Spoiling the fairies' sporting ground!

That bears not the slightest resemblance in meaning or verbal music to Dafydd's original. If I could only tax George with the conundrum of how someone who professes such affection for a subject can produce such doggerel in its praise! Though perhaps if it came to the point, and you kept company with his shade for a fast-striding mile or two along the dusk of a Welsh road, the criticism would only manifest itself in a degree of ironic mockery, and his vast enthusiasm for Welsh poetry would prevail. So with a more charitable view on this particular shortcoming, I took the road slanting down out of the mist into Glyn Ceiriog, recalling with fellow feeling the effect of the descent on his knees too.

Glyn Ceiriog is a sprawling old quarry village, not notably pretty but with an air of vitality about it. There are bakers and weavers and a Christian coffee shop (born-again, no doubt—all instant caffeine-and-conversion) where I would have stopped had I not been in haste on this short day to get to Pontymeibion. So I hurried along the road for a while before branching on to the Glyn Valley Tramway, restored as a riverside path by the National Trust and dedicated to public use. After a mile by the brown, flooding river the tramway crossed a track, and down to the right was '. . . a small bridge of one arch which crosses the brook Ceiriog—it is built of rough moor stone; it is mossy, broken, and . . . there is a little parapet to it about two feet high.' I crossed the river by it and sat on the parapet, along which, mewing frantically, came a black-and-white long-haired cat, which sat on my lap and butted moistly under my chin. A woman came by with two blonde children, one of them in a pram, the other pointing and laughing at the cat's antics:

'Are these the *meibion* of the *pont*?' I asked the woman.

'I'm sorry, I don't speak Welsh,' she replied.

Feeling vaguely embarrassed, I asked her if she knew where Huw Morus's Chair was?

'Oh, it's up here by the bend in the road.'

I sat a while longer on the parapet with the friendly cat, then made my way to the road, a few yards up which, at the entrance to a farmyard, was an ugly modern obelisk in memory of Huw Morus. Not what I wanted at all, so I went to knock on the door of the house, which is where he had lived though not, as Borrow was misinformed, where he was born. The woman from the bridge opened it. No, she didn't know where the chair was, but if I went down to Erw Gerrig, Ann Kynaston might be able to tell me. She could:

'Oh yes, it's in my garden. You're welcome to see it. Just go through the gate there and it's on your right in the top wall.'

This was easier than Borrow had experienced. He had been led through nettles and dripping shrubs by a serving-girl for half an hour before the woman of the house had come out to find it for him. Whereupon he'd installed himself in it and held forth on Huw Morus, recited his verses to the assembled company, '. . . all of whom listened patiently and approvingly, though the rain was pouring down upon them, and the branches of the trees and the tops of the tall nettles, agitated by the gusts, were beating in their faces, for enthusiasm is never scoffed at by the noble, simple-minded, genuine Welsh, whatever treatment it may receive from the coarse-hearted, sensual, selfish Saxon.'

The chair is set in a wall at the end of a short avenue of box and yew—a single seat between blocks of dull pink stone diagonally veined with quartz, and overarched with ivy. The slate slab which forms its back, and into which formerly were carved the initials H.M.B. (Huw Morus, Bardd), is delaminating now, with no lettering evident upon it. The whole runs with moisture, and is as dirty still as it was in Borrow's day, when the woman of that time offered to wipe the seat for him before he sat in it. I perched gingerly on its edge and talked with Ann Kynaston. No, I wasn't from *Cadw*—the Welsh ancient monuments agency by whom it was listed. Yes, it did look to me as if it needed urgent restoration work. She went back in to her lunch and left me looking out east— Borrow describes it as 'fronting to the west'—over her tidy garden to broken rocks on the opposite side of the valley. 'He read the songs of the Nightingale of Ceiriog when he was a brown-haired boy, and now that he is a grey-haired man he is come to say in this place that they frequently made his eyes overflow with tears of rapture' was how Borrow described his feelings to his listeners that day in 1854. Huw Morus, who lived from 1622 to 1709, has the

Huw Morus's Chair

sweet assonance and sentimentality of Burns (both men's work was written to be sung) at his most facile, but with little of the Scots poet's emotional range or intensity. His work is a triumph of form in concealing lack of content. I don't share Borrow's estimate of it, felt a distance as well as a closeness on this mutual seat over the gap between our times.

Thanking Ann Kynaston, I stepped back to the road just as a bus came straining up the hill. It lazed me over the three miles to Llanarmon Dyffryn Ceiriog, a small village with a self-possessed air of its own prettiness in a wide strath where the River Ceiriog starts to sweep round north-westwards to its source in the Berwyn moorland. There were two pubs. The car-park of one was full of Jaguars, Rovers and Mercedes, so I entered the other, the car-park of which was empty. This was, I suppose—being the older of the two pubs—the one in which Borrow had encountered the illiterate wagoner studying a newspaper: 'By looking at the letters I hope in time to make them out.' Go to an evening school, Borrow had told him, before passing on to an exchange of opinions about the Crimean War then in progress.

The conversation that took place during my visit, though less edifying, was equally representative of its time. I sat in a corner with my book and pint whilst two women of a certain age talked. Ginny and Trish they were called, from Putney and Barnes, dressed in oatmeal knitwear, silk scarves, slacks, and with highlights in their sculpted hair. They discussed tactics to secure property on divorce, how to enact insurance frauds, and the beachwear one might buy for cruises from Debenham's store in Telford. What, I mused, would Llanarmon's own poet—John Ceiriog Hughes, writer of three lyrics in particular that any Welsh person over the age of forty can happily quote to you, and who left the farm of Pen-y-bryn above the bend in the river six years before Borrow passed through here—have thought of their conversation? Narrow-minded and Anglophile in his later life, how disillusioning would he have found this sorry drift of talk (no doubt that of the respective husbands would be equally, if differently, dire)? I set myself to imagining the themes and quality of discourse he might have enjoyed in his Manchester exile with his fellow Welshmen R.J. Derfel, Creuddynfab and Idris Fychan. Ceiriog was a railway clerk, Derfel a preacher, dramatist, early Socialist and commercial traveller, Creuddynfab a literary critic and railway navvy whilst Idris Fychan was a harpist. Picture them together at the time, say, of Borrow's visit to the West Arms—a group of four young men conversing excitedly in a language not of their country of residence. Perhaps they're walking up and down Ardwick Green, factories and warehouses silent for once all around them. It's a warm Sunday, their talk even warmer on the subject of the Blue Books that have damned educational standards in the country of their birth and desired their native language's demise. (Why does Borrow never once allude to a subject paramount amongst the Welsh intelligentsia of his day? Did he never meet a schoolmaster or a Sunday school teacher?) R.J. is satirising, as he did forcefully in his 1854 play *Brad y Llyfrau Gleision*, the traitors who have sold out their own language for a mess of Gradgrindian advancement. Ceiriog and Creuddynfab set forth from this topic on to a vigorous exploration of the merits and limitations of writing poetry in the strict metres, and Idris Fychan steps in with special pleading for lyrics to be composed with the harp's musical accompaniment in mind. I've no doubt this conversation would have taken place, in that setting and others on scores of occasions between these men. And now the place of birth of their most eminent has to listen to how a husband can be incited to violence before a witness, the manner in which burglaries can be faked, and what factor sun cream to take to the Caribbean.

Back in the real world, I stole another look at the women from the South, gulped down my beer in rapid disgust and set forth. Mist was down on Cefn Hirfynydd. A raven harassed a heron along its border and flocks of fieldfares soughed past, windblown Maltese crosses. Lowing cows guided me down to Cae Hir along a track deep in mire. I thought of Borrow knocking on the door of the house and asking of the woman who answered whether she was alone there: 'Quite alone,' said she, 'but my husband and people will soon be home from the field, for it is getting dusk.' Nowadays a question like that would get you arrested. The farm-linking footpaths I'd intended following were policed by every kind of hissing, yapping, cackling, bellowing animal antagonism. I gave up on them, and followed Borrow's four long miles by lanes, where yellow leaves seemed to give out their own light and white streaks of lime mortar glowed from the collapsing chimney breasts of ruined cottages, to Llanrhaeadr-ym-Mochnant, where good fortune led me to the door of the Plas yn Llan guest house of Mrs Sheila Fleming, who took me in unannounced, bemired and bedraggled, installed me amongst her dogs with a pot of tea by the stove whilst she made up a bed; who fed me, entertained me and directed me on a tour of the town's amusements that evening which ended at an undisclosably late hour in a particularly friendly pub in heated agreement with the socialist Mayor of Llanrhaeadr. She turned me out next morning rested, Berwyn-bound and breakfasted with the laughing comment that I shouldn't interpret too anatomically Housman's description of this area as 'A country for easy livers, / The quietest under the sun.'

That sally alone made me grateful I'd lit upon her establishment rather than the Wynnstay Arms, where Borrow had stayed and to which I did have brief recourse during the evening. He noted that it '. . . seemed very large, but did not look very cheerful. No other guest than myself seemed to be in it.' The present licensee has that text framed on the wall as advertisement. I had a brief talk with a moustachioed 82-year-old who looked to be a fly-fisherman but vouchsafed that he'd scarcely missed a Liverpool game at The Kop in 60 years. At the next pub they were watching—and discussing in beautifully clear Welsh, the first I'd heard that day—the Manchester United game played that evening. For the rest of the night's talk, it and the beer flowed, and in the course of it I learnt a great deal about the economy of Llanrhaeadr, which is apparently based on an egg-packing factory and something that's 'green, gets you drunk, and comes on a Thursday'. Unpretentious little mellow brick town that it is, the most amusing incident in the whole of Borrow's long book happens during his two-night stay here. (On his excursion to Sycharth he meets two flaxen-haired Saxons whom he quizzes solemnly about church-going. They respond that they like ale. When he presses them further on what they like, he unwittingly describes them simulating sexual intercourse, and roaring with laughter at his puzzled response as they do so. It's an astonishing escapee from the book's presiding morality.) There is about Borrow's visit to Llanrhaeadr a puzzle. It was here that William Morgan between 1578 and 1587 worked on his translation of the Welsh Bible—a work of scholarship and linguistic power that more than any other single factor ensured the survival of the Welsh language. Yet Borrow records only an inaccurate comment about Morgan by the clerk who shows him Llanrhaeadr church.

It is the seventh-wonder-of-Wales cataract which draws people to Llanrhaeadr and from which the town gets its name. Borrow's often-quoted 'long tail of a grey courser at furious speed' description of it is as loosely impressionistic as his poetic translations. The fall is rather complex. A stream of no great volume spills in three columns that pulse and mingle down a blocky, dark cliff of perhaps 120 feet, efflorescing on the strata, rosetting white against the black rock before a right-hand mossy ridge obscures the water from view and it tumbles into an unseen pool, from which it jets out sideways through a remarkable round hole in the foot of the ridge to a series of lesser cascades beneath, the general impression being of less than the 240 feet that is the fall's total height. It is the hole and the strange spirit-bridge spanning it, that Borrow as a critic of scenery deplored, gives Pistyll Rhaeadr its uniqueness and oddly disquieting atmosphere. In the valley above the fall, I saw a stone circle and alignment Borrow had passed unaware by the little Afon Disgynfa; I saw too black grouse, a peregrine chase a skylark, the immediate texture of crystalled, frondy tussocks, red-bladed moor-grass and quartz pebbles amongst the peat as I navigated by compass in thick mist up to and across the high summits of the Berwyn, and I thought him a man who did not notice such things.

But as I waded through the morass that motor-cyclists and latterly mountain bikers have left all along the commodity-crest of these their smooth, high hills, as I collected their discarded high-energy drink-cans and chocolate-wrappers, I knew that Borrow's

Pistyll Rhaeadr

disregard is not as their disregard. And when I reached the Wayfarer Plaque to 'one who loved these hills' at the Nant Rhydwilym and looked inside the metal log-box to find it overflowing with mementoes, business cards, status reference ('Fourtrak', 'Frontera', 'Trooper') and language of the 4WD fraternity, I turned down towards Cynwyd with a sense that 'Wayfarer' would be ashamed of the changes wrought in his name, and that in this ruined, magical country Borrow's sense that landscape is also to do with lives and histories passed there is more fitting, more respectful, more aware.

Waun y Griafolen

Just beyond a bridge over Afon Fwy the path that had been nagging at my curiosity on the map for months assumed reality in the form of a break running in the wrong direction into a thick plantation of spruce. Within a few yards it swung round to the required reading and mounted the hillside. Worn rocks, fragments of broken-down wall amongst the trees spoke its age. It was pleasing to see how the Forestry Commission had preserved the route, and surprising too, for Coed y Brenin, of which this woodland is an outlier, is dire country for rights-of-way atrocities. Perhaps the planting of spruce hereabouts is a sufficient sin. I'd have far less quarrel with forest planters if the trees were larch, with its dusty-ginger autumn tones, and vivid feathery green of spring that always reminds me of Marty South's epitaph for Giles Winterborne in *The Woodlanders*—the most moving passage maybe in the whole of Hardy's fiction, and in its mood of quiet desolation and murmured remembrance perfectly suited to the landscape beyond this wood.

Something about journeying—not only on foot, but perhaps particularly then—directs you into metaphorical thought. As you travel, the ideas work their way inchoate into your mind and your observation of things in the natural world enriches and amplifies them until they resonate out into themes, excitements, images. A sort of rapture is accessible to those who walk alone. It was working for me along the path after the wood. It ran through a marshy *bwlch* with Arennig Fawr and Moel Llyfnant dominating the scene, rising from a cloud-filled valley to the north, the immediate texture of landscape—light-stippled moor-grass and shattered outcrops—counterpointing their simpler forms. In front, Y Dduallt—long a favourite of mine amongst Welsh peaks—was lifting into view, between us one of the great and powerful places in the Welsh hills, and one to which few go. I reached the gate

Castell Carndochan

THE BEREFT LUNATIC'S EMBRACE

before the descent into Waun y Griafolen, leant on it looking out, and wondered what it is about this place that I find so affecting.

The name means 'moor of the rowan tree' but there are none here now, though down amongst the peat groughs their embedded remains are clear enough. Its surface area is two miles long by a mile wide, a basin surrounded—on all sides but the one on which Y Dduallt rears up—by low ridges. It has a quite astonishing sense of space about it, and of emptiness. The vegetation—the heathers, rushes, mosses and grasses, have simply taken over, wiped the slate clean, started again in their slow way and produced a *tabula rasa*. There seems to have been an attempt made to drain it—ditches cross it regularly, for more forestry, no doubt, the presence of which here would be a manifest obscenity. But they too, futile as they are, are being filled in as frond, tendril, blossom uncurl, straighten toward the sun, bend in the wind, fall, rot and compact down to raise up this breathing organism, this simple place. The path marked on the map as crossing it is conceptual rather than actual. Down amongst the preserved rowan stumps are doubtless the smoothed rocks of old passage, but it has been erased, its line on the map now a dangerous one to follow. Afon Mawddach drains out in deep canals from reed-choked Llyn Crych-y-waun. Better to describe a prudent ellipse, avoiding the brightest green moss and heading for an obvious step low on the north ridge of Y Dduallt. The cloud from which I'd been freed spread down the valley of the Dee to England to keep chill and grey as their creed the heart of the Tory shires. Peaks were islanded amongst it, and all around were

The Flea on Y Dduallt

SPIRITS OF PLACE

the hills of Wales, clear and identifiable. Frost flowered the moss beneath the summit, where two grey falcons perched on rocks, watching. I ate lunch by the cairn whilst my dog crept into the rucksack for warmth. There is one finer viewpoint in in this region than Y Dduallt and we were bound for it—the neighbouring peak of Rhobell Fawr, from which on a clear day you can see from Snowdon to Pumlumon, from Garn Fadrun to Caer Caradog. We climbed it, and made our way sunwise down this 'noble mountain', as Patrick Monkhouse terms it, after half a mile picking up the path that runs down to Bwlch Goriwared. The sun set in the estuary of the river whose birthplace we'd traversed and in the afterlight, before we reached the col, this: on a cushion of emerald moss, a corona of pearl-grey down and feathers, a splash of bright blood at its centre. It was a peregrine's kill, fresh and savagely beautiful, the peace of the hills stilling it now, night fading its violence, a falcon chattering distantly on its rock, the long bulk of Cadair Idris in front acid-etched against a tangerine-and-eggshell sky.

Cadair Idris

Gloywlyn

When you are still amongst a landscape, and become an object fixed temporarily within it, the landscape itself starts to come to life around you. Those who have written about the Rhinog comment on what they see as its sterile and lifeless quality. Perhaps they were too busy passing through, too intent on destination to see what's here. I begin to be aware of how much is moving around my bed in the heather. From a rock behind me there is a fierce fluttering and chipping of small birds, as pipit and wren argue over territory, take up aggressive stances on prominent boulders before joining brief flurries of battle in the spaces between.

On the shining lake-levels there is a convergence which threatens more trouble. I see it all from this vantage point. A drake teal—a lovely small duck made shy and fearful by the depredations of the wildfowling fraternity—is gliding round the edge of a reed-bed, whilst unseen to him in the next inlet a moorhen jerks and bobs along. They meet in an explosion of wings, clattering away across the water, the teal airborne and wheeling back to alight in a clearing amongst the reeds before the more aggressive moorhen has even raised her trailing legs from ripples that follow her. A bemused fox comes down to the farther shore to drink, watches with one foreleg held aloft, points delicately to where the teal has landed, pricks its ears at the metallic, worn-bearing call of a snipe that rises from the sedge.

The accent of light falls differently now. Carreg y Saeth has become black, the stoney detail of its crags entirely gone. Its ridges serve as dark frame for the peak of Yr Wyddfa, twenty miles away and purple with coming night. The bright lake itself is a map, its countries sketched out in quicksilver, in wavering lines of rushes, reeds and sedge, in undisciplined clumps of bushy heather and the stirring, tawny grasses that catch the last rays. These light up also rock strata that dip at a steep angle into the water, bearing the scars of glaciation, erratics scattered across them from the yesterday of geological time. It catches too and glitters on the rings which surface tension has pulled up the brittle grey stems of reeds furred underwater by green algae and standing in soldierly groups. The hillsides, hitherto plain and dark, are glowing with rich greens of plaited bell-heather stems, and the dusty pink husks of last year's flowering in the common heather. Two ravens creak across the indigo sky. I imagine them as the 'twa corbies' of the old ballad, discussing in this stately progress their next meal:

> The one of them said to his make,
> Where shall we our breakfast take?

Gloywlyn

SPIRITS OF PLACE

'... the bright lake itself is a map'

Down in yonder greene field,
There lies a Knight slain under his shield
His hounds they lie down at his feete,
So well they can their master keepe,
His haukes they flie so eagerly
There's no fowle dare him come nie.

    A scimitar-winged peregrine flashes by. Colour ebbs away, then suddenly surges above the horizon again. An arc of robin's-egg-blue in the west modulates down through sunset's palette to a glisten of sea beneath. Above the rim of the cwm the lights of Criccieth and Pwllheli register, and beyond them the beam from Ynys Enlli pierces the haze. The moon is up, climbing above Rhinog Fawr, the lake still bright with its reflection. I watch the stars come out one by one, as though switched on. Across from my tent snipe are still drumming in the marsh. The sound is eery and yet comforting. Noises of the stream mingle, stilled momentarily by a breeze. As it traverses the hillside, on the farthermost ridge scarlet flames where the heather is burning leap as vivid and temporary within this landscape as our lives, tugging as they do so at the most primitive emotions. Streamers of livid smoke furl round the moon, extinguishing in their short sway the brightness of the lake.

THE BEREFT LUNATIC'S EMBRACE

Dyffryn Dysynni

I climbed the stile-like entrance to the enclosure and memorial on the site of the family home of Mari Jones at the head of Dyffryn Dysynni. It is a curious kind of memorial to a small event, a small human interchange, that had in its day considerable resonance. The roadside cottage of which it is built must have fallen into decay, but the walls were made good to shoulder height, the chimney-breast and hearth—the *aelwyd* which has meaning amongst any nation of exiles—rendered sound, and the floor paved evenly with slate, on which has been erected, above a plinth of native stone, a squat pillar of polished brown granite with an open-book motif carved on it. A plaque records the following detail in English and Welsh: 'In memory of Mari Jones, who in the year 1800 at the age of 18 walked from here to Bala to procure from the Reverend Thomas Charles B.A. a copy of the Welsh Bible. This incident was the occasion of the formation of the British and Foreign Bible Society.'

It also became part of the folklore—the Reverend Charles taking pity on the girl after her 25-mile walk across the mountains, giving her his own copy of the first cheap edition of the Welsh Bible, the rest having been sold. It was still part of the propaganda in the Sunday schools of my own Manchester childhood. I remember a print of the barefoot girl poised against the mountain wind, black curls cascading from beneath the hood of her cloak and looking to my ten-year-old eyes just as Kathleen Williams did, whom I sat next to in school and with whom I held hands sometimes in the playground. The extent to which the story has been pared down is striking. Its narrative detail is all moralistic—the girl's arduous devotion, the minister's charity. There is nothing by which to grasp an understanding of her life. That part of the story has been left hollow and empty as the hearth is now at which she read her Book. You learn more about her from her grave in Bryn-crug chapelyard, a few miles down valley, than you do from the shell of Tŷ'n Ddôl; that she married Thomas Lewis, a weaver, died in Bryn-crug on the 28th December, 1864 aged 82, and was buried above the flood plain of the river by which she grew up, her grave paid for by the Calvinistic Methodists. Bar memory in the region's pubs adds more—an unreliable sense of a woman whom celebrity had turned unpleasant and vain. I prefer to think of her, if indeed she was the agent by which the B&FBS came to be formed, as the instrument of Borrow's creation as a writer, for it was his experiences on behalf of the Society in Russia and Spain that gave us his masterpiece, *The Bible in Spain*.

I left Tŷ'n Ddôl, its beech-shaded stream and the old track over

Mari Jones's memorial

the mountain that had taken Mari Jones to unenviable symbolic celebrity behind and set off down the Dysynni. The valley's most intriguing site is Castell y Bere—the Kite's Castle, built by Llywelyn Fawr in 1221. It was to here that Dafydd ap Gruffydd retreated, after the death of his brother Llywelyn ('*Ein Llyw Olaf*') in December 1282 had spelt the beginning of the end for the Welsh stand for independence against Edward I. The castle was sieged by 3,000 men. The imminence of its fall obvious, Dafydd escaped—apparently to Dolbadarn—and Castell y Bere fell to the English on 25 April 1283. Dafydd himself was taken prisoner on the slopes of Cadair Idris on 28 June and put to death in the unspeakable manner the English inflicted on those they deemed traitors at Shrewsbury Cross, where a plaque still marks the spot, on 3 October.

Nowadays, no trace remaining of the atrocities of that time, the broken walls of Castell y Bere trail haphazardly around the summit of this surprising rocky outcrop, with its well from the mortared joints of which the ubiquitous spleenwort grows. A cool wind from the mountain was drifting through the gaps in them as I entered its green curtilage. Thyme was spreading and violets discreetly blooming. In months to come the delicate harebells would wave here. It is so still. Seven hundred springs having passed since the murderous commotions of war, since the siege and the fall, the blood and the cries at noon. Cloudshadow has passed over, the rain, snow and hail fallen. There have been mornings when the valley has been white with frost or filled with mist. Seven hundred times the woods have put forth green leaves, seven hundred times they

Castell y Bere

have grown tired, faded, burst suddenly into autumn glory and declined into dank miseries of winter. There has been human labour and mortality, birth pangs in the cottage by the church down there, in the garden of which today a brown-haired woman sits playing a guitar. The first mewling cries of infants have been heard tenderly or with resignation, and the last breaths of old men whose bodies putrefied and returned to earth to enrich the graveyard loam. The jittering wrens have nested in cracked walls throughout these years, cuckoos called and the cormorants returned to roost on their inland rock as the sea retreated from the valley. The dial on which this valley's time is told has subsumed, rendered insignificant, my time, Mari Jones's time, the time of those who worked, died, were betrayed here, and its hands still sweep on, so that time itself becomes insignificant, and there is only the great calm beauty of process, renewal, decay, the impersonal force and urge of nature in which all of us have our part.

Market Day in Machynlleth

The Wednesday market was in progress along Heol Maengwyn, as it has been every Wednesday since the thirteenth century, its traders outnumbering the town's population by all appearances, and doing little business on this hot day in their various wares. There were dapper Pakistanis with vivid, cheap clothes from Bradford, refrigerated counters of cheese and home-cured bacon from beyond Aberystwyth, a bookstall of the Welsh Christian Evangelical Fellowship, Hong Kong toys and Taiwan tools shouted up by strident Liverpudlians, long-haired women of faded beauty down from the valley sides where they'd been holed up and earth-mothering, digging potatoes and The Grateful Dead since 1967, presiding over jumbles of carved boxes, incense sticks, Indian scarves and packets of henna whilst sharing surreptitious, fat, sweet-scented cigarettes. I slipped aside from all this bustle into the Quarry Cafe, behind the bright primary colours of the façade of which is one of the singular institutions of the new Wales.

Thick soup with thick bread thickly buttered, and thick coffee in thick mugs that you eat and drink sitting on thick benches at tables made of thick boards—it's all designed, I think, to ground the place, introduce an air of solidity to offset the metaphysical yearnings of notices which line its walls and which are, taken together, an intriguing index to the preoccupations of the other Wales that's grown up in the last thirty years, beyond the confines of chapel, eisteddfod, and Cynddylan-on-a-tractor bleakness of the communitarian-past-seeking Anglo-Welsh literary coterie.

SPIRITS OF PLACE

My eye roves over sheet upon sheet of photocopied A4, lighting promiscuously on phrase, slogan, advertisement: 'Love isn't plastic—it's natural'; 'Drumming and Sweat Lodge'; 'Learn organic gardening'; 'a dynamic martial art based on co-ordination of mind and body'; 'Self-heal events summer-autumn 1995 (Selfheal is a beautiful little purple flower, underfoot everywhere)'; 'Peace Pilgrimage in Britain 1995'; 'Free Gendun Richen'; 'Come rock-climbing with other women'; 'Gandhi Foundation (Nurturing Ourselves and Others)'; 'Shelters, teepees, Celtic Huts, domes, yurts, made to order'; 'Ancient Pathways and New Directions—a residential weekend with Rob Lind of the Kwakiutl Tribe from West Coast Canada. Teachings on use of herbs and role of animals in Kwakiutl Healing. For information contact Jenni'.

The part of my mind not engaged on this odyssey through the alternative was picking up meanwhile on a conversation between the two women behind the wholefood counter about the effect of floods in South America on the price of walnuts. It would be so easy to mock the culture represented here, to scorn its frenetic reachings after new (and *ancient*) directions. My inclination is towards the sceptical—I'm quite sure the dupes and tricksters, the charlatans and hypocrites cluster as thickly amongst the exponents of alternative culture as they do in society's mainstreams. But I'm still left somehow with a sense of the good-heartedness and reverential nature of the enterprise, of its rejection (discussions on the price of walnuts aside) of materialism and its implicit acts of rebellion.

Hyddgen

Once you climb out of Glaspwll and reach the ridge of Esgair, an easy grass track, acrid with the smell of sheep and undulating through hummocks carries you three swift miles south to where a path, the marking of which across high ground by quartz boulders suggests its age, veers down eastwards to the old *tyddyn* of Hyddgen. Its former house is now a nettle-infested pile of boulders, of fallen roof-trees crumbling to tawny dust, but alongside it is a complex of wintering sheds crowned by a crazy-angled chimney and built of corrugated iron sheets, rust-red, surprisingly mellow and suited to the moorland colouring of grass and moss, stream, mine-spoil and peat all around. As a place to live, it is unimaginably remote, the nearest habitation perhaps four miles away. But then, no one has lived here for years. At shearing and dipping, lambing and gathering, the farmers and shepherds converge by Landrover and scramble bike. The stove flames and

Camp by Afon Hengwm

Afon Hyddgen

smokes, the kettle sings, sheep protest and the men laugh and curse until the work's done. Their vehicles sway off along the tracks, ash flakes and cools in the grate, a bat flickers from the shed's rafters, solitude orchestrates its *adagios* again. Thus Hyddgen, but there is another aspect to this name. Here's an account from the manuscript known as Peniarth 135, transcribed in the sixteenth century but from its language clearly dating to the first part of the fifteenth century:

> The following summer [i.e. 1401] Owain rose with 120 reckless men and robbers and he brought them in warlike fashion to the uplands of Ceredigion; and 1,500 men of the lowlands of Ceredigion and of Rhos and Penfro assembled there and came to the mountain with the intent to seize Owain. The encounter between them was on Hyddgen Mountain, and no sooner did the English troops turn their

backs in flight than 200 of them were slain. Owain now won great fame, and a great number of youths and fighting men from every part of Wales rose and joined him, until he had a great host at his back.

Walk the track from Hyddgen with the gleam of the Nant y Moch reservoir in front and you come in a mile or so to a little meadow of tussocky grass where Afon Hengwm and Afon Hyddgen join together. Its grass is spear-like, carmine-tipped. On the bank above, perhaps 80 feet apart, are two white blocks of quartz, the southerly one a four-foot cube, its neighbour a little smaller. 'Cerrig Cyfamod Owain Glyndŵr' they are called—the Covenant Stones of Owain Glyndŵr—perches now for the hawk and the quartering crow.

From outside my tent on the bank of Afon Hengwm I looked across to them as the gold disc of a full moon rose from behind Pumlumon. They glimmered a little, the grass waved in a fitful breeze, a peregrine traversed the dusk, stooped half-heartedly and sheered away. The bare facts recounted above are all we know from contemporary accounts of a day nearly 600 years ago when the longbowmen and spearmen of Glyndŵr prevailed against terrifying odds. What the covenant commemorated in those death-symbolising stones entailed is obvious: the terrible ferocity of warriors with nothing left to lose but life; the grim determination of their cause's last stand; recognition, slaughter and the raven's profit.

The vegetable life rises round the stones and my mind, running on this theme, turns to a historical curiosity. There is, in Kentchurch Court on the border between Herefordshire and Wales, a panel painting of an old priest called Siôn Cent. If widely known it would be recognised as one of the finest portraits from its time—the early fifteenth century. The representation of an old man, it is a work of exceptional power, is of an artistry far greater than would have been expended then on a mere parish priest. The house in which it's to be found was that of Glyndŵr's son-in-law, Sir John Scudamore.

Tradition has it that Glyndŵr, whose rebellion ultimately and inevitably was contained but who himself was never captured, came to the Scudamore estates of Herefordshire's Golden Valley in his old age, and died there. I believe he did. I believe 'Siôn Cent' is Glyndŵr, the skin puckered and lined, the hair on his high forehead receding now, the eyes sunk deep within the strong bones of his face. It's the same face as on the Great Seal. You cannot look into those eyes, that face, without understanding how, here, by this upland stream, desperately outnumbered, by force of spirit and will he prevailed. And you cannot but see, beyond his moment's necessity, the suffering endured and the waste of it all too, beneath the unchanging outline of the ridge from which his enemies descended, by the constancy of the stream's flow, amongst these now-quiet hills.

Pumlumon

The high summer sun had sucked the marshes dry, baked quaking bogs into immobility, desiccated even the floating foliage of bogbean as I walked by little pools which bejewel Fainc Ddu above the north-eastern arm of Nant y Moch reservoir—a geological curiosity by which a track curves round to the lake of Llygad Rheidol below Pumlumon's summit. As I rounded the spur into the cwm, two ravens flew overhead, making for a rocky bluff around which they revelled in a pouncing, tumbling, pirouetting aerial dance to the screaming distraction of a peregrine nesting there to whom their play was mischievous taunt. The lake itself glittered beneath sombre, heathery crags. Llygad Rheidol is tucked neatly beneath the dome of Pen Pumlumon Fawr, not much more than a quarter of a mile distant from the summit itself, but almost a thousand feet beneath. In 1854 George Borrow, in the course of his pilgrimage to the springs of the three rivers that have their sources on Pumlumon, descended this slope, and a memorable experience he found it:

'Yes, sir,' said my guide; 'that is the ffynnon of the Rheidol.'
'Well,' said I, 'is there no getting to it?'
'Oh yes! but the path, sir, as you see, is rather steep and dangerous . . . more fit for sheep or shepherds than gentlefolk.'
And a truly bad path I found it; so bad indeed that before I had descended twenty yards I almost repented having ventured.

Borrow must have made a very direct descent of the slopes above the lake from the ridge, for a brief detour round their western rim leads on to the smooth and swelling summit dome. The recurrent theme of these hills of mid-Wales is spaciousness, and Pumlumon expresses it to perfection. The quality derives from a general levelness of the mid-Wales plateau, the way it stretches away in rolling solitude, the tucked-awayness into deeply-incised valleys of human habitation, the fewness of the roads, the way soft outlines lead your eye inevitably into distances. On this fine August day, despite cloud to the east and an overall haze, I could still see

Conquistadore *of Pen Pumlumon Fawr*

the Longmynd and Brown Clee Hill in the Marches with England, and Cadair Idris stretched and reclined along the horizon to the north. Nearer at hand, little flashes of silver were Bugeilyn and Glaslyn, lakes of the eastern approaches to the hill around whose margins bog-oak starts from the peat. The valleys of Severn and Wye thread away along their different routes toward England; I followed mine to the dilapidated O.S. pillar and shelter cairn.

Borrow's description from 1854 is interesting. He scans round, reporting on the wilderness, the 'waste of russet-coloured hills', the lack of trees, and remarks to his guide that 'This does not seem to be a country of much society.' The guide's reported answer runs thus:

'It is not, sir. The nearest house is the inn we came from, which is now three miles behind us. Straight before you, there is not one for at least ten . . . Pumlumon is not a sociable country, sir; nothing to be found in it, but here and there a few sheep and a shepherd.'

It's a puzzling exaggeration. There were more farms and shepherds' dwellings in the valleys immediately to the north in Borrow's time than there are now. Hyddgen, for example, which Borrow may well have visited and drunk buttermilk at, was inhabited at his time, and on a clear day—which that of Borrow's visit was—would have been clearly visible less than three miles to the north. I wonder if, for all his physical prowess and perhaps as a result of his exceptional childhood reading, Borrow was short-sighted? That would explain the clarity of his close description and the extreme vagueness of his accounts of hill-shapes and distant views? If so, he might have found fellow feeling with the son whose conversation with his father I overheard as I sheltered in the cairn: 'So you see, Robert, there to the north is Snowdon and Cadair Idris, and out west, across the sea, the hills of Ireland. The Presely Hills are in that direction, and you can just make out the Brecon Beacons to the south.'

'But father,' the boy stated, with phlegmatic emphasis, 'I can't *see* any of them.'

Ystrad-fflur

I came out of the woods to the village of Cwmystwyth—half its houses for sale, some of the main ones in ruin, a sheep gathering in progress—and ran on over smoother slopes as yet unplanted to the complex landscape of the Teifi pools, from which a footpath leads along the bank of the Egnant and through a valley of haunting loveliness to Ystrad-fflur. The nearer I approached to Ystrad-fflur, the more excited I became. It has always been, throughout the years I've known it, to borrow Yeats's phrase 'one dear perpetual place'. I've sheltered from the sun beneath its graveyard yews, slept the length of summer nights on its green monastic turf, dreamed afternoons away with friends and lovers on my way from here to there. And so, in expectation, I arrived . . .

Plastic canopies, interpretation boards, admission fees, displays, galvanized steps—here . . . !

Ystrad-fflur, a Cistercian monastery founded in 1164, has claims on our attention other than the beauty of its setting. The main one's

Ystrad-fflur

SPIRITS OF PLACE

that it is reputed to be the burial place of Dafydd ap Gwilym, whom tradition claims to be buried underneath a majestic yew tree. Of all the lyric poets of late-medieval Europe, Dafydd ap Gwilym has the finest ear, the surest grasp of language's capacity for music. And he has also, as far as comes through in his poetry, an endearing, mischievous, sensual nature. On romantic love and natural beauty, on sexual play and cosmic jokery, he writes as well as any poet ever has written. For all my adult life I've loved his work, had him as one of the dozen poets I would not be without. Which made it the more wonderful when, as a teenager, I first came to this place, and found it so plainly lovely, so unstatedly holy. The heritage industry has now destroyed it—another example of the trend Robert Minhinnick defined in his fine recent essay, *A Postcard Home*. Tourism, 'Now the most important Welsh industry,' he suggested, 'is doing its level best to destroy what many people consider the two essential characteristics of Wales—its environment and its culture.' At Ystrad-fflur, the environment has been degraded, the culture reduced to slogans. Is that as much refinement and sensitivity as Cadw and the Welsh Tourist Board are capable of in their Cardiff tower block by the main line to Paddington?

Dafydd ab Gwilym's yew tree, Ystrad-fflur

Tregaron

I met a woman and she drove me away from the ruins to Tregaron, where we sat outside the Talbot Arms in the main square drinking excellent beer and watching the sun set behind the church's weathercock and cypress trees. The older Georgian houses had UPVC windows and the old cattlemen's bank was covered in ultramarine plastic signs. People next to us, up from London, talked with a second-hand car-dealer who had left the police force there about Maestros and Citroens. By the war memorial, old men in shorts, sunning themselves, shouted at youths in basecall caps whose ghetto-blaster was the size of a large suitcase and turned up to thudding volume. They sauntered away to a safe distance before tweaking the sound again, so that the gangsta rap of Snoop Doggy Dog thudded against the grey walls of the chapel. Black American street culture in the square of a Welsh market town! Laughing, I half-expected to see the walls fall. If these were vandals, what words are adequate to the foresters and heritage police, of whose insensitive thighs their generation was conceived?

Drygarn Fawr

Beyond Tŷ'n Rhos the track climbs north of the land ruined by conifers, past the moorland pool of Llyn Gynon the stream from which feeds into the Claerwen reservoir, and on to the long ridge of Esgair Garthen above it to the south. This is truly the great wilderness. The headwaters of the Claerwen drain the most extensive tract of wild country south of the Scottish border. The rough traverse of this Elan and Claerwen headwater country is the most satisfying (and arduous) approach to one of the best, strangest and most remote of Welsh hills, the taunting presence of which teases at your topographical sense from miles away. It is centrepoint, focus and definition of the Elenydd, presiding spirit of the once and future wilderness, and its name is Drygarn Fawr.

It's always intrigued me, the way in which some hills have a character out of all proportion to their height. Drygarn Fawr is a mere 2,115 feet above sea-level yet it still ranks with the great. Height isn't the primal quality here, and the lift of its ridge above the surrounding moorland is by no means remarkable. It has a rocky spine running north-east and south-west—attractive rock, too; a rough, stony conglomerate with quartz pebbles and seams—that rises just high enough to command. Bronze Age man augmented the feeling of the place by building here two huge burial cairns, perhaps a quarter of a mile apart (the third of the cairns that give the hill its Welsh name is a mile away to the south on the ridge-gable of Drygarn Fach). They are visible for miles around, beckoning, and when you arrive at them, neither of them disappoint. The one on the higher summit is perhaps ten feet tall and sixty in circumference, squat and powerful, dwarfing and looking down on the decayed Ordnance Survey pillar on a tump a few yards away. Beautifully built in drystone blocks, it's immaculately preserved.

The northern cairn is less well cared for, has an old Brecknock county concrete boundary post stuck into it irreverently, but has one striking feature. Its top is crowned with white, glittering quartz, and the effect is quite magical. To the south and east deeply incised valleys lead off to the lush country. Their sides are blotched with heather and patched with outcrops of pink-tinged scree. Beyond are glimpses of the border hills: villages in a folded landscape, fields of ripening wheat and barley, hedgerows, copses, half-timbered cottages. But this is not the land Drygarn Fawr inhabits. The carpet around its throne is of peat, seamed and cliffed and stratified, dark chocolate against sage, tawny and purple moor-shades. The whole of a ninety-degree arc to the north appears featureless, but the map is rich in names. For ten or fifteen miles there is no sign of

SPIRITS OF PLACE

Cairn, Drygarn Fawr

habitation or human activity other than the impinging forestry. It *appears* entirely featureless, but if you were to follow these vague long depressions where the streams start, there would be rocks with smooth green turf around them, pools of green or of bright ochre, emerald patches of sphagnum, and the sound of skylark, curlew and grouse. The skyline, lacking in striking individual notation, curves round in a slow, powerful, melodic sweep, very fluid, and across the whole scene there is the constant play of light and shade. As I look, it is khaki, but where the cloud shadow has passed, from amongst it glimmers a burnt-out, faint green that is almost grey. The cliffs above Claerwen are red. Suddenly, in the heart of the moor, a long streak of sun sketches in the underside of a ridge so that it looks like the belly of a recumbent animal. I'm reminded of prehistoric cave paintings. When the electric light goes out the guide holds a candle to them, your eyes accustom to the dark and because of the primitive artist's use of relief in the rock they flicker into magical life. That thought in turn reminds me that two thousand years ago this moor was inhabited. Five hundred years ago people lived here. Now it is empty. But as Hilaire Belloc wrote of a not far distant hill, it is '. . . like the continual experience of this life wherein the wise firmly admit vast Presences to stand in what is an apparent emptiness, unperceived by any sense.'

Llandod Cafe

The mid-Wales line is one of those miraculous survivors of Tory cuts from Beeching to whichever sneering anonymity is currently Minister of Transport. It serves a vast hinterland, runs through sublime countryside, and has the argument of social amenity as the main reason for its anachronistic existence. Four trains a day run each way along it between Swansea and Shrewsbury, passing through Llandovery and Llanwrtyd, Llangynllo and Knighton. There was an old woman I knew—widow of a railwayman—who used to travel on it every year from Pontarddulais to take her annual week's holiday in Llandrindod Wells.

'Oh, Llandod,' she used to tell me, ''Eaven on earth!'

When I first knew Llandrindod, in the latter half of the 'sixties, this old spa town, administrative centre for the old county of Radnorshire, was distinctly run-down. I used to come to the cinema here when I worked in Glasbury on Wye. It was called the Grand Pavilion—decaying Victoriana perfectly described by its name and opulent enough to have been an opera house. I saw *Woodstock* here when it first came out. There were three people in the audience and one of them was so stoned he fell off the balcony when Jimi Hendrix came on. The music caused pieces of plaster to fall from the roof. The usherette was in her eighties. She slept through it all. You could make love on the back row unnoticed during the film's *longueurs*. I don't think it stood a chance. Last time I saw it, it was boarded up, notices everywhere to tell you it was unsafe. Perhaps she's sleeping in there still, waiting and dreaming on the Valentino kiss that will restore her youth.

Nowadays the town is cosmopolitan, bustling, upbeat. Its large, redbrick Victorian terraces and pump-rooms still feel incongruous amongst the low green hills of Radnorshire, but it's manifestly more opulent now. The electronic cottage, in connecting people throughout the world, has liberated them from the cities and enabled them to move back into these dreamy places away from the world. The grocers and ironmongers may have gone, but there are the usual glut of delicatessens, antique shops and business consultancies along the high street, signifying new prosperity.

The old Llandrindod, meanwhile, maintains its presence as interested observer of this change. I went into a coffee shop for breakfast and—where else in untrusting Britain would this still happen?—was joined at my table by Joan from the Elan valley, who told me she was in town because her husband was away with the lambs at Rhaeadr market:

'He used to work on an experimental farm, increasing stock and improving yields,' she told me, 'but now it's all going back the other way to nature, isn't it? The farmers of my husband's generation, well, they don't know what to think, but the young ones now are talking to the very old ones for the knowledge they have, and that's a good thing, isn't it? He's from Llanddewibrefi, you know—they speak good Welsh there, but there wasn't much Welsh where I was brought up. But that's coming back too. My son, he learnt it at school, so now I'm learning it too, and it's easy for us—classes in every village, and friendly, isn't it? But it's all changing, and some things won't come back. The farm where I was born, well, that was sold for houses to people from Birmingham, and a company bought the land.'

As soon as Joan, a good-humoured, elegant middle-aged woman, had left, Alice came and sat in her place. She was under five feet in height and over eighty years old, but her eyes were the brightest blue. In an accent two parts cream to one of apple juice, she asked me if I was here for the convention at the Baptist chapel, told me that it had been going on since the revival of 1904, very popular, and the singing . . .! She was given a lift in every day from Newbridge where she lived by a relative who worked in the council offices, came in here for a cup of tea and a sandwich before visiting friends or sitting in the park, was I on holiday? She never went away, except sometimes for a few days to her sister in Shrewsbury, on the train of course, oh yes, the train, what would we do in Llandod without the train?

I left her there pondering that question, a distant smile on her face as though every remembered clack of its wheels along the line revived old memories. Llandod! Yes, time and the train still stop there . . .

Kilvert Country

There are some groups of hills of which memory never loses the sense. They needn't be high or grand, but they root themselves so as to call you back time and again. They are the places to which you return, in mind and body too, as a character in a romantic novel might turn at the story's end from obsession with beauty's drama to the plain, quiet charm of constancy. In my life, I always come back to The Begwns.

They are—or rather it is—a scarp of brackeny slopes, steep to the north, rising gently from the south to an altitude of barely 1,300 feet to swell out the rectangle of land enclosed south and west by the River Wye, to the north by its tributary the Bach Howey, and to the east by the border with England. It is an area that in itself you might pass a dozen times and disregard—just such another piece of high common pasture as you find throughout the middle parts of Wales, with the mountain ponies, sheep and the ranging crows, scattered rowans and thorns and the buzzard screaming its stately arc of flight overhead.

After an autumn in India I came back to exchange cacophonies

Radnor hill country

of Delhi—the street-noise and traffic, the beggars' heart-breaking importunities—for those of the Mawn Pool: seagulls and moorhens and the 'tsi-tsip' of the tits amongst the branches of dying pine trees. The night was bitterly cold, with a cracking frost and insistent east wind. I uncovered the hearth I'd carefully cut here and soon had a small fire's breathy leapings where the summer's flame had been. There are few things quite so comforting as a fire in night's solitude. I sat by it for hours with the moon flitting and glowing amongst rags of mist and my thoughts all quiet and fixed upon the man who'd brought me here, and whose personality infuses this landscape with complex and subtle blends of observation, sentimentality, personal tragedy, disturbing sensuality and profound human concern.

Maybe, I thought, there might once have been processions here as there were to his 'Wild Duck Pool' over at Newbuilding, to which '. . . the people used to come on Easter morning to see the sun dance and play in the water and the angels who were at the Resurrection playing backwards and forwards before the sun.' What, I wondered, would they do on a frozen night? Would they skate across in the moonlight under the pricking stars? On the glimmer of the ice-bound lake out there beyond the firelight, if I believed sufficiently, would I see them too?

Or the fairies, for fear of whom '. . . boys would wear their hats the wrong way round lest they should be enticed into fairy rings and made to dance'. I might not believe in them, but then, 'Walter Brown of the Marsh says that his grandfather once saw some fairies in a hedge. But before he could get down out of his cart they were gone.'

My own grandmother, born on the Welsh borders in the lifetime of the recordist of that memory, told me similar stories with complete conviction, and as I walked out of the fire's illumination and looked back from silvered shadows on my camp, as I observed a hare's leisurely staccato across the opposite slope, I would have to say that in me too, beneath the sceptical overlay of twentieth-century consciousness there is a yearning after the irrational and the magical that gnaws in times and places like this at its covering safety. And a yearning, too, for something at least of the—for us at times disturbing and difficult—innocence of the Reverend Francis Kilvert:

'The right conquered, the sin was repented and put away and the rustle of the wind and melodious murmurs of innumerable bees . . . suddenly seemed to me to take the sound of distant music, organs. And I thought I heard the harps of the angels rejoicing . . . I thought I saw an angel in an azure robe coming towards me across the lawn, but it was only the blue sky through the feathering branches of the lime.'

The Begwns, Clyro, Hay, Chapel Dingle, Rhos-goch, Colva and Bryngwyn Hill as they were in the 1870s, as the lives and concerns of the inhabitants of these wooded hillsides and secretive valleys were, are stitched through the tapestry of his daily record in the most vital and vivid colours. There is more of Victorian rural life and belief in the pages of Kilvert than can be gleaned from any other source I know.

Y Gelli Gandryll

From behind the house where Kilvert lived in Clyro you can cross the road and follow field paths most of the way to Hay, which you enter across a bridge over a stretch of the Wye where riverbank poplars are reflected in its unrippled waters. Hay is an idiosyncratic little town. It has a Welsh name, and an odd, evocative one at that—Y Gelli Gandryll—the shattered grove. Musing on it bookishly—and how can you not muse so in a town comprised entirely these days of second-hand bookshops?—it put me in mind of the agonising delicacies amongst the bombarded wood with which David Jones concludes his semi-autobiographical masterpiece, *In Parenthesis*, about trench-life in the Great War:

> The trees are very high in the wan signal beam, for whose slow gyration their wounded boughs seem as malignant limbs, manoeuvring for advantage.
> The trees of the wood beware each other
>   and under each a man sitting;

THE BEREFT LUNATIC'S EMBRACE

their seemly faces as carved in a sardonyx stone; as undiademed princes turn their gracious profiles in a hidden seal, so did these appear, under the changing light.

River Wye at Hay

Sitting in Oscar's Cafe in the upper part of the town, I thought to go to Capel-y-ffin in the Black Mountains, to make an excursion to it as Kilvert had done in 1870—he to see (and pass censure upon) the monks brought there by 'Father Ignatius', myself to visit the place where Eric Gill had set up the bizarre artistic community to which David Jones—whose poetry, prose and *character* I love more than those of any other modernist writer, and the mystery and magic of whose paintings and engravings no one should forego the opportunity to study—came to work in the mid-twenties.

It was a wet day for a pilgrimage, and I like idling hours away in cafes, particularly when they have good coffee and engaging, bright waitresses. A cafe is often the best index of its community. Oscar's was a fine expression of the *embourgeoisement* Wales has undergone in the last ten or fifteen years. There were prints of Moorish villas in the Spanish interior, of Citroen light fifteens in French provincial squares. There was a poster for Newlyn Art Gallery's last exhibition. There was much varnished pine, a soot-free spot-lit inglenook with vases of colour-coordinated dried vegetation, and blackboards with the menus chalk-written on them: Hot bacon & crouton salad; crevettes in a wine and garlic sauce; toasted brie with walnuts and orange; sorry, no elderflower pressé today. And then there were the women, two of them (do women in cafes and pubs always come in pairs?), who'd swept in from the rainswept street with a swirl of oiled cotton coats, a flourish of knitted scarves and a shake of broad-brimmed hats. They had sat down, they had patted their hair into place, they had run the index finger of each hand along delicately plucked eyebrows and flicked off the drops, they had loftily called for Earl Grey tea; and then, in a surprising London twang, they had begun to converse:

'She's got a hyperactive child—God he wears me out—excess energy basically—he lives near Chippenham with his new partner—you know what he did in Kilburn?—that's why he's called the butcher of Kilburn—half the teachers in the school gone—he was active in the Labour Party, of course, though he's rather taken a back seat now—Tufnell Park—that's north London, isn't it—yeah, but you know, the pits, the real pits actually . . .'

In fifty years' time a snatch of conversation like that will have become social history.

Black Mountains

All the way up from Hay I'd been scouring my brain for the names carved on two stones on a ridge of the Black Mountains that I'd seen for the first and last time nearly thirty years ago and the recollection of which, because of some conjectural romance, had inexactly stuck there:

'The first one,' I explained to Bill Bowker, 'was to an Irish-woman—Mrs O'Shea, Mrs O'Grady—something like that. And the second to a squire. And it's my belief that she was his mistress and they had natural children together and when she died he was so devoted to her that, because their relationship was illicit, he had her buried up there and himself close by her when his time came, in the wild, away from propriety and prying eyes.'

'That's just the sort of romantic gush you would believe, isn't it, Jim? Anyhow, I've never seen these stones, but I tell you where they'll be. They'll be on the Rhos Dirion ridge, and I don't fancy our chances of finding them today, but we'll have a look. Or at least we'll go as far as The Twmpa and see how we get on.'

'When you say The Twmpa, are you referring to what Allen Ginsberg mentions in his poem about Wales and what the O.S. one-inch seventh series map used to refer to as Lord Hereford's Knob, but which the 1:50,000 first series decided should go under a name without any such apparent—ah—oddity?'

'Ah, well, if you look at the map I have, which is the Landranger second series, you'll see that what your dirty mind insists upon and which the Ordnance Survey expurgated has been re-instated, to the delight no doubt of you and every giggling schoolchild west of Hereford—as well as Allen Ginsberg.'

'I've got it! It was Mrs MacNamara,' I butted in, before Bill could launch into one of his lengthier tirades against my character and personal morality.

'What was Mrs MacNamara?'

'The name on the stone . . .'

'There you are, you see—obsessed by Irishwomen! What you need is a long, cold shower, and that's just what you're going to get.'

With that, Bill turned south into the gale and I—grateful for full waterproofs, feet sodden already—plashed alongside him, snapping and sniping and chaffing away in the full, friendly flow of old acquaintance. For two miles we tacked along the whaleback ridge at twenty degrees to the wind, surfing a solid wall of rain with nothing to be seen beyond it.

'Good job I'm with a holder of the Mountaineering Instructor's Advanced Certificate, Bill, otherwise I might get lost.'

'Pity they didn't make them waterproof is all I've got to say to that.'

Occasionally we passed forlorn groups of ponies, long manes hanging sodden and string-like across their withers. Sometimes we veered yards wide from the path to avoid trampled bog. We entered into a disquisition upon why we both liked the Black Mountains but felt no similar affection for the Brecon Beacons. And then we came upon the stone.

It's a small slab of the local sandstone, its top rounded like a gravestone, heavily encrusted with lichens, measuring perhaps eighteen inches wide by thirty tall. Mrs MacNamara's name is still legible upon it, and a date, which appears to be 1825, but is difficult to decipher and in this weather we were not inclined to

Window, Capel-y-ffin

study it for long. Thirty years ago, I remember the stone as being intact and firmly rooted in the greensward. Now, it has apparently been vandalised, a large corner of it broken away, and it lists, supported by a heap of stones, in a mirey pool. I know nothing about it.* I wonder if Raymond Williams was constructing a story around it for the ambitious posthumous novel, *People of the Black Mountains* —a novel structured in part around a grandson's search for his grandfather in a storm along this actual ridge of Tarren yr Esgob? I wonder if this stone was part of his meaning in the last words he wrote for publication: 'Press your fingers close on this lichened sandstone. With this stone and this grass, with this red earth, this place was received and made and re-made. Its generations are distinct, but all suddenly present.'

That, I think, has something of the essence of this wonderful hill area's appeal. The long, high ridges and lovely valleys between are aesthetically appealing in themselves, but in their associative texture they pass beyond the merely recreational into a density of spiritual resonance. This is not just country of the geographical border—it is one of the rare places where time and historical moment shiver into concurrency. For our part we shivered too, and hastened along to Chwarel y Fan, too damp and dispirited to search for the partner to Mrs MacNamara's stone, before dropping off the ridge by the oddly-shaped stone called the Blacksmith's Anvil down a desperately steep and slippery hillside sentried with thorn, yew and whitebeam trees into the valley of the Honddu, or as Giraldus describes it, '. . . the deep vale of Ewias, which is shut in on all sides by a circle of lofty mountains and which is no more than three arrow-shots in width.' The aptness and reality of his image became even more strong as we turned north along the road and came to the tiny church of Capel-y-ffin.

Kilvert, on his two visits here, describes this 'chapel of the boundary'—the church of St Mary here is in fact a chapel of ease for the church at Llanigon, over the scarp to the north-west—as 'squatting like a stout grey owl among its seven great black yews'. The trees and the raised, circular churchyard are obviously older than the church that stands amongst them, and dates from 1762. It's easy to imagine the Welsh archers cutting their longbows here before departure for Crecy and Agincourt. And yet, despite so much of the association being of belligerence and war—the Third Crusade, border skirmishes, Sir John Oldcastle, Henry the Fifth, David Jones's masterpiece—the atmosphere is of simplicity and peace—an interior of whitewash and wood, without ornament apart from an east window that bears, in one of Eric Gill's elegant scripts, the text 'I will lift up mine eyes unto the hills, whence

*Since I wrote this, the guidebook authors John and Anne Nuttall have kindly informed me of the following. Prosaically, the name is simply that of a former local landowner, the stone a boundary marker.

cometh my help'. It is a church that has about it not the expression of power and aspiration through stone—the sort of architecture, as at Tewkesbury, Exeter or Chartres, to which I thrilled in earlier years—but the yearning for oneness and harmony that in a more true and unsullied way is at the root of religious experience. In one of his late fragments, *The Roman Quarry*, set on the hillside above, David Jones wrote of the 'place of questioning where you must ask the/question and the answer questions you'. Capel-y-ffin, with its stillness and lack of pretension or guile, turns your own outlook and desire back upon you to reconcile you with the elemental world of which you are inescapably and most happily a part.

Glasbury-on-Wye

There's a comfort in returning to a rural community in which you once lived to spend a night in its pub. I first arrived in Glasbury thirty years ago, as an instructor at the Woodlands Outdoor Pursuits Centre run by Oxford Education Committee. In the time I spent here, I came to know the paths and farms and hills of this discreet country. It remains one of my favourite areas, and because I once knew it so well, the changes register the more starkly. An evening's conversation in the slow, warm drawl that belongs more to Herefordshire than to Wales brought them powerfully home. In my time here there were three shops and two garages in the village, a dairy, a score of small family farms and a population infused with tradition and local knowledge and possessed of countless skills. I do not find it so now. Prairies spread across the Wye's flood plain. Death's taken some of the old faces. Progress has dispossessed many of those who remain.

I don't suppose many these days read the books of George Sturt ('George Bourne'), which is a pity, for his anatomy of social progress and change in titles like *Change in the Village* (1912) and *The Wheelwright's Shop* (1923) seems as applicable to present-day Radnorshire as it was to turn-of-the-century Surrey:

'We are shocked to think of the unenlightened peasants who broke up machines in the riots of the 1820s, but we are only now beginning to see fully what cruel havoc the victorious machines played with the defeated peasants. Living men were "scrapped"; and not only living men. What really was demolished in that struggle was the country skill, the country lore, the country outlook; so that now, though we have no smashed machinery, we have a people in whom the pride of life is broken down; a shattered section of the community; a living engine whose fly-wheel of tradition is in fragments and will not revolve again . . .'

Of course there is sentimentality and limitation in that view, but there is also truth and value. As for Farnham after the Great War, so for Glasbury in the 1960s. For my own part, I'm grateful for having been witness to a former way and a fading tradition, for having been able to learn from it and be affected (often in retrospect) by its attitudes:

'. . . no higher wage, no income, will buy for men that satisfaction which of old—until machinery made drudges of them—streamed into their muscles all day long from close contact with iron, timber, clay, wind and wave, horse-strength. It tingled up in the niceties of touch, sight, scent. The very ears unawares received it, as when the plane went singing over the wood, or the exact chisel went tapping in (under the mallet) to the hard ash with gentle sound. But these intimacies are over . . .'

Gun Hill

One of the delights about walking with Bill Bowker is the gift he has to explain with graphic simplicity the plan and detail of the landscape he's amongst. He has no training other than his own reading and acquired knowledge, but he's still the best teacher I know—as on a wet morning, standing on the banks of the Wye, picking up a stone and explaining its oddity here—limestone, fossils showing, not from anywhere along the river; or again, pointing out to me the evidence for the process of river-capture, but going beyond its mere mechanics when he tells of how, on crisp, blue-skied mornings, he's looked down from the slopes of the Black Mountains into the cloud-filled valleys to see all the former courses filled and flowing again. Listening to Bill at times like this, I'm reminded continually of the profound simplicities of Krishnamurti:

'A complex mind cannot find out the truth of anything, it cannot find out what is real—and that is our difficulty. From childhood we are trained to conform, and we do not know how to reduce complexity to simplicity. It is only the very simple and direct mind that can find the real, the true. We know more and more, but our minds are never simple; and it is only the simple mind that is creative.'

But to turn again to the river, it strikes me that such is its range and variety that I cannot begin to describe it except in terms of the power of feeling it elicits: 'The river is within us,' wrote Eliot. It's our awareness of time, of beauty, of process made actual in flooding green water, in a roar. Its course is memory, its time-scheme concurrency. My mind still bears the imprint of the pebbles beneath my feet in the summer bathing-place beyond Rhaeadr years ago; on my lips the sense of drops from when I drank at its source; the heron still stabs at eddies my canoe left behind coming down from Builth, and the rippling shallows keep the rhythm of Wordsworth's poem I learnt in my schooldays:

> Oh sylvan Wye! Thou wanderer through the woods,
> How often has my spirit turned to thee.

This reverie was sharply despatched when we came to the Wye's confluence with the Bach Howey, and chanced upon this sign: 'This has been designated a Site of Special Scientific Interest. Please do not walk up the stream nor disturb the area in any way. Thank you.'

Why should I not 'walk up the stream', as I have done times by the hundred in the past? Are my steps less careful, less reverential, less aware than those of the landowners and ecologists who collude in this prohibition, and whose unholy alliance is one of the most disturbing developments in the outdoors post-1979 (in which year the first Thatcher government began its campaign to bring to heel and corrupt the environmental agencies and curb by all manner of insidious means our legitimate rights responsibly to enjoy the countryside)?

It is not exclusion that is required to protect these holy places, but education, and an unoppressed populace whose spirit can appreciate them. Bill and I climbed in irritation past the sign to the top of Twyn y Garth—locally known as Gun Hill. It is barely 1,000 feet high, its top circled with a fine Bronze Age fortification, the views up the Wye, across to the Beacons and into Epynt majestically wide. It possesses a remarkable oddity—a 25-pounder

The gun

field gun from the Great War. The story goes that it was bought jointly by the villagers of Erwood and Llanstephan as a war memorial and placed on the village green of the former. Night raids and thefts of the gun by the youths of the two villages ensued until the compromise was reached of towing it to the top of the hill that looks down on both of them, and here it still stands, rusting, the wood-spoked wheels rotting away, pointing at the military ranges of Epynt across the Wye. I find it quietly moving, more poignant in its position and decay than all the phallic God-King-and-Country tokens to the same purpose across the land.

A squall of rain drove us from the hill's summit, and Bill and I became separated on the descent. I made my way down by the farm of Ciliau, curious to see whether this untouched seventeenth-century farmhouse had been gentrified in the quarter-century since I'd last enjoyed summer-evening hospitality here. It had not. A tortoiseshell cat sitting on the doorstep gave me brief hope, but no smoke came from the listing chimneys, no light from the kitchen within. Decayed machinery littered the yard, the cat fled to the barns at my approach. As I looked closely, I saw cracked window-glass and fissured walls. In the orchard, fruit trees grew mossy and unpruned. Round the front, where bean-frames still stood in the kitchen garden, the outer course of a gable had fallen away. These shales and mudstones are poor building material, do not long survive neglect. All will be ruin soon, where there was hospitality and warmth of human interest. I had stories here from the old man, mingling folk-tale and history: water-sprites on a green rock at Craig Pwll Du, cavaliers jingling two abreast along the Painscastle

Ciliau

lanes. Not for the first time in these Welsh travels, I was reminded of the great lament, *Stafell Gynddylan*, from the ninth-century Heledd cycle:

> *Stafell Gynddylan a'm erwan pob awr,*
> *Gwedi mawr ymgyfrdan*
> *A welais ar dy bentan.*

> (Hall of Cynddylan each moment pierces me
> With memory of great talk
> I witnessed at your hearth.)

Had it been restored, over what subjects would the hearth-talk—the dinner-table conversation—range now? Television programmes? Property prices? The National Lottery? Serial murderers? The Cardiff Opera House? I'm glad I knew it in a former time . . .

Epynt

Opposite the inn at Erwood, steps lead to a steep green lane, sunken and celandine-carpeted beneath its sheltering oaks, that climbs out of the Wye valley on to the long ridge called Twmpath. There was spring sunlight flickering fitfully across the bark of an oak trunk, the grains of apple-green lichen luminous upon it and a drift of crisp leaves around its foot. Resting my back against it, I stilled myself down into the lane's repose to catch at its former usage. The beef cattle from the green straths of Cothi and Tywi, from Llanddewibrefi and Llanybydder, from all the rich pasture-land between the Elenydd and Cardigan Bay once streamed and funnelled this way, bullocks bellowing, tar-shod geese hissing, boys yelling, dogs snarling and yapping, drovers hallooing '*Buwch! Buwch!*' as the whole furious precipitate tribe plunged and slithered down towards the crossing of the Wye and the tracks out to the smithfields of England. This was one of the main trade routes, one of the arteries of the west Wales economy for perhaps four hundred years, its livestock heading out by tens of thousands from the soft fields of their rearing to sharp steel and the town's appetite. Here's how one regional historian from the early years of the century, looking back on a way of life only recently defunct, pictured the scene:

'The track was ploughed by the hoofs of the cattle in the damp weather, and manured by the cattle as they passed over it. In the dry weather it would be harrowed by the hoofs of the cattle again. No bracken or fern has grown on it since and it is still today a green sward which has not been used since the black cattle went over it.'

The echoes of the last beasts' bellowings have long since dissipated across these long horizons. You breast the ridge of the Twmpath and come into a subtle-featured country of buzzard-mewed skies below the moors of Epynt. I followed little roads with cropped hedgerows, fields with wattle fencing and fat Kerry sheep, a continual dipping scurry of flycatchers, most characteristic of all Welsh birds, in front of me. By way of Nant yr Offeiriaid—the priests' dingle—dusty with the spring budding of hazel and willow and a place of so calm and unremarkable a loveliness that it puts you quite at peace (which is as well in view of what's to come) I came to the Griffin Inn at the head of Cwm Owen.

It's 1,200 feet up, dark-beamed and gas-lit, and I went in for a sandwich and a glass of beer to fortify myself against the next stage of this journey. I remember nights here thirty years ago when the farmers would drink through to the dawn, singing, telling stories, a prickling tension coming from them whenever any brash young soldier chanced this way pining for his lager. Now the landlord talked gratefully of the business from REME last month, the Paras last week. I kept my mouth tight-sealed, acknowledging economic necessity, and all the time the sound of gunfire beyond the door. For Mynydd Epynt, since the early years of the last war, has been the largest military range in Wales, the map spatched with red lettering: Artillery Range, Danger Area, Rifle Range.

You cannot move anywhere in the Elenydd or the valleys that intersect it without being conscious of the great hill-barrier of Epynt to the south. It has presence, its name carrying a talismanic charge, standing almost for the type of these Welsh hills. Its thousand-foot-high slope runs in a long wall from Llanfair-ym-Muallt almost to Llanymddyfri. I love the lines from Cynddelw Brydydd Mawr's *Rhieingerdd Efa* (maidensong of Efa) on Epynt:

> *Cyfleuer gwawr ddydd pan ddwyre hynt,*
> *Cyfliw eiry gorwyn Gorwydd Epynt...*

> (Bright like daybreak in the moment of its arriving,
> So bright is the snow-gleam on the wooded scarp of Epynt...)

But you cannot now walk freely along the crest of that scarp. From the brown moors above which Bronze Age man made his burial mounds, amongst which he placed the mysterious permutations of his stone circles, there comes the thud of howitzer shells, the stutter of automatic weapons, the ragged punctuation of rifle fire. There are rights-of-way, of course, used since prehistory, and you may still use them *by the book*. The battle range ordinances tell you that you may pass here when the red flags are not flying. That's a sour joke. The knots of their lanyards are sealed with moss and algae, the gates' hinges rusted shut. These scarlet prohibitions are never taken down. For the public good, no doubt, but to me it seems dishonesty and sleight of hand.

If you imagine that there will ever be any change in this situation, then you are more sanguine about it than I would dare to be. I cannot see the Ministry of Defence ever being prepared to relinquish its tenure here. In the history of its land acquisitions, which generally take place in the heightened emotional climate of wartime, often as not there are promises stated or implied that the land will be returned to its rightful occupants on cessation of hostilities. Invariably, that contract is dishonoured. It is justified, of course, in the interests of national security and defence. Training is necessary, especially as other countries grow increasingly sceptical about our military presence on their soil. It's also, you'll be pleased to learn, environmentally friendly. All manner of plants, birds, animals, are grateful for the respect accorded them by the army during its training routines, its live firing across these landscapes. The case for this was argued in the MoD's tasteful and persuasive study of its own impact on the landscape published several years ago—to near-universal scepticism amongst concerned bodies—as *Defence and the Environment*. The arguments go back and forth: the *Report of the Defence Lands Committee* (the Nugent Report) of 1973; the Countryside Commission's study of *The Cambrian Mountains Landscape* and the UK Centre for Economic & Environmental Development's extended discussion paper on *Military Live Firing in National Parks*, both from 1990. In all this languishing verbiage, Epynt is the ghost at the feast. It is a huge hill area, and a forgotten one:

'Let's ignore Epynt, and then we can get on with the more popular and significant campaigns to be fought for access to Dartmoor, to Castlemartin on the Pembrokeshire Coast, to Otterburn in Northumberland', goes the argument. I'm not inclined to accept it, nor the idea that Epynt is barren, dreary, treeless, insignificant. It is not. It is one of the key places in the Welsh uplands, and if it were not for the surly presence and dishonest prohibitions of the military, it would widely be recognised as such. What I would like to see in the short term, and what I cannot imagine anyone might reasonably oppose, is the reaching of an accommodation with the army: at weekends and holiday periods, in accordance with its own ordinances, the flags are taken down, the public rights-of-way which have existed for millennia opened up,

SPIRITS OF PLACE

The Drovers' Arms, Epynt

the Drovers' Arms up there on the Upper Chapel to Garth road which the MoD land agent hereabouts, to his credit, has recently restored, turned into a cafe and perhaps even an exhibition centre on the history of these moors. Let them lease it out to private enterprise, let them put in for lottery money for the project, but above all, *remove the barriers, let the public in*.

I do not believe that individuals within the armed forces are unaware of the amenity value of this land. On the contrary, as I walked across it recently, I came across a very poignant example of just that. At the Drovers' Arms an old woman and her daughter drew up in a car, climbed out, bunches of snowdrop plants in their hands. We talked. She was the widow of a REME officer who'd driven the first military roads across the ranges on their acquisition in 1940: 'After he'd retired, he often used to say to me, "Let's drive up on to Epynt." He loved it up here. When he died last year we scattered his ashes from that knoll, which is where I'm going to plant the snowdrops now.'

I hope they flourish for her. I hope the army opens its heart a little too, and abandons its harshly exclusive deceits. Meanwhile, I cannot, of course, advise you to trespass there. But let's conjecture. If, in the course of this journey, I had found myself, having made a four-mile detour by road down from the Griffin and back up to the Drovers' Arms, able to sneak round the cordon of soldiers—Dutch in this case, on a training exercise—and had managed, furtively, camouflaged, hiding in hollows, hunted by Landrovers and buzzed by helicopters, to traverse this great moor where there was once school, chapel, community, but where the houses now are blind-windowed shells; if—and I must stress that this is conjectural, because I don't wish to get anyone into trouble with the MoD—I'd been able to rise above the fear and threat to walk this finest of moorland ridges along from the Drovers' Arms to Tri Chrugiau (which cairns, I'm sad to say, the army have treated with scant respect—how interesting it would be to have some properly independent archaeological and environmental studies carried out on the army's impact here), what would I—or you, whom I cannot possibly recommend to follow my conjectural example—have found, before dropping down to that last outpost of empire which is Llangamarch Wells? I'll tell you: despoiled land; a sad absence of peace and freedom in a place where those qualities alone are the rightful inhabitants.

Llangamarch Wells

The first living creature I set eyes on as I came down off Epynt and into Llangamarch Wells was, I think, made of steel. She had steel-rimmed glasses and steely-grey curls, wore stockings of worsted steel wire which glinted up and down as, steel-spined, she pedalled her bike uphill. It was a Raleigh. In its front carrier, proudly displayed, was a copy of the *Daily Mail*. I looked down, to register what I'd just seen, and when I looked round she'd gone. I felt I'd been accorded a glimpse into the soul of the place, and went looking for a cafe to ponder it.

There wasn't one, nor a pub either, it seemed, unless you counted the bars of grand hotels on the outskirts of town. There was an odd and ungainly church, into which the steel lady may have disappeared to arrange *immortelles* on the altar and read her *Daily Mail*. There was a bookshop. I looked in the rack outside: *The Story of the British Empire in Pictures*; *Painting as a Pastime* by Winston Churchill, and a volume of Patience Strong. Inside, the proprietess and a customer who was so dusty and foxed he might almost have been part of the stock were having fun with an English-Hindustani dictionary. I would have liked to have bought it, but it seemed rude to intrude. There was a distant rumble of gunfire from beyond the hill. The military were active on their ranges again. The colonels pensioned back after '47 to a country they'd not known since their schooldays would have felt at home. Not so much as a B-road runs to Llangamarch Wells. It exists in lane-obscured oblivion somewhere to the west of Llanfair-ym-Muallt. There's a station on the mid-Wales line, in the window of one of the shops a picture of its platform, a porter on it and a cat.

,'The station in 1936' reads the caption, 'Not many more people about in those days!'

Even then, I'm sure most of them were colonels. The countryside writer and broadcaster S.P.B.Mais, when he stayed across the valley in grander and more popular Llanwrtyd Wells just after the Second World War, mentions hiring a Welsh cob from a former colonel of the Gurkhas. It fits perfectly, but the nearest I saw to it was a lithe young woman washing a small red car on the main street with the same brisk strokes by which, in an earlier decade, she'd surely have groomed her cob. Mais refers to the misuse of Epynt as well:

'Shooting on the big range at Mynydd Epynt all day at minute intervals was a sharp reminder of the rate at which the Government spend my income tax. I'd rather they let people have petrol. It would bring more cheerfulness into men's hearts.'

The bookshop proprietess and her customer had finished their discourse on Hindustani and for purposes of comparative study were looking for a dictionary of Gujerati. I bought a copy of *The Siege of Krishnapur*—giggling at the notion of how Farrell's ironies would have raised the colonels' eyebrows—and headed out of town.

Cefn Brith

I'd come out of idle curiosity to Llangamarch to see the house where John Penry—the Blessed John Penry, Presbyterian martyr—had been born in either 1559 or 1563. I've long admired Penry for the colour and vigour of the abuse he employed in what was, in its time, a righteous cause. In tract upon tract he excoriated the venery of the absentee clergy of Elizabeth's reign, and its consequences in the backwardness of his fellow-countrymen, their idolatrous beliefs, as he saw them, in fairies and magic, their ignorance of the Gospel. His publications bear snappy titles like *An Exhortation unto the Governours and people of his Majestie's country of Wales, to labour earnestly to have the preaching of the Gospell planted amongst them.* Or again: *A Treatise addressed to the Queen and Parliament containing the Aequity of an humble supplication in the behalfe of the countrey of Wales, that some order may be taken for the preaching of the Gospel among those people. Wherein is also set downe as much of the estate of our people as without offence could be made known, to the end (if it please God) that it may be pitied by them who are not of this assembly and so they also may be driven to labour on our behalfe.*

Don't be misled by those genteel and deferential forms of

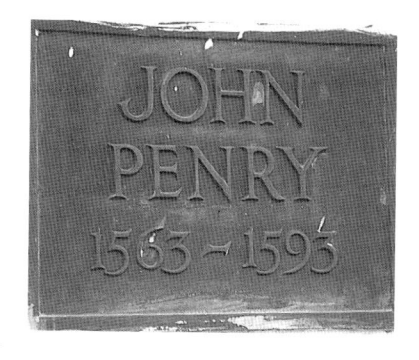

address. What lay within these and also the famous 'Martin Mar-Prelate' tracts, for the printing if not the authorship of which Penry was responsible, was biting rancour, savage sarcasm, crude wit at the expense particularly of the bishops, and the bishops bit back. His books were banned, he was arrested, released, fled to Scotland, returned after three years, was re-arrested, tried, refused to recant and was sentenced to death by a court that did not have the power to impose that penalty, for an offence that did not carry it. A week later, whilst at dinner, he was ordered to prepare for execution. He spent his last hours writing to his four young daughters, the eldest of whom was only four years old, and to Lord Burghley, to whom he describes himself as '. . . a poor young man born and bred in the mountains of Wales . . . the first since the last springing up of the Gospel in this latter age that publicly laboured to have the blessed seed thereof sown in these barren mountains.' At five p.m. in the churchyard of St Thomas-a-Watering in Surrey, Archbishop Whitgift, the brutal incumbent of Canterbury, had his revenge for the slights and insults visited on his gracious personage by the Mar-Prelate tracts, and Penry was hanged.

Plaque, Cefn Brith

It seems at odds with the peace of the place that one of the fiercest chapters of religious dispute from the Reformation should locate here, under the scarp of Epynt. I made my way up to Cefn Brith, his birthplace. It's two miles from Llangamarch by the Tirabad road—a long, low, whitewashed building, still primitive, the byre next to the house, rock ribs of the hillside breaking through the mire of the yard and a lowing of bullocks from barns where they await the order for their slaughter from a higher authority. The great beech trees that surround the house are bowed away from the west, the wind blusters along the mountain wall. I'm reminded of what the great educationalist Owen Morgan Edwards wrote of the atmosphere of Cefn Brith: 'To look at the beautiful ridges of Mynydd Epynt was rest for the mind, not the rest that leads to idleness but the rest that leads to activity. This is rest like that of heaven, rest that awakens the mind and strengthens it for work. No wonder that John Penry's mind was alert and active . . .'

The incantatory rhythms have little in common with the harshness of Penry's own utterance. I suspect 'O.M' is simply trying to resolve in his own mind the indecipherable enigma of land's power over mind: 'How could a scene as soft, mellow and lush as that of Cefn Brith produce so fiery and intransigent a character, so firm and convinced an idealist?'

Maybe that's simply to misinterpret. Look again, beyond the greenness of this spring afternoon, at the beeches' testimony, at the lowness of the house on its rock foundations. There's force in plenty beneath the softness—the latter just a title, like those of Penry, that belies the underlying text. Look north and west across the Irfon into the kite-country and the headwater gorges of Pysgotwr and Cothi, up to the bare prominence of Drygarn Fawr behind which the midsummer sun sets. There's wildness in abundance here. How much, anyway, would Penry have known of the place where he first drew breath? The carefree child gambolling through the meadows whom we'd like to place here, imbibing peace, harmony and a sense of beauty, is a later, post-industrial social construct. Perhaps it's more realistic to construe his character as modelled by cottagers' poverty and the pedagogue's lash in the seventeen years before he left for the fens of Cambridge and the crises of conscience around the spiritual puberty of ordination. I don't find the religious tenets to which Penry held particularly attractive. Divorced from historical context, they have a narrowness and a pungency which alienates. But to honour is not necessarily to agree, and as a Welshman whose strength of character was forged, whether by landscape or heredity, amongst these hills, who came to fear no earthly power or title, whose steely witness to individual conscience was paid for at the highest price, he is one of this small nation's great exemplars.

As I rested against the stone-and-turf wall of the farmyard, the door of the byre opened and the farmer came out. We exchanged greetings. His dog circled round behind me, manoeuvring for the nip to the calf:

'*Dos adre'r diawl uffern*,' I hissed at it—very useful vocabulary, this, for Welsh farmyards, and at least as effective as a stick.

'She don't speak Welsh, don't Fly,' the farmer smiled, offering me a cigarette and calling her off in the rich, amused drawl of the border country. 'Where are you from, then?'

We got to talking—an intense conversation about BSE to the accompaniment of the bellowings of his Hereford beef herd from barn and byre, of which the main exchanges certainly can't be reproduced here and the mildest were animadversions against a 'Teflon-coated bloody Government' every member of which deserved John Penry's fate. We talked about Penry himself. Many visitors to see his birthplace? Very few, but they were welcome. Was he of the family? No, his forebears only went back here into the last century, but his descendants would hold on if they could. Only beef cattle? Sheep as well, on the ranges, but you could only get up there to tend them on Sundays, and not every Sunday at that. His cattle looked healthy and well-cared-for, and the yard, beyond the inevitable mire, was tidy and clean. He was a big man, face weather-beaten under a cap and with a direct gaze. Large hands, very strong, unlatched the gate for me and invited me into the yard with a surprisingly delicate gesture:

'Oh, don't worry, it's not deep,' he said, catching my grimace at the mire. 'We're on rock here!'

Campers

I've nothing against Llanwrtyd Wells. It's an admirable little town, enterprising, entrepreneurial, thriving. The pony trekkers and the mountain bikers and even a few gregarious hill-walkers throng in every weekend to its cafes and pubs and excellent independent hostels. It feels youthful, brimming with life and energy. Its temporary residents rush around excitedly at their fashionable exertions in their shiny clothes, and I, in consequence, feeling myself to be a shabby, quiet man of a certain age in this brilliant company, am obliged to leave town by the fastest mode available and head into calmer pastures. So I took the train through the tunnel and a stop down the line to Cynghordy, whence it's a couple of footpath miles over the hill to Rhandir-mwyn, where I made for the camp-site of the Camping and Caravanning Club. Campers and caravanners! I'd never been at close quarters with these people before. An anthropologist would have a field day amongst them. *Witchcraft among the Azande* pales into insignificance alongside caravanning at Cil-y-cwm.

As far as I know, such rules as there are on C&CC sites are pretty understated, to do with courtesies and consideration, and are faultlessly adhered to in an affable way. It's not the rules, it's the tribal rituals that are startling. There is, for example, the question of regalia. I had imagined a certain gaudiness would be the vogue in matters of equipage. I was wrong. Every trailer (I gather this is the experts' name for caravans), every pavilion, every piece of bunting adorning the latter, and candy-stripe on a folding chair and glimpse of a zip-together sleeping bag on a double inflatable mattress is of one or other of the two sole hues—a sort of light, muted tan or subdued sage green.

The habits of the people too are equally reticent and understated. Foremost is the occupation of territory, between which and that of the neighbour a clockwork gap of twenty feet. Within the territory, activity—or rather inactivity—takes place. There are three phases to this. The first lasts from early morning to early evening and—breakfast and ablutions apart—is characterised by complete motionlessness. At seven o'clock this ends. It's followed by ritual charring of flesh—steaks, sausages, other things on the provenance of which I dare not speculate—on collapsible braziers. These are

SPIRITS OF PLACE

allowed to be black, and the men officiate at the ceremony with long silver forks. Thereafter, handicaps increased, it's back to the collapsible-chair endurance test, though playing *Scrabble* and drinking wine are now allowed. Each territory is guarded by a dog. These also come in two colours. There are black labradors and golden retrievers. They enter into the spirit of the inactivities and sleep all day. The signal for the end of the daylong competition is for the dog to wake up and take the winning male of the group— the chief supine—on patrol along a fenced perimeter footpath round the whole site, after which darkness and silence supervene.

On Sunday mornings those who have lost the motionlessness competitions go to church, five minutes' walk up the hill. It is exactly halfway between the camp-site and the pub. The latter is very good, called the Royal Oak, has a terrace looking out over the valley, serves excellent food, keeps its beer well, stands amongst a grove of laburnum trees, and introduces us to new factions amongst the valley visitors. Firstly, there are defaulters from the ongoing camp-site competitions. They are for the most part heavy men with heavy Birmingham accents, their heaviness accentuated by the T-shirts and long shorts they wear. They trail up the hill behind worn, slender women in cotton print dresses with Empire waistlines, drink several pints of Burton ale, and in the mothy twilight roll back down again. They do not say much, but sit at tables on the terrace quietly, and the breathing peace, the breeze in the chestnut trees, the rustling of oak-leaves, the stream's sound, seeps in to them and now and then they intone little prayers to it in the rounded nasalities of their native town. I've seen the same effect, as of a congregation waiting on the immanent, at the Taj Mahal. It is here. It is undefinable. It makes you wistful-happy. So silently within yourself you celebrate.

The second faction comes in garrulous, intense groups, eyes quick and darting. They wear trousers with an infinity of zips, and waistcoats multi-pocketed, and their conversations are catalogues of species and places. These are the 'twitchers'—the travelling fraternity of bird-watchers. Not many sisters amongst this brotherhood, whose talk is as seriously competitive and self-unaware as any body of salesmen discussing the lettering on their company cars. Ever since the days when Rhandir-mwyn was the last British stronghold of the red kite, the valley has been a lodestone to them. The kite is now more numerous almost everywhere else in the Elenydd than here, yet still the birders come. I saw a trio of them by the Doethïe. A kite soared over the ridge and never was activity more fervid and agitated than these three diplayed. A clashing of tripod legs and swinging of astronomical telescopes and raising of binoculars and waving and gesticulating

Twitchers

and hallooing must have terrified every shy brown hedgerow bird within a hundred yards. The kite sailed serenely back behind its ridge. The birders performed a shaking, uncoordinated dance like *post mortem* muscular involuntaries. I don't think they take up residence on the camp-site, being too unquiet.

Finally, there are the locals, and once you have come through that tunnel to Cynghordy, you cross a linguistic watershed as clearly defined as the physical one from which the rivers now drain not eastwards to England but west into the Celtic Sea. On the lips of the men and women in the pub—the solid stratum of permanent residents with their easy manner, farming talk and allotted seats—there is the good Welsh of Carmarthenshire, *iaith pur Pantycelyn*, exotic, resistant and wonderful to hear after the long miles of Anglicisation.

Ystafell Twm

The *Dictionary of Welsh Biography*, in the stuffy manner characteristic of such publications, notes of Twm Shon Cati that '. . . apocryphal tales have been associated with his name, but his manuscripts show that he was not devoid of scholarship, and official records accord him the status of a country gentleman.' In *Wild Wales*, Borrow has a memorable conversation with a cattle drover as he walks into Tregaron. The drover introduces Tregaron's most famous son to Borrow with a catalogue of folk-tale roguery and drollery that has Borrow intrigued, and when he finds in Tregaron a copy of 'a kind of novel called *The Adventures of Twm Shon Catty, a Wild Wag of Wales*', he's enthralled. The episode

Ystafell Twm

SPIRITS OF PLACE

germane to the Tywi valley is given thus by the drover. Twm has rescued and charmed a rich lady, returned her to her husband, and extracted a promise that on the latter's death she will become his wife. In due course the news comes that this sad event has taken place:

'. . . but the lady, who finds herself one great and independent lady, and moreover does not quite like the idea of marrying one thief, for she had learnt who Tom was, does hum and hah, and at length begs to be excused because she has changed her mind. Tom begs and entreats, but quite in vain, till at last she tells him to go away and not trouble her any more. Tom does go away, but does not yet lose hope. He takes up his quarters in one strange little cave, nearly at the top of one wild hill, very much like sugar loaf, which does rise above the Towey, just within Shire Car. I have seen the hill myself which is still called Ystafell Twm Shone Catty. Very queer cave it is, in strange situation: steep rock just above it, Towey river roaring below. There Tom takes up his quarters . . .'

He manages to trick the lady, who retains a sneaking fondness for him, on the pretext of going away forever to fight in France, into extending her arm through the iron bars of her window that he might bestow on her hand one last kiss. When she does so, he seizes her by the wrist, draws his sword, and threatens to sever her arm if she doesn't hold to her promise—hardly politically correct behaviour, but the lady succumbs, Twm's fortune is made and his character reformed.

It has to be said that the facts known about the life of Twm Shon Cati don't lend much credence to the story. The lady in question, widow of Thomas Rhys Williams of Ystrad-ffin, he married when in his seventies—hardly an age for passionate adventurism or fighting wars in France. Still, the cave was surely worth finding, and on the old one-inch map I used when I first came to this area it was clearly marked as Ystafell Twm Shon Cati, in Gothic lettering, on the north-west side of Dinas above the confluence of Afon Tywi and Afon Doethïe. So I thought to look for it. On current 1:25,000 and 1:50.000 maps, in plain lettering, the word cave appears—no mention at all of Twm. Since Dinas is now an RSPB reserve, I have the shadow of a suspicion that the link is being played down to discourage frivolous visitors—myself for example—who are attracted by the suggestion of villainy and venery. However, I set off along the path to see what I could find. It runs through a bluebell wood above the river. Wood warblers were singing in the trees, but only the first trilling run of notes and not the plaintive *diminuendo* of its conclusion. Occasionally I caught sight of a flash of bright yellow high amongst the oak-leaves. There were signs

Graffiti, Ystafell Twm

Confluence pool of Afon Tywi and Afon Doethïe

along the river bank warning of the coming perils of the path above its gorge, but these only consisted of a step or two over boulders, a descent here and there. At length I saw a fainter path rising into the trees, followed it, and came to the cave.

It's a landslip amongst the Ordovician rocks of the hill's summit. You squeeze through a narrow cleft to arrive in a chamber—the *ystafell*—perhaps twelve feet long by eight feet wide, a skylight leading up out of it, the rocks polished by the passage of decades of visitors, initials carved into every square inch. The earliest date is from shortly after publication (1828) of the book Borrow saw, which leads me to suspect an element of fabrication—of story-location to tease the tourist imagination—similar to that of Gelert's grave. But it would certainly be a fine hideout for an outlaw, and as I came down from the hill to the deep confluence pool beneath, a lovely young woman with long blonde hair in a black bathing costume stretched her limbs in the sun before plunging into cool water, and I imagined the ghost of old Twm looking on from his hill-top and smiling in approval.

SPIRITS OF PLACE

The Doethïe valley, June

The Drowned and the Saved

There are many places in Wales of which I am fond, all of them entrancing in their different ways and at their proper seasons. But if I were asked by a stranger to this loveliest of all countries which place is the most beautiful, then I would tell of the pleasure in walking up the Doethïe valley on a fine day in the high spring of May or June when hawthorn blossom beacons the hillsides and bluebells shimmer like low flame amongst the woods.

It's reached from Rhandir-mwyn by walking up towards the new reservoir of Llyn Brianne, the disfigured hand-shape of which grasped too much of Wales's beauty when it drowned the infant streams of Camddwr and Craflwyn, Tywi and Nant Gwrach. Those culpable surveyors looked, no doubt, at the adjacent valleys of the Doethïe and the Pysgotwr, and I don't for a moment disbelieve that they are capable of looking there again. The Pysgotwr, from Pwll Uffern where Pysgotwr Fawr and Fach meet, down to where it joins the Doethïe, has been ruined by insensitive plantation of conifers. Miraculously, the Doethïe, apart from a marginal encroachment of dark trees over the brow of one ridge and the slash across a low-down hillside of a Eurotrack, remains unmarred. It has its source in the forest pool—lonelier and sourer now than it ever was when it shone across the wide moorland—of Llyn Berwyn, five miles up from Tregaron in the Great Wilderness. From there it zig-zags crooked as a snipe's trajectory eight miles in direct map-distance before, in the great dark pool under Dinas, it calms the rage of the Tywi and together they flow down to Llandeilo.

You enter its valley by lanes beneath Gallt y Bere, their verges flowery with red and white stars of stitchwort and campion, walls braided with herb Robert, a musky scent of hawthorn on the air and a heavier, richer one too of rowan blossom. At first the road is metalled, but after the farm of Troed Rhiw Ruddwen it becomes a rutted track from which, purposefully, an old green path sheers off round the shoulder of a hill, contouring, alluring, beckoning you into the delights of its own secret place. There is an excitement about this valley of the Doethïe. It plays on your anticipation. You see just so far into it, and then a bend obscures, a craggy bluff juts out above the stream and you follow ledges above the falls and pools, the mountain ash, the holly and the small, twisted oaks that cling to their riparian steeps. Beyond, there is the haven to which your curiosity has led, the rose of your desiring that unfolds for you alone: a bushing of sweet ash and oak woodland in the valleys' divergent thighs, distance too in the sight, that takes beauty beyond its admirers; and there is old memory—in the broken-down walls of those who lived here, in the summer pastures of years ago.

The ache of it can be unbearable. Camus wrote of the Aegean that 'If the Greeks knew despair, they did so through beauty and its stifling quality.' Perhaps it's here, in the nexus of emotions when faced with temporal heavens, that you find cause for the developers' urge to destroy the loveliest places. Do we, as human beings, lack the magnanimity to stand back and love? Must we always give in to the urge to possess, and if that proves impossible, through envy to destroy the essential nature of what we cannot possess? You cannot wear the summit's evanescent snow-plume in your cap, even your ego knows such acquisition to be falsehood; and so—*the loveliest women lead lives savagely threatened; the highest mountain is the most despoiled; the most perfect places are the most vulnerable . . .*

I escaped over the hill to Nant Llwyd, the grey stream—the name of which inconsiderable tributary of the Camddwr is taken by a small hill farm where old brothers still follow their sheep on horseback, and from which today they were absent, ponies grazing the in-bye land and oiled saddles hanging in the stable, for there was a service a mile away at Soar-y-mynydd.

Soar-y-mynydd is one of those places it astonishes you to come across. The whitewashed simplicity of chapel and chapel house are so congruent here with plainness of stream and green hill. Chaste front of the house harmonises with the chapel's two doors, high windows between them rounded and lancet-framed, three red panes through which the sun shone at the back warming those inside. I went through the gate, and from open doors into the blue brightness of the day, these words of Pantycelyn's:

> *Pererin wyf mewn anial dir*
> *Yn crwydro yma a thraw,*
> *Ac yn rhyw ddisgwyl bob yr awr*
> *Fod tŷ fy Nhad gerllaw.*

> (I am a pilgrim in the wilderness
> Wandering near and wide
> Watching, hoping every hour
> To be at my Father's side.)

A woman came out. She wore a floral print dress and the frames of her glasses swept ornately heavenwards. She offered me an order of service and asked kindly, in high, fluting Welsh, if I would step inside. I excused myself. '*Sgidiau budr*', I told her, with a shrug—dirty shoes.

But really, it was because I could not—not even into the fine honesty of that place and company. Because if I had gone inside, what would I have done but gaze out through the high windows, watch the mottled light on the trunks of tall pines and the tree-creepers in their intense search across them, and my attention, praise and love would be directed on to them. If I could only have told her so that she would not have been offended, I would have let her know that *my* chapel is not Soar of the mountain, not some Carmel or Hebron transplanted here, but the mist on the mountain and the fitful sunlight and the star-vaulted sky and all things that move innocently beneath it. These are the things in which I exult; and to Calvinism I can accord only an anxious respect.

So instead I sat amongst the small graves of minimal record, the tiny mounds amongst the tree roots that bespeak harsh historical reality, and watched the house-martins' vibrant rhythm of wing-beat, fold and glide.

Yet inside, where the old brown varnish is thick over the wood's living grain, the minister's strong voice sings out too, his congregation listens to him with full and proper respect, and behind them the sun streams through the coloured lights and its rays transformed to bright artificiality of garnet and amethyst fall on grey curls and bald heads alike; and where one red pane broke and its shade could not be matched, a clear shaft slants down. *They are His flock, attentive, hopeful, welcoming, though their breeding seasons are past.*

And I, I suppose, have strayed and gone wild, and am too mistrustful of civilisation, congregation, society, ever to want to come back. Yet I cannot hear these old hymns, of Pantycelyn's in particular, without an irresistible surge of uncritical emotion, and at times like this in the chapel yard of Soar-y-mynydd, it brings me close to tears. There is an essay by D.H. Lawrence entitled 'Hymns in a Man's Life', in which he writes that '. . . all these lovely poems which after all give the ultimate shape to one's life; all these lovely poems woven deep into a man's consciousness, are still not woven so deep in me as the rather banal Nonconformist hymns that penetrated through and through my childhood . . . They live and glisten in the depths of the man's consciousness in undimmed wonder . . .'

I remember myself the wonder listening to hymns as a child induced in me: the swelling rhythms, the fervour of the singers, the mystery of language and name, for these were Welsh hymns in my grandmother's Manchester chapel, and in the memory of them, the distance from mid-century Chorlton-on-Medlock to Soar-y-mynydd at the millenium's end becomes in the moment of

Soar-y-mynydd

recollection only a sounding board to the echo's intensity. And I'd take issue with Lawrence, too, over the idea that there is a necessary banality in these hymns. Is he willing to dismiss Isaac Watts or Charles Wesley so easily? Certainly, the *Welsh* hymns of my childhood, of Ieuan Glan Geirionydd or Ann Griffiths or William Williams Pantycelyn, even in the light of the growth of intellect, do not seem to me thus. They seem—and none more so than Pantycelyn's—suffused with passion, sensuality, the desire for knowledge and an ardent social commitment, and I cannot hear them without being moved by them still.

I walked at length a little way from the chapel and sat on the edge of a marsh for some time, very still, with the music permeating the air, and one of those small miracles which come to us only when our being is thus quietened then happened. From out of the clumps of brown sedge, darting on stiff legs, came a snipe, shyest of birds, slender, long-billed. In a brief flurry of sharp wings, it alighted on my palm, upturned on a knee, its feet a pricking roughness soon lost in moist warmth of its down as it nestled there. I scarcely dared breathe, and have never felt more blessed.

Dinas and the Tywi valley from Mynydd Malláen

After this communion, I made my way back to Rhandir-mwyn by way of the dead pastures of Nant Coll and Banc Du—lost rill, black bank; past Pwll Uffern and Cors Pwll y Ci—the hell pool and the marsh of the dog's pool. Lonely Drygarn Fawr lent her cairned presence eastwards to keep me company, and low diagonals of the sun across Allt Maesymeddygon made incandescent the fields of bluebells—so late and burning still this spring. To welcome me back to the secular world, at the Tywi Bridge Inn where I stopped for beer a bold peacock with a dry rustle shook out his tail feathers in vain and alien display.

Afon Cothi

It's difficult to imagine a place more agrarian than the Cothi valley. As I came down from the hill a huge tractor with all the contrivances and safety equipment of modern agriculture was ploughing a field of astonishing steepness on Banc Maes yr Haidd, and looking in need of a wizard's protection. In former times the ploughman, without legislation and roll-cages to safeguard him, would no doubt have had it from the inhabitants of the fine old farm of Pant-coy that I passed on my way to Cwrtycadno. For this place was home to the most famous of all Welsh conjurers, astrologers, medicine men.

John Harries and his son Henry died respectively in 1839 and 1862, and before those dates both of them had been renowned as wise, mysterious doctors, conning their knowledge from an extensive library that ranged from all the medical textbooks of the day to Latin and Greek authors. The collection's now in the National Library of Wales. Their working methods are less accessible to us, though the content of Henry's prospectus of 1838 suggests they'd have plenty of takers, and not just amongst society's alternative sectors, if they were still plying their trade today: '. . . to calculate nativity; to tell fortunes; to tell friends and enemies the trade or profession best to follow; whether fortune will attend in speculation, viz. lottery, dealing in foreign markets, etc. etc.'

It sounds to me a profession perfectly suited to the new Dark Ages of post-Thatcher Britain, with its commodity brokers, futures marketeers, management-and-consultancy cohorts, and Mystic Meg. Perhaps some business school should run a course in it alongside their more usual curricular schemes: mastery of acquisitiveness & greed, language abuse, snout-alignment & trough-draining, *nativity-calculation and lottery-prediction* . . .? Other modern professions might jib, however, at some of John

Harries' cures. In his 'water treatment', for example, for the nervously afflicted, he would take the patient to the bank of the river above a deep pool, discharge a flintlock pistol by their ear and cause them to fall in. It sounds only a mite less barbaric, and was probably as effective in cowing the patient, as electro-convulsive therapy. Then as now, the wisest course of action's probably to stay away from society's self-styled *healers*.

The walk along farm lanes by Afon Cothi is anyway healing enough. This is one of the loveliest of Welsh rivers, and to rest by it in a field-verge fragrant and filmy with meadowsweet, watching dippers work their way against the current between mossy boulders pearled with wood anemones, is to hold for a moment to the paradise place. I love the delicate complexity of meadowsweet. *Blodau'r mêl* it's called in Welsh—honey-flowers—and the name's so apt for this elegant field-rose, creamy-coloured and heavily aromatic, the defining flower of Wales and summer.

The Cothi itself may appear pastoral-idyllic, yet two millennia ago the Romans tapped its waters and channelled them by way of a seven-mile leat that's now a scheduled ancient monument, clearly discernible on the southern slopes of the valley, to fill washing tanks for the crushed ore extracted from the goldmines of Dolaucothi. I remember years ago climbing the upper gorge of the Cothi, a mysterious place of waterfalls, sculpted rocks, rare ferns jewelled with spray and green, dappling light, to arrive at the point from which the leat takes water—Pwll Uffern Cothi, the Cothi hell-pool—deep, circular and bell-like, with the moorland stream dropping vertically into it. It's one of those landscapes-in-miniature that imprint on the consciousness, and to which you should perhaps never return lest you disturb the power of the retained image.

Caio

An old dog slept in the sun on a mat in front of the former post office, whilst another slunk away panting into the shade. Petunias trailed from hanging baskets. The notice board offered a *Noson Carioci*—Japan, after all, sustains the culture of south Wales—in Rhydaman on behalf of *Plaid Cymru* . . . As I looked at it—notice-boards, village shops and local papers are good indices to any community—a woman of thirty or so with a sharp, amused face came out of one of the neat cottages opposite to pin on it yet another notice—the party had a monopoly here across the board—advertising a *Plaid Cymru* event. 'Are you from India, then?' she asked, and without waiting for a reply and in the singing accent of her native place lilted on, 'Of course we don't get many from your

SPIRITS OF PLACE

'An old dog slept in the sun'

part of the world down by 'ere, still it's very nice to see you, I'd be inviting you in for a cup of tea but I'm down to Llandeilo to pick up the children from their *nain* . This chap 'ere, of course, 'e knew a thing or two about India,' and with a gesture at the church porch and a plaque she sped off, leaving me to puzzle over this new nationality.

This was less easily solved than the identity of the man who 'knew a thing or two about India'. The plaque revealed him as General Sir James Hills-Johnes, a formidable old India hand of Victorian times who fought in the Indian Mutiny, won his VC at the siege of Delhi, served in Abyssinia, in the bloodbath of the Second Afghan War of 1878-1881 was second-in-command to General Roberts at the battle of Kandahar against Ayub Khan ('although weakened by illness, Roberts commanded the entire operation from the saddle, taking occasional sips of champagne to keep up his strength'), and was briefly appointed military governor of Kabul before returning home laden with honours in 1881 to marry the heiress of the Dolaucothi estate and spend the four decades left to him as a Welsh country gentleman. After the rigours of playing the Great Game on behalf of Empire in the wilder regions of Asia, Caio must have been balm to his dauntless old soul.

I went in to the yard of the fine, double-naved church, where inscriptions on the grander marble monuments were in English, on the humbler ones in Welsh. One angel with raised finger and trumpet at the ready above a child's grave reminded me that somewhere in the vicinity of Caio was born the fifteenth-century poet Lewys Glyn Cothi, whom Borrow mentions as 'the greatest poet after Ab Gwilym of all Wales'. We're spared in *Wild Wales* one of Borrow's doggerel translations, and that was something for which I was profoundly grateful as I stood by this child's tomb and there came into my mind lines from *Marwnad Siôn y Glyn*—the poet's elegy for his five-year-old son which is one of the most profoundly poignant and unexpected—because expressive of personal emotion in an age of stylised tribute—achievements of medieval Welsh literature. Here's an extract:

> *Afal pêr ac aderyn*
> *A garai'r gwas, a gro gwyn;*
> *Bwa o flaen y ddraenen,*
> *Cleddau digon brau o bren.*
> *Ofni'r bib, ofni'r bwbach,*
> *Ymbil â'i fam am bêl fach.*
> *Canu i bawb acen o'i ben,*
> *Canu 'ŵo' er cneuen.*
> *Gwneuthur moethau, gwenieithio,*
> *Sorri wrthyf fi wnâi fo,*
> *A chymod er ysglodyn*
> *Ac er dis a garai'r dyn.*

A literal translation might run:

> (A sweet apple and a bird
> The little fellow loved, and white pebbles;
> A thorn-twig bow,
> A frail wooden sword.
> Frightened of the pipe and scarecrow,
> Pleading with his mother for a little ball,
> Singing out every inflection of his thought,
> Crying 'Oh!' for a nut,

> Playing sweet, flattering,
> Turning sulky with me,
> Reconciled by a bit of wood
> Or a dice the little man loved.)

But in instances like the elegy for Siôn y Glyn, translation asserts the untranslatable dimension of the poem, literal meaning underwrites mystery and suggestion, the rhythm of thought is the native tongue's alone. Yes, the transcribed meaning does convey some aspects of the whole. It evokes character and fragility, the father's awed sense of childhood's vulnerability, his watchful love and fastening grief. But when that meaning comes through in the tremulous conjunctions of the original, it achieves something more achingly complete. The lines I whispered on the warm Carmarthenshire breeze were the echo of too common a pain and longing down the centuries—of the agonised comfort of recollection that resonates from so many sparse epitaphs, and to which, in honouring this bright, brief flame of life extinguished over five centuries ago, Lewys Glyn Cothi gave the solace of brave memory and heartfelt expression.

Llansawel

I'd walked down lanes from Esgairdawe and was in a pub in Llansawel. It was The Angel on Pen Cnwc Square—for its very small size Llansawel has a lot of pubs—the shelter of which had helped temper the wind for the Carier Bach, on his way back from selling the neighbourhood's butter and eggs at Neath market, with his black mare tethered outside, a century ago. I was listening to the Monday lunchtime conversation whilst the sun baked the deserted street. Two old-timers, one weighty, the other a meagre scholar, were at a corner-table lamenting the changes at the Arms Park, bewailing the politics of it and the way rugby had gone. I caught the scholar's drift first: 'Nowadays, it's just a man coming in, taking 'is coat off, and doing a job of work. There's a spark 'as gone from the game, 'e's not fighting on 'is own territory any more, and when 'e climbs into 'is Jaguar to drive the 'undred miles 'ome, 'ow much money 'as 'e got in his boots these days?'

That last question prompted the fat man into his own threnody for the scrum on the five-yard line, with the Welsh pack attacking, the inside-half poised, waiting. And since I was poised and waiting too, as he drifted off into contemplation of his golden-age sporting dream I came flying in with a question of my own: 'Since you two gentlemen are so fond of the old ways, I wonder if you might be able to tell me where I'd find Penrhiw Fawr, which is the *Hen Dŷ Ffarm* around his early life in which D.J. Williams wrote the sharpest and loveliest expression of nostalgia, the clearest statement of the value of community, in the whole of the prose literature of Wales?'

I thought that convoluted formality would be likely to produce a positive response from this scholar and his poetic friend, but no such luck. They looked at me askance; they shook their heads; they appealed to the landlord, who was from Surrey; they implied that even the smallest detail I might wish to know about the sporting career, on or off the field, of J.P.R. Williams was within their gift. But *D.J.* Williams . . .? Sorry—never 'eard of him.

Now I didn't have a map, so I thought that if I were to go into Llansawel's only shop, even if they couldn't provide that commodity they would be able to give me the information I needed.

I could have had a map of Shrewsbury or the Llŷn peninsula, or even a motorist's map to take me from John o'Groats to Land's End, but a large-scale map of Llansawel—no, they had no such thing. Galvanised buckets, hen-coops, vanilla slices, wellington boots, cattle-drench, chocolate ice-creams or four-star petrol—Llansawel's combined general store, petrol station, agricultural merchants and medicinal dispensary could supply them all, but not the plan of the region which makes use of its comprehensive facilities. I asked the woman who seemed to be in sole charge of this great barn behind its rusting metal-framed windows. Did she know of a farm by the name of Penrhiw Fawr? She cocked a careful ear: 'Penrhiw Fawr,' she repeated, 'I wonder if that's the same as Penrhiw? If it is, then go back to the end of the road, turn up for Esgairdawe, and it's first on the left at the top of the hill after you've left the village.'

I bought an orange lolly and thanked her, walked out into the furnace of the street sucking on the ice and thinking myself in luck. The right track was surely the road to Esgairdawe, where his mother had been a member before her marriage of the Congregational Chapel, and where DJ himself had not often been taken, because for short young legs it was *dwy filltir faith dros gaeau serth, a gweundir ac afon y rhan gyntaf o'r ffordd*—two long miles across steep fields, with a moor and a river on the first part of the way. At Penrhiw a cascade of puppies and assorted other friendly dogs lapped, deluged, tumbled and yapped around my lower legs. A dark, plump, pretty young woman in a bathing costume came through the gate of the yard, and they frothed and foamed round her legs instead. No, this wasn't Penrhiw Fawr. That

Hen Dŷ Ffarm

was on Maes-y-coed land, but it was no use my going there because the place was in ruins now, nothing left of it. Yes, it was the place about which D.J. Williams had written his book, but no, she hadn't read it—too much to do in running a farm, you know. The sound of tractors throbbed down from the hayfields. She gave me directions for Maes-y-coed.

There were starlings in the wires and honeysuckle hanging sweet and rich-scented in every hedgerow. I descended the lane to Maes-y-coed, past a new bungalow into the empty yard. I knocked on the door of the farmhouse. No reply. I looked into the sheds. Nobody. As though from the heart of the valley, the steady rhythm of haymaking pulsed on. I heard an engine approaching, and soon a small Daihatsu jeep whined into the yard. I went over to greet the driver. He was in his seventies, his shirt collarless, his braces red and his eyes cornflower-blue. His wife sat beside him with a couple of young children on her lap, a riot of older ones in the back of the jeep: 'Grandchildren,' she explained, 'we've been down by the river.'

The old man, after we'd exchanged pleasantries on the good weather for cutting silage and I'd told him why I was there, climbed out. 'Come by 'ere,' he beckoned me, walking slowly over to the fence, 'I'll show you where Penrhiw Fawr was.' We stood looking west across the valley of the Marlais brook: 'See the roofs by those tall trees, up at the top of the red field—that's where you'll find it. But it's down now—it's down—just the barns left.'

Was it on his land? Might I go there?

'You're welcome, boy. Walk down by the river. Shut the gates. It's good that it's not forgotten, the old place.'

THE BEREFT LUNATIC'S EMBRACE

Hen Dŷ Ffarm

I struck down the hill beneath a spruce plantation, passed an incongruous renovated cottage where a lonely cavalier spaniel howled from behind satin-aluminium double-glazed windows, and wondered if I was on the right track. At length it curved round to reach the Marlais brook, which I crossed on stepping stones. A grey heron, surprised in its fishing, lumbered into the air and flapped slowly away. At the top of the steep field above were the trees. I climbed towards them in mounting excitement. For this was the red field of Cae Dan Tŷ, as a result of running down which on hearing that a cow was stuck in the bog of Cae Du when her time was near, DJ's mother's first-born was delivered still-born, his tiny corpse for over a century now under one of those unmarked mounds which stipple the margins of the chapelyard at Esgairdawe. Rutted and grassed-over, the approach slants across then steeply round the barns in a final twist before entering the top of the sloping farmyard. I had arrived at Penrhiw Fawr, at *Hen Dŷ Ffarm*.

Generally, the visiting of literary monuments doesn't much appeal to me. I'd no more wish to seek out Chawton or Abbotsford or Haworth parsonage than I'd desire to go to Disneyland or Alton Towers. Penrhiw Fawr is somehow different. In a sense, it's the main character in the book for which it provides a title. Within its walls, across its fields, on excursions from its secure base, all the action of *Hen Dŷ Ffarm* takes place. If you asked what this book is about, I could tell you that it's an account of life on an up-country Carmarthenshire farm towards the end of the nineteenth century. But that's as informative as saying that *Paradise Lost* is about the big boss sacking an under-manager. *Hen Dŷ Ffarm* is one of those uncategorisable masterpieces which discomfit academics because they refuse steadfastly to fit into their neat schemes of things, and are hard to teach, but which the reading public of Wales (an English translation by the great modern Welsh poet Waldo Williams was published 35 years ago, and has long been out of print) continues rightly and instinctively to love. The nearest equivalent in English, and from a very similar period, is Flora Thompson's *Lark Rise to Candleford*, but D.J. Williams's is the more complex, witty and accomplished piece of writing. Its working premise is that the eye of the child is of the utmost clarity. As DJ—it's a measure of the affection in which he's held in Wales that he is always referred to by his initials—writes early in his book, 'I've long been of the opinion—quite apart from everything the psychologists say to confirm it—that a child's memory and observation of what's going on around him in his earliest days are

SPIRITS OF PLACE

'An undershot water-wheel made by T. Jones, Priory Foundry, Carmarthen'

very much deeper and more intense than people in general have believed them to be.'

The remembered child-observer of *Hen Dŷ Ffarm* becomes recorder of community, society, individuality and entrenched value and belief. At one level this is a self-deprecating stratagem that attempts to conceal the gathered wisdom of a man's life and the developed skill of his art. This book is not the work of a child of six-and-a-quarter-years-old—DJ's age when he left Penrhiw Fawr. When it first appeared in the October of 1953, its author was sixty-eight-and-a-quarter years of age and had been gone from Penrhiw Fawr for a decade more than the century was old. But the record he recreated from those earliest memories, and the values he underpinned by them, are extraordinarily vivid and persuasive. It teems with anecdote, oratory, folklore, song, incident, character of women and men and horses—if you wish to understand the importance of the horse in agrarian societies before the invention of the internal combustion engine, here's your source-text. Most of all, though, it glows with the character of its author.

There is a phrase in Welsh, *dyn ei filltir sgwâr*—'a man of his own square mile'—that in a sense defines D.J. Williams's literary project. It might sound simple, but the web of interdependence, knowledge, role and responsibility implicit in that phrase is intricate and profound. Its design is comprehensible, the individual's relationship to it defined. It's not some web-site you can log in and out of at will, gaining information, understanding—what? As a literary work *Hen Dŷ Ffarm* was the expression of a historical moment and a nation where scale was human and appropriate—where the *filltir sgwâr* could both contain and satisfy aspiration. Perhaps the reason why I so passionately love this small country is that the diminishing echo of that moment remains.

No doubt but that DJ knew it was passing. And as I walked down through the farmyard, the evidence was all too plain that in the material manifestation DJ knew, it had gone. I looked in the barns: an axle, an old, steel-tyred hay-rake, a three-bladed plough; an undershot water-wheel made by T. Jones, Priory Foundry, Carmarthen, the leat feeding which had entirely collapsed; a roofless hayloft where rotten floorboards were ribbed and latticed with sunlight. Of the house, the only traces were a mound of rubble where nettles and foxgloves grew, a pile of slates stacked against a tree. And yet—this fallen place, looking up the valley to Esgairdawe where his parents worshipped, is real in a way that the Roman cartoons, say, for the tourists at the goldmines of Dolaucothi can never be real. Because of DJ's attention and memory, we know the specifics of work and thought, words and values that directed and defined this place. Because of his writing and his example, something still adheres. Because, out of a selfless and communitarian moral conviction, he wrote *Hen Dŷ Ffarm*, for all its ruin and neglect Penrhiw Fawr remains a place resonant with meaning.

Look—high up in the ash tree's bole! Is that the scar from where Uncle James the idler and joker, tolerated, loved for his gift of song, mocked for his unsteadiness, tried to shoot the dancing squirrel and succeeded only in raising white splinters from the living bark, so bad was his aim, with a gun, in life . . . ? Maybe I like to think it is—as indeed it may be—because it gives me something tangible, some actuality to reconcile myself to the subtle, quiet force of DJ's moral convictions. This was, after all, the man who so passionately believed his cultural web to be worthy of preservation that he served a sentence in Wormwood Scrubs in 1937 for burning sheds at an RAF bombing range on the Llŷn peninsula, the construction of which had caused the destruction of Penyberth—a house, in the words of another Welsh icon, Saunders Lewis, that '. . . belonged to the story of Welsh literature . . . a thing of hallowed and secular majesty . . . taken down and utterly destroyed a week before we burnt on its fields the timbers of the vandals . . .'

As I sat amongst the ruins of Penrhiw Fawr, there came to me W.J. Gruffydd's definition of the cultured man as '*y dyn sy'n cyffwrdd â bywyd yn y nifer luosocaf o fannau*'—the man who touches life in the greatest number of places—and of D.J. Williams' variation on that theme: 'I do not think there is any occupation in as favourable a position to answer this requirement as that of those who dwell on the land and obtain their living out of it. In this work one has to do daily with one's fellow creatures, man and animal, and with nature herself in every aspect. From cradle to grave, the inheritors of the earth are in closest touch with all the secret powers of life.'

I left Penrhiw Fawr regretfully, knowing that the life of its day had passed into the words, the *logos* of the man who was born here a hundred and eleven years ago, where its perceptive loving-kindness will endure as long as we give it attention and understanding. I crossed over Cwmcoedifor Bank, came down to Rhydcymerau where DJ and his wife Siân are buried in the chapelyard. By chance, as I rested amongst warm graves, eating lunch, scanning the day's paper, I read of the acquittal of the heroic women in Lancashire who'd rendered temporarily harmless Mammon's Harrier jet destined for use against the innocent people of East Timor. And I knew in that moment the strength of the community of the spirit, amongst whom D.J. Williams is an honoured guest.

SPIRITS OF PLACE

The grave of D.J. Williams and his wife Siân, Rhydcymerau chapelyard

Rhydcymerau

DJ had stood up and spoken here at a meeting before returning to his pew, where the life had passed from him as he sat amongst his own people to whom his last words had been addressed. Realising he'd gone, the congregation offered up a prayer and sang a hymn before his body was taken away. There's something about this story that, to me, is both affecting and satisfying—the return to the native place, the peace, the respect. It has an atmosphere of deep-rootedness that few of us can identify in our lives. Here in Rhydcymerau, taking up the journey again in a raw wind and the shortening days, the spruce plantations were darker under a dark sky and only the dulled ginger of the larches lightened the gloom. The gimcrack portico of the Red Dragon caravan site, rotting wood and faded paint of the chapel windows, tell the usual tale from unvisited rural Wales, of change and neglect.

This is not country through which the recreational walker often passes. From Rhandir-mwyn to Aberteifi and Caerfyrddin, no *ways*, no *trails*, few paths. It is a sort of waste land, its few small towns—Llanybydder, Llansawel, Llandysul—workaday little places with a scattering of taverns, a butcher and baker, banks, a cattle mart maybe, hardware stores with goods spilling out across unhurried pavements. It's not picturesque landscape. Nor is it entirely nondescript and nor was it entirely useless. In *Hen Dŷ Ffarm*, D.J. Williams described the genesis of the rural scene of his time, the loving and unremitting activity those like his father who lies in a nearby grave in Rhydcymerau chapelyard put in to rendering productive the rough land that had lain fallow since the first settlers whose cairns star the hill-tops and moorland ridges had turned the sod and manured the ground millennia ago:

'. . . in their day these made a cultivated land out of the steep hillbreasts of the north of Carmarthenshire, turning them into grassland and cornland and into a hedgerow-knitted net of tamed country up as far as the mountain heather.'

In 1951 a government spokesman made the following comment: 'We intend to plant 800,000 acres in Wales. We intend to change the face of Wales. We know there will be opposition but we intend to force this thing through.' The effect of this chilling assertion's enactment upon the Welsh landscape has been the biggest environmental catastrophe in Britain this century, and one that is only now—as the conifers approach maturity—becoming apparent. Unthinkably large tracts of land in the upland areas of the most beautiful region in Britain have been laid waste. From viable, if marginal, agricultural land that, properly managed, was a national resource and in human terms was far more than that, a future desert has been created, its onset assured by tax concessions to the most wealthy in our society, its reality concealed for the moment beneath dense coverage of trees, its occurrence showing that we've learnt nothing from the examples of Oklahoma, the Amazon, the Himalaya. Once these trees, dark-suited, upright and indistinguishable as Tory politicians and as dire in their effect on the land, have been clear-felled, the true extent of damage is revealed. The ground beneath is soured, its earth washed away down the ditches by which it was first drained to cloud the rivers and silt the lakes. A law of diminishing returns operates. If it can be planted again, it is with less success, and less again beyond that. Conifer plantation apart, it is rendered unusable. Do the wealthy few of our regenerative species have any right in the pursuit of short-term financial gain to treat the planet we must share with our descendants in this manner? For in fifty years time those descendants will view what our generations have allowed to be done with outrage. A new Mercedes, life membership of the local golf-club, or whatever else these self-centred gentlemen desire are not worth the merest fraction of the cost at which they were bought.

That cost was made entirely clear in one of the great Welsh poems of the century, published in the same year as the infamous pronouncement of the government spokesman quoted above. It's from the collection *Eples* ('Ferment') by Gwenallt—the bardic name of the poet David James Jones (1899-1968). He was a cousin of D.J. Williams, one whose family, like many others, moved from rural Carmarthenshire to the industrial towns of south-west Wales. His father was incinerated by molten metal spilt in an accident at the steel-mill where he worked. Gwenallt himself rebelled against the Calvinism and industrial brutalisation of his background, was imprisoned in Dartmoor for his pacifism, faltered his way through Christian Socialism and Marxism, on a visit to the Irish *Gaeltacht* encountered the idea of nationhood, and emerged to a reconciliation between Christianity and social justice as radical as it is rare. A profoundly interesting writer in many genres, his organic perception of the nation as cultural entity—not properly subservient to the requirements of the state but often, and most particularly in its stress on individual human creativity, superior to the latter's mechanical uniformity—strikes me as being of crucial importance within our society. The poem, on its most obvious level, is about the effect on a small rural Welsh commmunity of that 1951 government spokesman's infamous edict. I was in Hungary recently, lecturing at the university in Budapest on the tradition of political dissent in Britain, and read this poem—both in Welsh, where the language builds from grave, calm, humorous recall to spitting, apocalyptic ferocity—and in English to the audience. The response to it, from students in a country conquered and subject throughout much of its recent history that has yet managed stubbornly to practise the forms of cultural resistance and maintain cultural identity, was heartening, overwhelming. I hope you, as readers, understand that the project of cultural nationalism, around which hovers much of the material I've presented you with in this journey through Wales, has a singularly effective and enabling dimension. It takes from the past, without being unaware of the past's shortcomings, in order to apply the worthwhile aspects it finds there as critique of the uniformity and exploitative basis of the culture of the present. This visit to Rhydcymerau for me was a dual pilgrimage—if a nation's culture is the root, the act of pilgrimage is one of palpable respect—to the place that produced two texts the coming-to-terms with which has taken me many years. Both generate complex resonance from apparent simplicity. With both, the character and history of the writer adds immeasurably to the depth of the writing. The first was *Hen Dŷ Ffarm*. Here, in my inadequate translation, is the second, Gwenallt's 'Rhydcymerau':

> They have planted saplings for the third war
> On the land of Esgeir-ceir and the fields of Tir-bach
> By Rhydcymerau.
>
> I remember my grandmother in Esgeir-ceir,
> Pleating her apron as she sat by the fire,
> Skin of her face yellowy-dry as a Peniarth manuscript
> And on her old lips the Welsh of Pantycelyn.
> A piece of last century's puritan Wales she was.
> My grandfather, though I never saw him,
> Was a character—small, vital, tough, lame,
> Fond of his pint;
> He'd wandered in from the eighteenth century.
> They brought up nine children,
> Poets, deacons, Sunday School teachers,
> Leaders each of them in their little sphere.
>
> My Uncle Dafydd farmed Tir-bach,
> A country poet, a local rhymester,
> His song to the bantam cockerel famous around:
> 'The bantam cock goes scratching
> Round and round the garden . . .'
> I went to him each summer holiday

Of shepherding and sketching lines of *cynghanedd*,
Englynion and eight-line stanzas in 8-7 measure.
He too brought up eight children,
The oldest son a Calvinist minister
Who also wrote poetry—
In our family a nestful of bards.

And now there is nothing there but trees,
And their insolent roots sucking the ancient earth—
Conifers where once was community,
Forest in place of farms,
Corrupt whine of the southern English where once was
    poetry, was divinity,
A barking of foxes where lambs and children cried,
And in the central darkness
Is the den of the English Minotaur,
And on the branches, as on crosses,
Corpses of poets, deacons, ministers, Sunday School teachers,
Bleaching, rain-washed, desiccated in the wind.

'Bleaching, rain-washed, desiccated in the wind'

It is a good thing, I mused, as I made my way up the lanes which led once to Tir-bach and Esgeir-ceir, that within proper limits desecration of the land and its community can rouse this strength of feeling. Up on Llanllwni mountain in a clawing, steel-cold wind, the cairns from 4,000 years ago nestled beneath the police masts and Wales hunched its patient shoulders under the burden of time. I ran down to Llanybydder, caught a bus, sat on the back seat and at some rainswept spot Sheba jumped aboard, on her way to sign on in Llandysul. She had hair of bright henna hue and rings in eyebrow, ear and nose. She huddled into a parka on the back of which was scrawled 'New Model Army', and rolled up small herbal cigarettes, shared them in conspiratorial ritual with me as we bumped along. I couldn't help but smile at the thought of what one puritan sect might make of its precursors, or the other of its supplanters, but she was a pleasant, dreamy young woman who smelt faintly of woodsmoke and goats. Her conversation was ripe with vague, sweet ideals, and before she caught her return bus we idled away some time over food and a beer in Llandysul, which was home to another writer—in English this time—of entirely different complexion.

Llandysul

'Sheba' gave me a discomfitingly frank and garlic-hued kiss on the lips in thanks for lunch, and with a shake of henna plaits boarded the bus back to Llanllwni, leaving me alone to contemplate the delights of Llandysul. It has them, too, though readers and admirers—if any still exist—of the works of the town's most famous ('Infamous!' contends time's whisper) son might have been led to doubt it. It's a pretty little place stacked up above its battlemented church and looking down on to water-meadows through which the Teifi flows. Beloved of anglers, it seems more suited to Izaak Walton's century than to ours—footpaths along green banks, kingfishers, trout rising—and it still feels curiously remote and lapsed from time's rattling needs and pieties. The cultural texture of the place suggests this sense of peace to have been illusory. At one time it was epicentre to an early form of football hooliganism. On *Dydd Calan Hen* (Old New Year's Day— the day on which New Year fell before the calendar change of 1752), a football match called *Y Bêl Ddu* was played between the youths of Llandysul and those of Llanwenog, eight miles away. The goals were the two parish churches. The local historian W.J. Davies, writing in 1896, tells that '. . . they began early in the morning and by nightfall the lads were drunk and had given each other many clouts and nasty kicks. Many a lad came near to being killed too.' When, in 1833, the Llandysul vicar decided to set up a Church Sunday School festival in quiet competition, local opinion was deeply divided, and didn't swing behind the new event until a fatality finally did occur in the football match, which the religious festival had caused to be pursued with even more fervour. The latter still follows its catechising, choir-singing course, whilst the football has long been defunct.

Despite its demise, the Llandysul area this century has been a fruitful gathering ground for students of folklore and folk-customs: harvest customs, Valentines, divination—Llandysul has supplied its oddities in each, none more striking than the marriage-prophecy ritual where a contestant was blindfolded, had to dip her hand into one of three bowls, each of different import. If she chose the one filled with soil, a death would follow; dirty water signified a vexed relationship; pure water success through life. When I'd told Sheba of this, she'd held up a grubby hand, wryly.

The Bereft Lunatic's Embrace

These customs which survived amongst rural people in the secret, unvisited country along the borders of Cardiganshire and Carmarthenshire until at least the close of the last century bring us inevitably to one of the most startling and bizarre works of literature produced in these islands this century. When *My People: Stories of the Peasantry of West Wales* was published in 1915, its author was duly elevated to the rank of 'most hated man in Wales'—a position he held secure until ousted by Winston Churchill in 1926. Even today, Caradoc Evans' first book retains its power to shock and disturb, its psychotic presence. Glyn Jones, in *The Dragon Has Two Tongues*, wrote of its author that 'He was regarded in Wales as the enemy of everything people of my upbringing and generation had been taught to revere, a blasphemer and mocker, a derider of our religion, one who by the distortions of his paraphrasings and his wilful mistranslations had made our language and ourselves appear ridiculous and contemptible in the eyes of the world outside Wales.' So who was he, and what did he write about, that so angered this forbearing country and community?

He was born David Evans in the village of Llanfihangel-ar-arth, east of Llandysul, in 1878. His father died when he was quite young, leaving his mother to bring up five children. They moved to Rhydlewis, just to the west of Llandysul, where he spent what appears to have been a poor (his mother was expelled from chapel for not paying her dues) and unhappy childhood, falling foul of the Cymrophobic education system of the time. He was apprenticed to a draper in Carmarthen, moved on to London where he spent years in poverty and servitude before breaking into journalism and finding eventual literary fame at the age of 37, when *My People* was published—after which he became malignant icon to the emergent modernism of Anglo-Welsh literature. Dylan Thomas made a pilgrimage to visit him in 1934, when he was living in relative affluence in Aberystwyth, and has one of his characters refer to him as 'the great Caradoc Evans'. His influence, mediated through Thomas's more genial character, is pervasive in the latter's play for voices, *Under Milk Wood*. Even today, amongst the Welsh literary establishment he causes discomfort—a necessary and unloved footnote.

The root problem is a profound misanthropy that finds expression through the grotesque and malevolent characters who drive his stories. Essentially, these are horror stories of a peculiar psychological bent, claustrophobic and sadistic, unredeemed by any glimmer of humanity, recounted in parodic Bible rhythms and a sneering, lisping patois which is one of the author's most extraordinary achievements. They're at once utterly distasteful and comically, horribly fascinating, their theme religious hypocrisy, and no author ever flayed the souls of his characters more completely than did Caradoc Evans. The plot of the first story in the collection, 'A Father in Sion', gives the flavour. Its main character is Sadrach Danyrefail: 'He was a man whose thoughts were continually employed on sacred subjects. He began the day and ended the day with the words of a chapter from the Book and a prayer on his lips.' He marries an older woman, Achsah for her good farm, sires eight children on her, she appears to lose her sanity and he locks her in the saddle-loft: 'Once a week when the household was asleep he . . . threw a cow's halter over her shoulders, and drove her out into the fields for an airing.' He moves another woman into the house, is elected to the Big Seat of Capel Sion. Six of Achsah's children die: 'Rachel developed fits; while hoeing turnips in the twilight of an afternoon she shivered and fell, her head resting in the water-ditch that is alongside the hedge. In the morning Sadrach came that way with a load of manure . . . Rachel was silent. Death had come before the milking of the cows. Sadrach went to the end of the field and emptied his cart of manure. Then he turned and cast Rachel's body into the cart, and covered it with a sack, and drove home singing the hymn which begins "Safely, safely gathered in . . .".' On the wedding day of Sadrach and Achsah's first-born, the wife escapes her loft, watches the marriage procession go by, wonders at the absence of six of her children, finds their graves in the chapelyard. When the son returns with his wife to Danyrefail, the latter is embraced by a lunatic.

Caradoc Evans country! He's the Hieronymus Bosch of the printed word, and Wales still rightly shivers at mention of his name—as I shivered next morning on the outskirts of town, glaring vacantly upon the map in a state of indecision as to which route I might take onwards. At which point there drew up alongside me the small blue Peugeot belonging to Mr Harri Pritchard Williams, retired schoolteacher, on his way to Synod Inn if I wanted a lift. Which is how I came to be regaled with stories of Rebecca: 'If you'd been passing Pont-tyweli down by 'ere, boy, 'undred and fifty years ago, you'd have run into a rough gang of women, if women they were. You 'eard of the 'osts of Rebecca?' he demanded of me, and without waiting for reply went on, 'Because this is the place they got up to their mischief, if mischief it was. They pulled it down twice, the toll-gate there, and the second time, who d'you think they got to do it but the constables 'ad been set to guard it. Of course they arrested this boy on suspicion of being Rebecca, but he got off. Doesn't change, does it, boy? Rebecca, Meibion Glyndŵr—nobody knows 'oo they are, in a country where everybody knows everything. What do you think . . .?'

With this shot, he wheezed into coughing spasms of laughter that left me in no doubt where his sympathies lay and lasted most of the way to Synod Inn, where I thanked him and climbed out just as a bus arrived to take me on to Ceinewydd—Newquay, Welsh version, and not entirely unlike its Cornish cousin. It's more clustered, less bleak, but there are the same red-brick-and-white-render bungalows with pampas grass in the gardens; the same names—*Sparkie, Artemis, Hurlybird, Bojangles*—on the sterns of the summer boats drawn up and draped on the quay; the same obsessive recording on menu-boards outside hotels of the weight of what you might eat and the novelty of what you might eat it with: 'Twelve-ounce chicken breast in a garlic and black cherry sauce', 'Four-ounce gammon steak with peach, madeira and cream'. I had a glass of bitter and a cheese sandwich amidst the electrified antique lamps, framed shipwreck posters and Admiralty charts of an off-season pub where a bored and querulous barmaid who'd drifted ashore here from Ongar engaged me in conversation about the responsibilities of child-rearing ('. . . I don't care what she wears, so long as it's not indecent, because the fashion's not going to last, but I tell her it's her responsibility and if it gets her into trouble she'll have to pay the consequences and she can't look to me for help though of course I would if it came to that because you can't turn your own daughter out can you but she's got to learn . . .'). From this cascade of moralising—Heaven knows what Caradoc Evans's venom would have made of it—I escaped to a noon of mist and buoys and apricot clouds, walked round the headland past the fish-freezing plant and arrived on one of the least-known and best stretches of coastline for walking in Britain, running down south-west for twenty-five miles from Ceinewydd to Aberteifi.

Like most British landscapes it's significantly marred—in this case through electro-optical tracking stations to monitor commercial weaponry trials taking place on the 2,600-square-*mile* range of the Royal Aircraft Establishment at Aber-porth. There were objections to their installation and its effect on land newly acquired through the Enterprise Neptune appeal, and newly designated as Heritage Coastline, in the 1980s. Their installation went ahead—Mrs Thatcher, after all, couldn't allow anything to stand in the way of her son making his millions or Saddam getting his hands on decent weapons. They fit ill with the beauty and peace of the place and the most prominent of them is sited within the ramparts of a promontory fort, Pen Dinas Lochdyn, dating from about the time of the birth of Christ. If you divert a little from the path which traverses this gorse-flamed coast, and from the more discreet promontory fort of Castell Bach climb up through lanes bordered by corbelled banks and wind-angled thorns, you arrive at a little church dedicated to St Tysilio.

It's one of those rare locations where you can imagine the life of former centuries taking place. The church is twelfth-century in origin, but restored. Two sections of semi-circular bank delineate the former round churchyard, outside which to the north on sloping ground is a tiny stone well. Lingering here in the fading light, I can almost feel the activity of the *clas*. A fence of wattles resolves out of holly and hawthorn, sheep call, pigs grunt, children laugh, women banter, the crow wings past and it falls silent again, bent oaks in the valley brooding down into night and the sea running beneath. According to tradition, St Tysilio spent seven years of solitude here, praying. Across the headlands, the last sun glints on a dome of white perspex, monitoring tamed oceans with a savage heart. Perhaps Caradoc Evans was right? Insufficient and self-interested in the vitality of our love for the land, some of us conscience-stricken, others graspingly unaware, hypocrites all, we endure the bereft lunatic's embrace.

The Great Outdoors, 1995-1997

THE BEREFT LUNATIC'S EMBRACE

Shape-shifter, Silkie, what do you see in the seal's eye?

Acknowledgements

My thanks for permission to reprint articles and broadcasts to: Hywel Gwynfryn, Arfon Gwilym and BBC Radio Wales; Dave Sheasby and BBC Radio Four; Roger Alton, Ian Mayes, Polly Pattullo, Bill Smithies and *The Guardian*; Cameron MacNeish, John Manning and *The Great Outdoors*; Tom Prentice, Garry Thomas and *Climber*; Ed Douglas and *Mountain Review*. Thanks to the Arts Council of Wales for generous financial assistance in the publication of this book; to Sally Baker of the Taliesin Trust for friendship, encouragement and guidance; to the subjects of the character-pieces for their time and co-operation; to Denise, Lady Evans, and Asta Wathen for photographs of their husbands; variously to Elizabeth Ashworth, John Barry, Phil Bartlett, John Beatty, Martyn Berry, Rob Collister, Bill Condry, Martin Crook, Rhian Davies, Steve Dean, Ed Douglas, John and Pauline Earle, Robbie Fenlon, Mark Goodwin, Laurence Gouault, Tony Greenbank, Dave Gregory, Sarah Gregory, Harry Griffin, Antony Griffiths, Leo and Claire Hallissey, Mike Harding, Stevie Haston, Peter Hodgkiss, Alistair Hughes, Jo Longland, Alistair MacDonald, Sylvia Meschke, Breeda Murphy, Richard Bonner Pritchard, Val Randall, Ioan Bowen Rees, Medwen Roberts, Tony Shaw, Dermot Somers, Joan Rix Tebbut, Mick Ward, Ray Wood (to whom thanks also for the perfect muse of his cover photograph) for faith, friendship and companionship. Especial thanks to Dafydd Elis-Thomas (*Yr Arglwydd Elis-Thomas*) for his foreword, and above all to Mairwen Prys Jones of Gwasg Gomer for grace, sly good humour, the delight of trips to Llandysul and the inestimable privilege of this book's going out under the same imprint as those of Waldo, Gwenallt, and T.H. Parry-Williams. And beyond all these, apologies for the inevitable inadvertent omissions.